Your Towns and Cities in the

Stafford
in the Great War

Your Towns and Cities in the Great War

Stafford
in the Great War

Nick Thomas

Pen & Sword
MILITARY

First published in Great Britain in 2017 by
PEN & SWORD MILITARY
an imprint of
Pen and Sword Books Ltd
47 Church Street
Barnsley
South Yorkshire S70 2AS

Copyright © Nick Thomas, 2017

ISBN 978 1 47386 033 9

The right of Nick Thomas to be identified as the author of this
work has been asserted by him in accordance with the Copyright,
Designs and Patents Act 1988.

A CIP record for this book is available from the British Library

All rights reserved. No part of this book may be reproduced or transmitted
in any form or by any means, electronic or mechanical including photocopying,
recording or by any information storage and retrieval
system, without permission from the Publisher in writing.

Printed and bound in England
by CPI Group (UK) Ltd, Croydon, CR0 4YY

Typeset in Times New Roman by Chic Graphics

Pen & Sword Books Ltd incorporates the imprints of
Pen & Sword Archaeology, Atlas, Aviation, Battleground, Discovery,
Family History, History, Maritime, Military, Naval, Politics, Railways,
Select, Social History, Transport, True Crime, Claymore Press,
Frontline Books, Leo Cooper, Praetorian Press, Remember When,
Seaforth Publishing and Wharncliffe.

For a complete list of Pen and Sword titles please contact
Pen and Sword Books Limited
47 Church Street, Barnsley, South Yorkshire, S70 2AS, England
E-mail: enquiries@pen-and-sword.co.uk
Website: www.pen-and-sword.co.uk

Contents

✦

Foreword by
Patrick Farrington,
Leader of Stafford Borough Council

The first guns were fired in the Great War more than 100 years ago. It was a war that shaped the twentieth century itself and affected every family up and down the land.

Until now, however, there has never been a comprehensive study of Stafford's role in this monumental conflict.

Years of painstaking research by Nick Thomas have resulted in this detailed account of every aspect of the county town's contribution. From Stafford men's involvement in the battles that consumed Europe, our naval and RFC/RAF heroes, local women's contribution and much more, the book is packed with information.

Stafford in the Great War contains many first-hand accounts based on contemporary letters, interviews, diaries and news reports. It also contains over 150 images, including many rare photographs of local servicemen.

The book – which is a companion to Nick's history of Stafford in the Second World War – provides details of the 200 local men who were presented with gallantry awards, along with information on the town's casualties. Over 1,165 Stafford men lost their lives during the Great War, including the 430 casualties whose names do not appear on the Borough War Memorial.

For anyone interested in our town's history and the wider story of the Great War, the book is a must read. It's also an important resource for local schoolchildren studying the First World War as part of the National Curriculum.

Most of all, though, *Stafford in the Great War* is a wonderful tribute to the people from our town who gave so much for their country during those dark years.

Introduction

❖

For over a generation Europe had maintained an uneasy peace through a series of mutual defence pacts. On the one side sat the Central Powers of Germany, the Austro-Hungarian Empire, Bulgaria and Turkey (Italy had entered into a mutual defence treaty with Germany, but this need not come into effect if another signatory was the aggressor; in the event Italy fought on the side of the 'Triple Entente'). Opposing them were the members of the 'Triple Entente': Great Britain, France and Russia. Great Britain, however, was not necessarily committed to declare war in support of France.

During the late nineteenth century Germany had looked to expand its own influence. One-third of the globe was already a part of the British Empire, while Portugal and France dominated much of the remainder. As early as 1905 a plan was formulated by Field Marshal Alfred von Schlieffen which, it was hoped, would lead to Germany's rapid conquest of France and the annexation of her colonies. Russia was the secondary target, the conquest of which might also be achieved if France was quickly subjugated – Germany should avoid fighting on two fronts. If the plan was to succeed in its entirety, then the German army's advance needed to be swift and decisive. It was considered that the Russian Army would take several weeks to mobilize by which time France would be subjugated; this should be achieved in thirty-nine days.

A munitions worker's badge, 1915.

A munitions worker's badge, 1916.

The assassination of the heir to the Austro-Hungarian Empire, Archduke Franz Ferdinand, in Sarajevo on 29 June 1914 sparked a sequence of events over which politicians lost control. On 5 July the Austro-Hungarian government gained Germany's assurance of her support for a war against Serbia in the event of Russian militarism. The Austro-Hungarian government then issued a ten-point ultimatum to Serbia, which they claimed was not met (actually only one minor amendment was requested by the latter). In vain the Russian Tsar

Nicholas II pleaded with his cousin, the German Kaiser Wilhelm II, for restraint before it was too late. But the Kaiser was driven by expansionism. A month after the assassination of the archduke at the hands of the Bosnian Serb Gavrilo Princip the Austro-Hungarian Empire declared war on Serbia.

Meanwhile, a Berlin newspaper anticipated actual events by reporting that Germany had mobilized her army and forced the issue. Consequently, on 31 July, Russia began mobilization to fulfill its role as Protector of the Slavic Nations and to stand by its commitments to Serbia. This was taken as an act of aggression, leading to Germany making a pre-emptive strike by declaring war on Russia on the following day; upon which France immediately mobilized. Germany's ambassador in London sounded-out if Great Britain would go to war in defence of France if she were invaded. The response was not a decisive 'yes'.

On 2 August, Germany swept into Luxembourg and on the following day declared war on France (claiming to be retaliating against a fictional French air raid on Nuremberg and Karlsruche), which was treaty-bound to support Russia. In vain, Belgium denied Germany the right to cross her borders on 4 August. Germany wanted to invade France via the Belgian border and avoid her heaviest defences which were further south along the German–French frontier.

Great Britain protested at Germany's violation of Belgian neutrality, which she was treaty-bound to guarantee under Article 7 of the First Treaty of London (1839). Germany's Chancellor, Theobald von Bethmann-Hollweg, described the treaty, to which both Austria and the German Confederation were also signatories, as a '*chiffon de papier*' ('a scrap of paper'). While Great Britain gained little from the treaty, it was nevertheless duty-bound to honour its terms. And so at 4.30pm on Tuesday, 4 August the order was given to mobilize the army. Meanwhile, an ultimatum was sent to Berlin; the use of the English Channel as a 'Home Base' by the German navy could not be tolerated, while they must indicate a willingness to withdraw from neutral Belgium. There was no reply and so at 2300 hours GMT Great Britain, Ireland and the British Dominions beyond the Seas declared war on Imperial Germany and her allies.

Great Britain had long planned for war and every scenario had been considered and was documented in the *War Book* which, when consulted, provided the route map for every official to follow in order to mobilize the army and organize it for war. A pre-prepared telegram would be transmitted to all parties concerned, setting the plans into motion: 'IN THE CIRCUMSTANCE THAT GREAT BRITAIN IS AT WAR WITH [space to be filled in accordingly], ACT UPON INSTRUCTIONS.' By 'act upon instructions', the communication meant, refer to the *War Book*.

Anti-German feeling had been high in Great Britain for nearly a generation, despite the blood ties of the monarchy – King George V and Kaiser Wilhelm II were first cousins. For years there had been the threat of '*Der Tag*' or 'The Day', which was an allusion to the moment that Germany would release its war machine on Europe.

War had been declared over a bank-holiday weekend. With all railway timetables cancelled and rolling stock put at the disposal of the military authorities, the streets were unusually busy. Patriotic crowds thronged outside Stafford's Shire Hall, which become a recruiting centre. All talk was of the war and scores of young men took the 'King's Shilling', eager to do their bit. Many said 'it will all be over by Christmas'.

Staffordians served in every theatre of the war, from the Home Front to France and Flanders to Italy, also fighting against the Ottoman Empire in the dry heat of Egypt, Palestine, the Dardanelles, Mesopotamia and Salonika. Local men fought in the air too, and on the high seas, keeping the vital shipping lanes open for the Merchant Navy.

Local volunteer units and militias had been abolished in 1907/8 as a part of the review of the army. These disparate units had been replaced by the Territorial Army and the Special Reserves, which came into being on 1 April 1908. The local gentry, politicians and factory owners held high rank in the county's pre-war Territorial units, also stepping forward and acting as figureheads for various fundraising campaigns and initiatives during the war. For instance, the Earl of Dartmouth became the Chairman of the County Committee for providing comforts for troops. In 1916 Lord Stafford was appointed temporary lieutenant colonel and County Commandant of the Staffordshire Volunteer Regiment. The sons of local dignitaries and factory owners fought as junior officers at the front, while their grand homes and their factory's recreational facilities were made available to servicemen for recuperation or entertainment.

The Great War became the first 'total war', involving every home in the Empire. Every man who was of service age, and not in a reserved occupation, was encouraged to join the forces. Those who did not meet the criteria or who were medically unfit for armed conflict were to work as volunteers in the various newly formed home-defence and recruitment bodies.

Women played their part too, raising funds for comforts for the troops or undertaking nursing and non-combatant roles, both in Great Britain and behind the lines in France and Flanders and elsewhere. Schoolchildren collected paper, scrap and old rags for recycling as well as picking blackberries or helping with the harvest (under direction from the Food Production Department). Those girls who were good at knitting and sewing crafted gloves, balaclavas, socks, scarves and nightshirts as well as making sandbags when they were in short supply. The younger boys were also put to work, unravelling old knitwear for recycling and making simple mittens.

Among the local industries that played an important part in the supply of military hardware was Siemens Brothers Electrical Engineering Works (later English Electric Co.), who manufactured a variety of munitions and held major contracts with the Admiralty. The boot and shoe manufacturers also turned their production to war work, as did the heavy engineering works of W.G. Bagnall Ltd, W.H. Dorman & Co. Ltd and Universal Grinding Wheel Co. Ltd; all produced shells of various calibres. From 12 July 1915, W.H. Dorman & Co. Ltd came under government control and practically all of its resources were devoted to the production of munitions and locomotives for the war effort.

Some businesses found new outlets. For instance, Irish linen manufacturer Major J.C.B. McFerran, of Rickerscote Hall, became one of the main suppliers to the aviation industry. Fixed into position over a rigid frame and painted with dope, once dried the linen became taught, forming an aerodynamic wing.

Naturally the local press, including the *Staffordshire Advertiser*, *Staffordshire Chronicle* and *Stafford Newsletter* (all weekly issues), carried war news. There were regular war-time columns which included the stories of local volunteers, fundraising events and general war reports, along with bulletins regarding the mobilization of the country's military and civilian forces. Later weekly casualty lists, war honours and details of those who were wounded, or were home on leave, became more prominent. From time to time the papers carried reports on medal and other presentations made at the Borough Hall, the Assizes Court, local factories and public gatherings.

Much of the information regarding the exploits of local servicemen originated from letters from the front. The War Office had been quick to understand that the morale of the men in the trenches could be maintained through frequent contact with home. From August 1914 it was free for servicemen and woman to post letters, while post to the front cost 1*d*.

The press frequently made appeals for their readership to share correspondence from men on active service, which was published in regular columns. The content of most communications followed the same basic form; acknowledging the receipt of recent letters or parcels, requesting items that were in short supply, predictions for when the next Home Leave was due, and passing on kisses to family members. A few letters were more descriptive and provided more colourful accounts of life in France, but were consciously composed for the eyes of the intended reader and therefore the facts were often modified accordingly. The underlying tone and the content of these letters, which usually contained only oblique references to casualties, changed noticeably as the war progressed, becoming less gung-ho and more poignant.

By early 1915 post was taking so long to censor that the military authorities introduced an official postcard which became almost the only method of communication from the trenches. These cards were pre-printed with a series of options which the sender had to delete in order to convey the most appropriate message. This was limited to expressing their current health and whether or not they had received a recent letter or package from home. Nevertheless, waiting for any news from a loved one at the front dominated many people's daily life. Every fortnight or so, soldiers were allowed what was referred to as a 'Green Letter' (so named after the cover, which included a declaration the serviceman had to sign). It was taken on trust that these letters contained no information that would be useful to the enemy, and they were not censored.

As warfare became more terrifying and industrialized, the people at home had less and less of an idea of the true nature of the front; and it became impossible for those who had experienced the carnage first-hand to tell them.

There were a number of military units with strong affiliations to Stafford. Since its foundation in 1794, the Staffordshire Yeomanry had a troop based at Stafford. In 1914

A 'Green Letter'.

it regularly trained at the Drill Hall, Bailey Street. The 6th (Stafford) Staffordshire Battery (later 'C' Battery, 232 Brigade, RFA, before sections joined 'A' and 'B' Batteries) trained on King Edward VI Grammar School's playing fields.

'B' (Stafford) Company of 1/6th Battalion, North Staffordshire Regiment was another of the local Territorial units originally formed for home defence. To a man, the company volunteered for overseas service. From March 1915 they fought in France and Flanders; at Loos in 1915, most notably at the Battle of the Somme the following year and at the crossing of the St Quentin Canal in September 1918.

On 31 July 1915, the 3/5th Battalion, North Staffordshire Regiment, which included many local men among its ranks, arrived in Stafford from Stoke by train. The battalion, command by Colonel Bliszard of Milford Hall, was billeted at the Corporation Street School, with a soldiers' institute springing up in the street, courtesy of the Stafford Federation of the Church of England Men's Society.

The battalion carried out much of its drill and training on Stafford Common, where they excavated a trench system. Up until their transfer to Belton Park, Grantham, on 9 September 1915, the men could often be seen in full kit undertaking route marches to Newport and further afield, occasionally bivouacking on Cannock Chase. With bandsmen at their head, their presence was heralded by popular marching songs including 'It's a Long Way to Tipperary'.

A number of military establishments took advantage of the county town's rail links. Two vast army training camps were built on Cannock Chase, one near Rugeley and another at Brocton.

A POW camp was also constructed at Brocton, opening on 10 April 1917. When labour became scarce German prisoners were allowed out of the barbed wire compound to work on local farms on licence.

Stafford Gaol was turned over to the military authorities and became the temporary accommodation for German and Austrian nationals, later housing British servicemen under detention. With the outbreak of the Easter Rising in Ireland, however, its role changed temporarily and on 1 May 1916 the first intake of Irish Rebels (including two women dressed in men's clothing) arrived, a further 300 joining them a few weeks later. The prisoners included Michael Collins, who was to become highly influential in the rebel movement. At the end of June the prisoners were transferred to the purpose-built Frongach Camp in Wales, from where most of the detainees were released on 22 December 1916.

The protracted campaign of trench warfare resulted in terrible casualty figures. Many of the less seriously wounded and those requiring long-term care were sent to Stafford General Infirmary. The first casualties arrived in May 1915. Other serviceman convalesced at Sandon Hall, which housed a 100-bed Red Cross Auxiliary Hospital. In the meantime, a temporary sixteen-bed Red Cross Military Hospital was established at 21 Foregate Street, providing beds for men of the 3/5th Battalion, North Staffordshire Regiment, during 1915. Here the nursing staff, all volunteers, administered first aid and vaccinations. Further down the road, at 40 Foregate Street, members of the Stafford (40th) Voluntary Aid Detachment (VAD) were housed. Stafford's Royal Brine and Turkish Baths, known for their curative waters, were used by invalided servicemen for whom a course of brine bathing had been recommended. Further afield was the Sister Dora Convalescent Home at Milford which, from February 1915, received discharged wounded soldiers via the Red Cross.

A number of servicemen's clubs were established across the town, including the

No.

The British Red Cross Society.

INCORPORATED BY ROYAL CHARTER, 1908.

STAFFORDSHIRE BRANCH.

Received the _28th_ day of _July_ _19 17_

from _Mrs Pyett_ the sum

of _Fourteen_ _Pounds_ _Shillings_

and _Three_ _Pence, being_ donation ~~subscription~~ _for One Year_

as _proceeds of Gitano Concert_ _for the above Branch of_

THE BRITISH RED CROSS SOCIETY.

£ 14 : — : 3

Isabel Blumer

Honorary Secretary, or Treasurer.

A Red Cross event paying-in slip.

Empire Welcome Club at St Chad's Schoolrooms (the use of which during 1917–18 is remembered on a plaque set high on the south wall), while from January 1915, the newly built Carnegie Free Lending Library, on the Green, became a Welcome Club for soldiers and sailors. Other reading and games rooms were provided at the Friends of the Soldiers Club, the Stafford Wounded Soldier's Institute, the Discharged Soldiers and Sailors Club, the School Room at the Wesleyan Church, the Siemens Brothers' sporting facilities and Bostock's Pavilion, to name but a few.

Regular free concerts were held for the troops, while there was a plethora of fundraising events. The first of these were staged in 1914 in aid of Belgian refugees and the Red Cross. One of the many volunteer concert parties that toured the area was that established by Hixon farmer Wilmot Martin, who became known as the 'Staffordshire Harry Lauder'. His inspiration, the real Harry Lauder Pipe Band, composed largely of servicemen, had visited Stafford on 7 June 1915, towards the end of a fundraising tour of sixty towns, which had begun in January of that year.

Many of the town's factories had war savings groups which collected for their own adopted charities as well as supporting national campaigns. The town's efforts were orchestrated by the Stafford War Savings Committee.

While the role of the Home Front is covered in part within these pages, the main focus remains the local soldiers, sailors and airmen who fought during the Great War.

The stories of a number of individuals are recorded in depth and may be seen as representative of thousands more, many of which have been lost to history.

While many Staffordians were gassed or wounded several times over and survived the war, around 1,165 were killed in action or died of wounds or as a direct result of military service. The names of the dead are recorded on the Corporation War Memorial and elsewhere within the town. A full list was published by the author under the pen-name of John Quintaine in 2001, while their memories are preserved by the Commonwealth War Graves Commission. For the sake of posterity, the names and service details of the men not recorded on the Corporation War Memorial are remembered here.

This volume is intended as a tribute to all who served their country in what was dubbed 'the war to end all wars'.

CHAPTER 1

The War on the Home Front

❖

On learning of the declaration of hostilities Staffordians from all walks of life came forward to contribute actively to the war effort. This was reflected in the plethora of volunteer groups that quickly emerged.

The Volunteer Training Corps

The first of these units, established by 15 August, was the locally inspired Civic Corps (re-named the Volunteer Training Corps from 1 December 1914), later commanded by Lord Stafford. The Corps' role was initially to assist with recruitment drives. They ran their own munitions shop and rifle range, which helped to foster marksmen needed in the services.

Men of service age who did not volunteer for active service risked being accused of being 'shirkers'. Across the country men were pressured into the forces, and those who were believed to be trying to avoid their 'duty' were presented with white feathers, an accusation of cowardice. In September 1915 the *Staffordshire Chronicle* reported:

> Strict limits are being put on those who wear war workers and other badges. If a man is seen wearing a Volunteer Training Corps badge he has been proved either under or over military age, or unfit for military service.
>
> Every man you meet should be either in khaki, wearing an official war workers badge, a Volunteer Training Corps badge, or a Special Constable's badge.

The article added a warning note: 'Wearing unauthorized badges may mean incurring heavy penalties, and men of military age should take serious warning.'

The Stafford Volunteer Battalion

The drive for volunteers for the pseudo-military units continued throughout the war and Staffordians were rarely found wanting. However, the momentum could not always be maintained and, very late on in the war, on 9 March 1918, the *Staffordshire*

Chronicle carried an appeal by the mayor of Stafford for more men to come forward to support a unit known as the Stafford Volunteer Battalion. Stafford was apparently significantly short of its anticipated complement of 250 men. The feature noted that the county had four Infantry Volunteer Battalions at Stoke, Walsall, Wolverhampton and Stafford. The mayor was reported as saying that if the shortfall was not made up, then: 'The Commanding Officer would be under the painful necessity of reporting to Field Marshal Lord French that the people of Stafford and district were not prepared to resist an armed invasion of this country by the Germans.' The terms of service in the Home Defence unit were said not to be onerous: 'A man upon joining puts in 14 drills of one hour each per month, or two more drills might be performed on the same day. After being passed as efficient, which 99 per cent of the men could do in two months, the number of drills was reduced to 30 in three months, a very valuable concession.'

The Cadet Corps
Field Marshal Lord Kitchener predicted a three-year war. If the early rate of attrition experienced in 1914 was to continue, then the military would require a vast pool of the country's youth to reinforce and maintain the army at full strength.

Stafford had a thriving Cadet Corps. This was formed in April 1915, and was for 15 to 18-year-old boys. From 12 June it became attached to the 6th Battalion, North Staffordshire Regiment and was known as the Territorial Cadet Corps. With two companies, the Corps, which met at Corporation Street School, had 125 cadets in its ranks by September 1915.

The Cadets received military instruction under Captain Kidder and wore khaki military style uniforms. The boys underwent drill and made route marches carrying 28lb backpacks, building up their fitness levels, and undertook battle training at Hopton Heath and Stafford Castle.

Twice a year members of the Corps were assessed by a regimental sergeant major from the 6th Battalion, North Staffordshire Regiment. He selected individuals who could be fast-tracked into the services. The boys received an official letter from the War Department six months before their 18th birthday, giving them an appointment with a health inspector at a regimental centre. Those who were passed as A1 immediately received a call-up for military service.

The *Staffordshire Chronicle* of 19 February 1916 reported that a joint parade of the Stafford and King Edward VI Grammar School Cadets was held in the Market Square before both units marched to the Brocton Camp for a demonstration of the use of Mills bombs:

> On arrival at the camp the Cadets entered the trench system, and a most interesting demonstration as to the value of bombs was given to the Cadets, this practical demonstration being accompanied with the explosion of many of the bombs now being used at the Front.

The demonstration also included the blowing up of a railway line, the bursting of mines, and the breaking down of barricades between trenches, all by the means of high explosives.

After the bombing demonstration was over, Captain Janion and Lieutenant Dexter personally accompanied the Cadets through the trenches, explaining how they were dug, and the reasons for their formation, and the use of the various dug-outs, communications trenches etc.

One former cadet, Percy Smith, recalled the demonstration: 'One was a hand-held grenade, from which you had to withdraw the pin, and then throw it. The other was one that you placed in a trench catapult.'

The *Staffordshire Chronicle* of 15 August 1918 reported that the Cadet Movement in the county proposed that the County Volunteer Regiments should be re-designated the 1st or 2nd Volunteer Battalions of the North or South Staffordshire Regiments, as the case might be (instead of being referred to as the 1st, 2nd, 3rd or 4th Battalions of the Staffordshire Volunteer Regiments). Under the existing format 'A' detachment of the 2nd Battalion met at Stafford's Newport Road Drill Hall.

The Volunteer and other Corps

Another, quite separate, organization was the Volunteer Corps. This eventually comprised three battalions: the North Staffordshire (Stoke), the Mid-Staffordshire (Stafford) and the South Staffordshire (Wolverhampton) Volunteer Corps. There were two local companies: No. 1 (Stafford) Company Mid-Staffordshire Volunteers was composed of 18–30-year-olds, while No. 2 (Stafford) Company was made up of 30–55-year-olds.

Other organizations mentioned in the press included the West Stafford Corps, which had a rifle range at Kingston Hill and was served by a munitions factory on Lloyd Street, and the Staffordshire Volunteer Regiment. Filling the void left by the posting overseas of the Territorials was the Stafford Volunteer Training Corps. This unit was essentially a forerunner of the Home Guard. They had an indoor range at Backwalls.

Fundraising for the War Effort

The country had gone to war to uphold the neutrality of Belgium. Consequently the papers were full of stories of atrocities committed against Belgian civilians. One of the town's earliest fundraising campaigns was for the relief of the Belgian refugees, some of whom were re-housed in Broad Street in late 1914: 'Hospitality is being extended to seven Belgian refugees in Stafford. Large numbers of Belgian subjects, driven from their homes by the ruthless Germans, whose inhumanity to unoffending people is a standing disgrace to civilization.' By April 1915, the Stafford Refugee Committee had housed fifty-eight Belgian citizens, mainly along the Newport Road.

Meanwhile, on 7 August 1914, Her Royal Highness the Princess of Wales made an urgent appeal in *The Times* for a national fund to provide financial support to the dependants of Reservists who were called up. This effectively launched the first nationwide appeal and the people of Stafford were quick to join the fundraising efforts, co-ordinated by the town's mayor. Public support for the troops was overwhelming and by midnight the Palace had received £250,000. Within a week what became known as the National Relief Fund had reached £1,000,000 (a staggering amount of money, when you consider that £1 in 1914 is the equivalent of about £60 today).

Naturally, the troops in training and at the front were high on the agenda. When it came to fundraising on their behalf, money and comforts were forwarded via official channels. In Stafford fundraising was carried out by numerous individuals and groups. One early example was the Castle Tavern's proprietor who asked his regulars for tobacco and cigarettes which were distributed among Stafford men serving overseas. In advance of Christmas 1914, local bakers provided cakes and Christmas puddings for the troops.

There were frequent appeals in the press for families to supply details of men who might welcome a parcel. Batches were sent to the 6th (Stafford) Staffordshire Battery, as well as to local men serving in the 1/6th and 2/5th Battalions of the North Staffordshire Regiment and the Staffordshire Yeomanry; all were still at that time on home soil.

Fundraising continued throughout the war, and when there wasn't a particular national campaign to support, Staffordians came up with their own ideas for good causes. Meanwhile, with troops convalescing or under training locally, there were always opportunities to provide home comforts, leading to weekly articles in the press headed 'Entertainment for the Wounded' or 'Soldiers Entertained'. One such event was reported in the *Stafford Newsletter* of 20 November 1915, and it may be seen as representative of the hundreds held in and about the town during the hostilities:

> The Baptist Church at Stafford held a Tea Morning for soldiers, 150 of whom attended, enjoying refreshments and entertainment. The get together was organised by ladies of the Baptist Church and the refreshments provided at cost.
> A concert was to be held at the Borough Hall in aid of wounded Belgian soldiers. The event was sponsored by the Mayor of Stafford, while the majority of the performers were themselves Belgian.

Fundraising usually took the form of auctions, tea mornings, dances, concerts and jumble sales. Occasionally, however, war-related artefacts formed part of an exhibition which the curious paid to view. In September 1916, the press carried the following story: 'The original letter written by Lord Kitchener, making his historic appeal to the nation for a million men for the British Army, will shortly be on view in Stafford, proceeds to the Red Cross Fund. Also on display were curiosities from the battlefields loaned by locals.'

War Relief Funds
Stafford's factory workers were prominent in raising money for war charities, setting

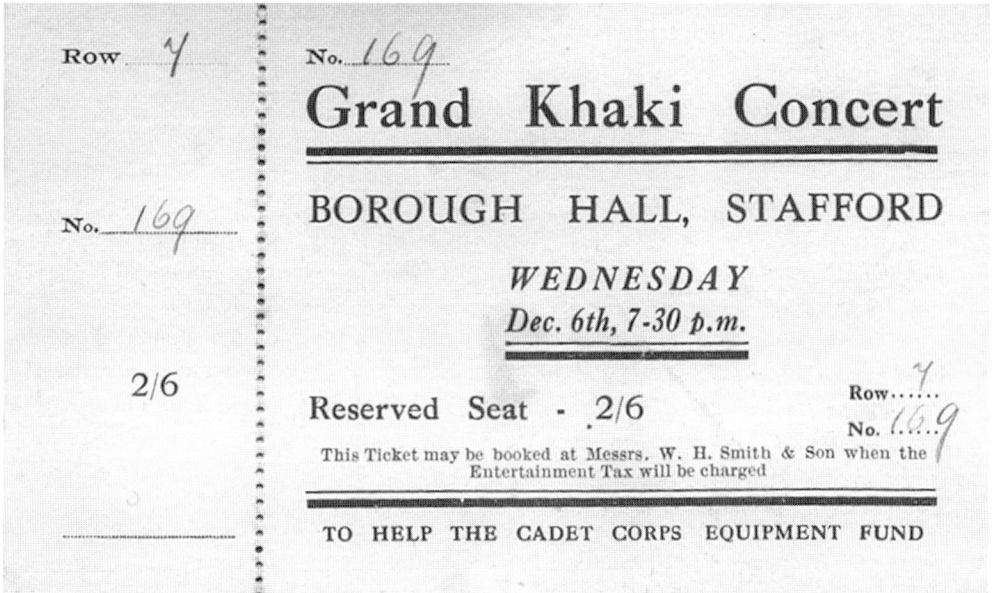

Row 4   No. 169

Grand Khaki Concert

No. 169

BOROUGH HALL, STAFFORD

WEDNESDAY
Dec. 6th, 7-30 p.m.

2/6

Reserved Seat - 2/6

Row......4

No. 169

This Ticket may be booked at Messrs. W. H. Smith & Son when the
Entertainment Tax will be charged

TO HELP THE CADET CORPS EQUIPMENT FUND

A concert ticket for a Grand Khaki Concert held on Wednesday, 6 December 1916.

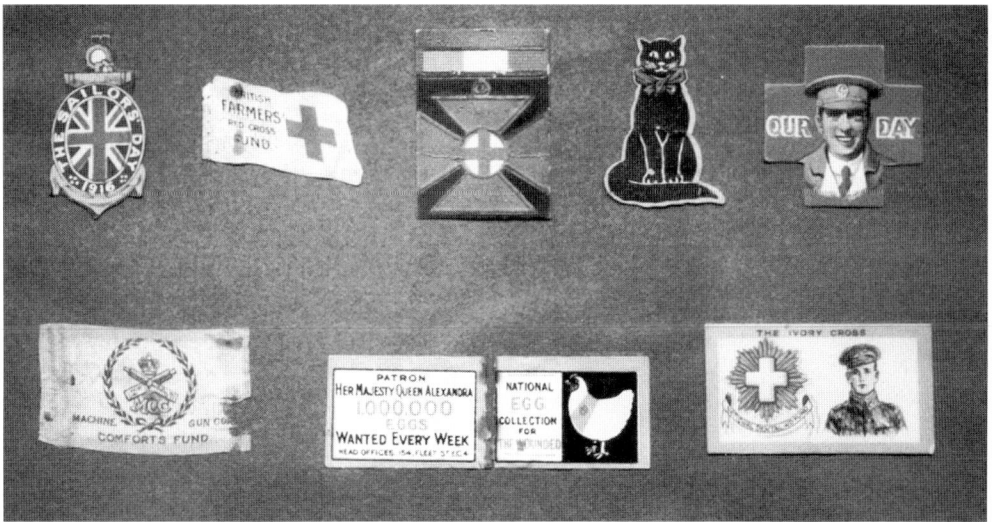

A selection of flag day pins.

up and administering their own funds. Most notable among these were the Dormans'
War Relief Fund, the Bostock's War Relief Fund and that of Siemens Brothers. This
did not stop their workforces from collecting for their own adopted charities and
contributing to the national campaigns.

By January 1916, Edwin Bostock & Co., boot and shoe manufacturers (later Lotus
Shoes), employees had contributed nearly £500 to the National Relief Fund, with a
further £400-plus to the Red Cross, Hospital Fund, Allied National Relief and other

war funds. The company had put £200 aside to give assistance to workers invalided out of the services who were no longer able to provide for their families.

Special flag days were held throughout the war. These raised money for all types of military and other charities. The press fostered friendly competition between factories or streets to see who could raise the most.

War Savings Groups

While fundraising brought in hundreds of thousands of pounds for charitable work, another source of revenue for the war effort came from war bonds, which could be redeemed for a modest profit to the investor once they matured.

The sale of war bonds and certificates was a vital part of the government's fundraising drive. Factory workers were encouraged to invest part of their wages in the government bonds, all of the town's bigger establishments taking part in the scheme. There were many drives throughout the war, one following close on the heels of the last, but all received a warm reception with the people of Stafford hitting their targets.

Stafford Aeroplane (Tank) Week was part of a national campaign held between 4 and 9 March 1918. The idea was to feature a British Mark IV tank, still something of

An Aeroplane (Tank) Week meeting in the Market Square.

SOUVENIR EDITION.

THE BOOM-WEEK BUZZER

Edited by A. TANQUE, Jun., W.S.

| No. 1 (and only). | STAFFORD, MARCH 16, 1918. | PRICE ONE PENNY. |

STAFFORD'S AEROPLANE TANK WEEK.

SCENE AT THE OPENING CEREMONY.

Photo—   Pearce, Stafford.

After visiting the "TANK" and purchasing your War Certificates, call at

BROOKFIELDS
(Messrs. Smith & Tomkinson),

Greengate, Stafford.

GENTS' and BOYS'
UNDERWEAR & OUTFITTING.

Ladies' and Gents'
Raincoats a speciality

Lotus, Delta & "K" Boots & Shoes.
"Standard" Boots now in stock.

Previous to Stocktaking

Messrs. W. H. Smith & Son
are clearing a large amount of
Stationery at less than Pre-
War Prices.

Now is the time to purchase
note paper and envelopes.

Bargains in all Departments.

W. H. Smith & Son,

GREENGATE, STAFFORD,

Where War Savings Certificates
may be purchased.

OUR BUZZERETTE.

Things have got to buzz, to hum, to fly, in Stafford this week.

Like the little busybee (when it is free from D.O.W.), we have to improve each shining hour. We have to gather nectar from the opening flowers of War Bonds and War Savings Certificates. By the same operation we store up honey for the nation.

What is it we are asked to do? Provide 27 Aeroplanes at a cost of £67,500!

Prodigious! you will say. It is not impossible. But there must be a jolly lot of buzzing about. When you get tired of buzzing you must begin again, and keep it up.

It will have to be a big buzz. Something like that of Siemens' buzzer—equally penetrating, but of longer duration.

Talk alone is no use. Actions, determination, a buzzing disposition, self-interest, national interest will "boom" "Boom Week."

Let there be no redundant chatter. Scoot off to places where War Bonds are in bond. And take the shortest cut.

Do not wait and think. Go at once and invest, and then send in a coupon.

Pack up your margarine troubles in the drawer of the kitchen dresser and
Fly! Fly!! Fly!!!
to the nearest Bank or Shop. The longer the queue there the better.

Our Airmen want 27 Royal Staffordia Aeroplanes with which to fly over Northern France and elsewhere. And when that happens, the Germans will fly—away.

So Buzz around! If you cannot fly to the Bond Booth, walk. If you cannot walk, take a Tank. But get there.   —W. G.

THE SHOPS SCHEME.
THE TRADER'S OPPORTUNITY.

The Country needs the help of every Shop-keeper. The majority of Shopkeepers value what the fighting men have done for them and are anxious to render their quota of "personal service" in the great cause in which we are bending our national energies.

This is made easy for them. Hitherto the privilege of selling War Savings Certificates has been limited to the Post-offices, Banks, and War Savings Associations. Now Stafford Shop-keepers have an opportunity of becoming "Official Agents" for the sale of the same securities to their customers and the public.

Already over 5,000 shopkeepers and licence-holders have made application to the National War Savings Committee to become "Official Agents." The results of this scheme will probably astonish those who have not realized the possibilities.

The time will come when it will be a distinction for a Shopkeeper to refer to the fact that he was one of those appointed an "Official Agent" of His Majesty's Treasury for the sale of War Savings Certificates or for the sale of the "Easy-to-Buy" £5 War Bonds.

"I congratulate you on your enterprise in producing the 'Buzzer,'" writes Mr. Wareham Smith, Hon. Organizer, Business Men's Week.

No increase in Price owing to shortage of Paper.

The programme for Aeroplane (Tank) Week.

a novelty, to help raise money for the war effort, but not necessarily to purchase tanks, as the title implied.

Stafford's goal was set at twenty-seven aeroplanes (each of which cost £2,500) with an overall target of £67,500, or £2 10s. per head. As usual the people of Stafford

An Aeroplane Week endorsement stamp.

were not found wanting and exceeded their target and raised over £145,000. The *Staffordshire Chronicle* noted: 'This week all classes in the town who have a spark of patriotism in their constitution have come forward to contribute the money they could spare for the purpose, as the street motto puts it of "saving those who are saving them." They have "stumped up" well.' The editorial explained how during the evenings throughout the week there had been a slide-show in the Market Square 'for the most part treating of aeroplanes and their work in the war'.

The National Savings Committee had access to only eight tanks (six of which were: 113 'Julian', 119 'Old Bill', 130 'Nelson', 137 'Drake', 141 'Egbert' and 142 'Iron Ration') and these toured the country during 1917–18. The tanks were already committed elsewhere and so 'an excellent imitation of one of these modern novelties of warfare' was manufactured by Siemens Brothers Electrical Engineering Works. This was displayed in the Market Square throughout the period of the bond drive. All of the war bonds and war savings certificates purchased during the week were impressed with a special commemorative stamp of a Bleriot-type monoplane.

In addition, in keeping with the town's goal to supply the RAF with new aircraft, W.H. Dorman & Co. Ltd arranged for an aeroplane to be displayed in the Market Square, while Royal Flying Corps (RFC) photographs were exhibited at the Borough Hall on the Tuesday, along with a searchlight and other military hardware.

The *Staffordshire Chronicle* of 2 March 1918 reported:

The first day's business amounted to £11,275. The Post Office authorities had established an office in the Corn Exchange at the Shire Hall, and certificates have been on sale at tradesmen's shops and licensed houses during the week.

On Tuesday evening a large audience assembled in the Borough Hall. A lantern lecture on the history and work of the aeroplane was given by Sergeant Chateris, of the New Zealand Rifles.

The first two days of the drive had raised a total of £31,434. During the lecture given on Tuesday evening Dormans' management 'issued a challenge to the workpeople of other concerns in the town, including the boot operatives, to raise a larger sum in War Saving Certificates (in proportion to the number employed) than any other works in the town'.

Crowds gathered in the Market Square on Wednesday, when the mayoress, Mrs Young, addressed the ladies present. Mr Young, also present, revealed that he had laid down the challenge to the Mayor of Newcastle, stating that 'Stafford would do better than Newcastle'. One of the guest speakers at the rally was 'Ray Bee, the holder of the DCM and the French War Cross, [who] made a spirited appeal on behalf of "the boys at the Front." The day's events (Wednesday) and activities raised a further £9,459.' The report continued:

> On Thursday evening further addresses were delivered from the summit of the 'Tank.' The total received at the close of business for the day was £51,143.
>
> We understand that Messers Dormans employees had, up to yesterday, subscribed about £6,000 and that Messers Bostock's employees had contributed £5,000. Messers Siemens' employees are also going strong, the firm have themselves subscribed £50,000 during the week [across their various factories, not just in Stafford].
>
> Meanwhile, Edwin Bostock & Co. offered ten £5 war bonds and 200 £1 war savings certificates in a lottery, tickets being issued with every certificate sold. 'The returns from different schools in the town show that a sum of £5,750 has been contributed; but the returns have not all been received, and it is expected that over £6,000 will be subscribed.'

The Daily Return:

Monday	£11,275
Tuesday	£20,159
Wednesday	£9,459
Thursday	£10,251
Friday (5 o'clock)	£8,700
Total	**£59,844**

An Edwin Bostock & Co. plaque (in the name of Lotus Shoes Ltd).

As a footnote to this and the many war bond campaigns carried out in the county town, after the war it was announced that Stafford was to be one of the towns 'awarded' a tank in recognition of its fundraising. Like many other towns, Stafford does not appear to have ever received its reward.

Comforts for the Troops

Women and children played a key role in the volunteer sector. Local women led a number of funds, including the Stafford District Comfort Fund, the Stafford Ladies' Comfort Pool, the Berkswich Women's War Association and the League of Honour. Assisted by local schoolchildren, they collected reading material, clothing, cigarettes etc. for the troops, POWs and for those invalided out of the services. Groups worked together to knit woollen mittens, scarves and balaclavas, which were collected and sent off to troops.

All of the local factories regularly collected cigarettes, chocolate, clothing, books and other items to send to the troops at the front and to those held as POWs, the press regularly announcing their safe delivery to the troops.

Women's Units

The war was a massive drain on the nation's resources, particularly its workforce. In order to combat the effect of the loss of often skilled industrial and agricultural labour, women were encouraged to take on jobs that for decades had been the male preserve. These included roles in heavy industry and farming. Over 950,000 women undertook dangerous work in the munitions factories, many of which were in Stafford. This figure was eclipsed by the number involved in agriculture.

The *Staffordshire Chronicle* of 10 April 1915 carried the following announcement:

The scheme which has been devised by the Board of Agriculture has met with a ready response in the Midlands from women who are prepared to take the opportunity of making themselves useful on farms in order to help make up for the very serious shortage of workers on farms all over the country. The first course of instruction which has been arranged by the Harper Adams Agricultural College commenced on Wednesday.

All the women are resident in the college, and the work milking, dairy-work, feeding stock, rearing caves and pigs, field-work, and poultry.

The first who have entered the course look a very efficient and capable set of women who should put the information they acquire at the college to useful account.

The need to replace the agricultural workers lost to the services eventually spawned a number of organizations: the Women's Forage Corps (WFC), established in 1917 to produce forage for horses, the Women's Land Army (WLA), the Women's National Land Service Corps (WNLSC) and the Women's Legion (WL), all of which had an agricultural focus.

The WLA was formed in 1917 to meet an urgent need to replace the tens of thousands of farm labourers who had been conscripted. It has been said that at the time Britain only had provisions for three weeks and was potentially on the verge of starvation.

An advert appeared in the *Staffordshire Chronicle* of 4 May 1918:

Women's Land Army. Women of Britain! The nation's Food Supply depends

*A Land Army
advertisement.*

on You! Enrol today in the Women's Land Army, and help to secure food for
all. Women's Land Army Appeal for 30,000 women will be held in the Borough
Hall, Stafford, on Wednesday, 8 May at 8pm.

Women had a major part to play in uniform too. A number of women's
organizations operated directly alongside the services, sometimes within shelling range
of the enemy. These included the First Aid Nursing Yeomanry (FANY), which assisted
the RAMC and had members serving in France from October 1914. Seventeen
members of the FANY earned the Military Medal for gallantry under fire.

Other women's organizations existed to support the war effort. The Volunteer Aid
Detachment (VAD) ferried the wounded and worked in hospitals, both in Great Britain
and overseas. The Women's Auxiliary Army Corps (WAAC) was established in 1917
and its 57,000 members carried out a variety of military ancillary roles, 6,000 of them
seeing service in France. Similarly, the Women's Royal Air Force (WRAF) and
Women's Royal Naval Service (WRNS) performed an ancillary role for the air and
naval forces.

Stafford's Industry and War Work

By 1914, the Siemens Brothers Electrical Engineering Works was the single largest employer in the county town. Naturally as a German company there were several German nationals among the senior managers and foremen working at the factory. A number of German Reservists from the works were interned in York for the duration of the war.

The *Staffordshire Chronicle* of 8 August 1914 reported that the company's works, which had been closed during the previous week for annual holiday leave, would reopen as usual on Monday (the 10th). It was further noted that a number of Germans were employed by the company, including Mr E.O. Keiffer, general manager, and Mr Donati. In a potentially damaging blow to the factory Mr Keiffer, a lieutenant in the German reserves, had left on Tuesday, 4 August to rejoin his regiment.

There was initially some controversy surrounding the firm, particularly as they manufactured instruments for Royal Navy vessels. Mr Keiffer had overseen the company's important Admiralty contract and consequently there were concerns raised that this might have been put in doubt.

An open letter, addressed to The Right Honourable Winston Churchill, First Lord of the Admiralty, was published in the *Staffordshire Chronicle* of 5 September, giving assurances that the Admiralty work would not be compromised and that the non-naturalized German managers and members of the workforce were no longer working in the factory.

The Siemens Brothers' works, like other businesses within the town, faced another pressing issue – a drain on its skilled workforce. During the first fortnight of the war over 300 workers had enlisted. These losses must have damaged production figures, something that was reflected across the country. Consequently, measures were later taken to make some roles 'reserved occupations'. This meant that workers in these jobs would only be allowed to enlist under very special circumstances.

Agriculture

The German fleet was deployed to blockade Great Britain and deny the country food and munitions. Agricultural production was therefore just as important as the manufacture of arms and ammunition. Local farmers formed meat, poultry, egg and vegetable production committees, regulating the collection and distribution of produce. While farmers supported many local charities, collectively they formed the British Farmers' Red Cross Fund.

Rationing

Rationing was introduced on 1 January 1918, with ration books being issued from 15 July of that year. The Stafford Food Control Committee, following government guidelines, brought in regulations governing the sale and stockpiling of many foodstuffs. From 25 February tea was officially rationed to 1¼oz and butter or margarine to 4oz (per person, per week). Everyone had to be registered with a single butcher and had a weekly allowance of 1s. 3d. worth of meat.

In 1917 the game laws were suspended, meaning that tenant farmers could shoot any game on their land. While wild rabbits and other game were off ration, the committee heard a number of cases of over-charging. Unfortunately, the public were reluctant to make their complaints official as they were registered to individual butchers and grocers. One case which did go before the committee fell at the first hurdle because the evidence (i.e. the rabbit) had been eaten.

Horses

The British Army relied heavily on horses for transportation as well as for their cavalry and artillery units (according to the *War Book* 200,000 horses would be required on mobilization). Because of the importance of horses to the country's economy a regular census of stock was taken. The government knew how many of every class and age of horse there were, and in whose ownership. Notices went up in and around the town 'impressing horses' for military service. Locally, the requisitioning of both work-horses and thoroughbreds for the Stafford Battery, the Staffordshire Yeomanry and other military units meant that no one's stables were spared. It was reported that 'in one case the stables of a prominent gentleman, who resides a mile or two from Stafford, were depleted of every animal, with the exception of a pony and an aged horse'.

The *Staffordshire Chronicle* of 8 August 1914 reported that horses were rounded up and temporarily paddocked on the Grammar School field. Here they were branded with the government stamp, before being put through their paces and assessed: the better quality horses being selected as 'mounts', the remaining serving as beasts of burden, hauling wagons, various types of transport and field-guns. As many as 6 million saw service during the war. Very few of those donated or requisitioned for the war effort ever returned to Great Britain.

Lord Sandon, of the Stafford Battery, took his own horse, Christ Church, to war. In pre-echoes of the story behind the film *War Horse*, Lord Sandon wrote a letter to *The Times* in February 1934, shortly after Christ Church's death (on 15 December 1933), extolling the virtues of his mount. He remarked that while other horses panicked when under fire, Christ Church remained calm. On one occasion a field gun became bogged down and the gun crew was under fire. Lord Sandon recalled how his horse 'was standing very still with head erect and ears cocked, listening to the bullets whining all around him'. His mount was not, however, without faults. In his letter, Lord Sandon recollected that he used to eat anything that came within reach, while keeping its master on his toes through the habit of unseating him without apparent reason. Christ Church was buried in the grounds of Sandon Hall, his head, tail and hooves being preserved in the entrance to the hall.

CHAPTER 2

The British Expeditionary Force, 1914

❖

Across Europe, on both sides of the conflict, mobilization evoked great waves of almost euphoric patriotism, with each nation believing that they were following a just and noble cause. Along what was to become the Western Front, seventy-two German divisions led the assault on sixty-eight French. Meanwhile, between 12 and 17 August, the British Expeditionary Force (BEF) of 80,000 Regular soldiers and Reservists (half the entire British Army) landed at Rouen, Boulogne and Le Havre and were transported to the Le Cateau–Maubeuge area. To his credit, Lord Kitchener had seriously questioned such an advanced deployment of the whole of the BEF, but had been over-ruled.

In response to the German attack through Belgium, the French launched an all-out assault to recapture Alsace-Lorraine, territory lost during the forty-four-day Franco-Prussian War of 1870. Their advance followed the French Plan XVII, which had been anticipated by the enemy and played directly into their hands. Under the command of General von Kluck, the German 1st and 2nd Armies, following the Von Schleiffen Plan, swept all ahead of them in a wide arc through neutral Belgium, to strike at the rear of the French Army. This became the catalyst for a widespread retreat which threatened to outflank the BEF, which was forced to withdraw from positions they might otherwise have held.

In his Order of the Day, 9 August 1914, the German Kaiser, whose conscript army numbered some 5 million men, had commanded: 'It is my Royal and Imperial Command that you concentrate your energies, for the immediate present upon one single purpose, to exterminate first the treacherous English; walk over General French's Contemptible Little Army.' Meanwhile, with the BEF in their advanced position and ready to implement Plan XVII, Sir John French's Order of the Day, issued on 20 August, was equally robust in tone:

Our cause is just. We are called upon to fight beside our gallant allies in France and Belgium in no war of arrogance, but to uphold our nation's honour, independence and freedom. We have violated no neutrality, nor have we been false to any treaties. We enter upon this conflict with the clearest consciousness that we are fighting for right and honour.

Using this trust in the righteousness of our cause, pride in the glory of our military traditions, and belief in the efficiency of our arm, we go forward together to do or die for GOD – KING – AND COUNTRY.

The BEF's first major conflict came three days later at Mons. Here the comparatively small force fought a heroic defensive action before being obliged to begin a tactical withdrawal. A temporary halt was made at Le Cateau where, on 26 August, a rearguard action was mounted by the British II Corps. This gained valuable time for the remainder of the BEF to regroup.

The press remained bullish, despite the loss of ground and men. On 30 August *The Times* wrote:

BROKEN BRITISH REGIMENTS BATTLING AGAINST ODDS

Forced backwards and ever backwards by the sheer unconquerable mass of numbers. Our losses are very great. I have seen the broken bits of many regiments. To sum up, the first great German effort has succeeded. We have to face the fact that the BEF which bore the great weight of the blow has suffered terrible losses and requires immediate and immense reinforcement.

The BEF has won in deed imperishable glory, but it needs men and yet more men. We want reinforcements and we want them now.

The French, who with their Reservists had an army of 3.5 million men, withdrew to the River Marne, from where a counter-attack was launched. There then followed the Battle of Aisne, which was fought between 12 and 15 September, the enemy retiring only to hold high ground, from where they could easily halt a British counter-offensive. In October and November, the Germans launched an attack in the Ypres Sector where they had seen a weakness in the defences. The *Staffordshire Chronicle* later (9 January 1915) reported one of the town's earliest fatalities, which occurred during the Battle of Ypres: 'There was during the week a rumour in the town that Mrs. Moore of [8] Backwalls South, had received a postcard informing her of the death of her son.' Unfortunately, the rumour was correct, as Corporal Henry Moore, 3rd Battalion, Worcestershire Regiment was killed in action near Bethune on 27 October 1914.

On 31 October, the temporary British HQ at Hooge was shelled, with the loss of a number of key commanders. With the chain of command broken, the British front was only saved by the bravery of the infantrymen who fought to the last man, knowing that they were the final line of defence.

The 2nd Royal Worcester Regiment made a bayonet charge over open ground at Gheluvelt, pushing back a far superior German force. This engagement was typical of the dogged determination of the ordinary Tommy, who fought heroically against tremendous odds. Field Marshal French later wrote of the Battle of Ypres: 'No more than one thin and straggling line of tired-out British soldiers stood between the Empire and its partial ruin as an independent first-class Power. When all has been said, it was their courage and endurance which spoke the last word.'

By the end of November 1914, the BEF, which by then had been reinforced by Reservists and the first of the new recruits, had suffered 89,864 casualties, in what H.G. Wells had already coined 'The war to end all wars'. These losses, which would soon be eclipsed by such battles as the Somme and Passchendaele, represented the near destruction of the best trained, best equipped and best organized army that had ever left British shores. Typical of the Regular units was the 1st (Guards) Brigade, which formed a part of the 1st Division. It had landed in France with 4,500 men, but by 12 November (and despite reinforcement) could only muster 473 officers and men:

	Officers	Other Ranks
1st Battalion Scots Guards	1	69
1st Battalion Black Watch	1	109
1st Cameron Highlanders	3	140
1st Coldstream Guards	0	150

Among the first British regiments to have been heavily engaged were the Coldstream Guards. The 1st Battalion formed a part of 1st (Guards) Brigade, while the 2nd and 3rd Battalions were a part of 4th (Guards) Brigade.

Staffordians Private Alphonso Bird and Charles Churchill were two of the Regulars serving with the Coldstream Guards. During the initial advance they passed through a number of villages where they were given a hero's welcome, with locals offering them wine, cigarettes and food. In a letter home, Churchill explained that: 'anything we wanted we could have'.

A Coldstream Guards cap badge.

Arriving at Mons on the morning of Sunday, 23 August, Churchill's battalion was initially held in reserve. The troops could hear the sound of a distant battle as German artillery pounded villages in advance of their position. That evening, before they were able to be deployed, Churchill's company was ordered to cut down fences and remove barbed wire entanglements, clearing a path for retreating troops. Suddenly the mood changed as shells began exploding close by.

Soon Churchill's battalion joined the retreat, marching throughout the following day before taking shelter in an orchard. Here the men snatched 3 hours' sleep before being awoken by a sergeant who crept silently among them saying, in hushed tones: 'Get up lads, and don't make any noise.' The Germans were hot on their heels and there wasn't a moment to lose. Charles Churchill explained that after only marching 3 miles, shells began falling to the rear of their column, landing short despite the gunners adjusting their aim: 'We went as fast as our legs could carry us until three o'clock in the afternoon when we arrived at Landrecies, where we got into a hole.'

It was at Landrecies where the 2nd and 3rd Battalions fought a heroic rear-guard action during 25/26 August. The men, who had halted in the drill square of an old French cavalry barracks, were allowed only a moment's respite before they were ordered to 'Stand To', when the enemy was sighted on the approaches to the town. One company was sent forward to establish a perimeter defence. They had about 1½ hours to 'dig in' and prepare their positions.

Churchill's company was stationed on the crest of the hill, and as the open ground was only about 50ft wide the men were arranged in a 'V' shape, 'by that means it was possible to get a firing line of 150 men, and it was done to deceive the enemy with regard to the strength of the British forces'. The enemy, who were several thousand strong, was only about 400yd away, and the Guardsmen inevitably began to take casualties.

Churchill's company was held in reserve behind the firing line during the first 2 hours of the engagement. He later described how two Maxim machine guns were set up 'occupying a spot similar to the entrance to Stafford at Rising Brook'.

Positioned towards the middle of the firing line, Charles Churchill described the scene:

We kept up a steady fire from ten o'clock that night till three the following morning. I didn't expect to get out of it alive, but I was lucky and they didn't get me, despite the gun-fire and heavy shelling. It was so intense that we were unable to bring up reinforcements. By this time the enemy had closed to within 200 yards.

With the Coldstream Guards' position under a terrific fire, a runner was sent to request artillery support and a Royal Field Artillery (RFA) team was brought up. The gun crew quietly manhandled their field gun into position, unseen by the enemy. Firing over their sights, the gunners' first round 'entered the muzzle of the German gun that had been causing havoc amongst the Coldstream Guards and blew it to pieces'. Their spirits lifted, the men around Churchill exclaimed 'Thank God for that!', and put up a rapid rifle fire which further weakened the enemy's resolve.

Despite outnumbering the Guardsmen, the Germans suffered heavy casualties in the attack. Churchill recalled how they had advanced against the British lines shouting 'Hock Kaiser!', only to be mowed down by the withering rifle fire. According to

Churchill's account, the Germans retired under the cover of darkness, allowing time for the whole British division to fall back from Landrecies unmolested. The Coldstream Guardsmen performed many acts of gallantry, with Lance Corporal George Wyatt winning the Victoria Cross.

Charles Churchill estimated that the British firing line had accounted for nearly 300 of the enemy, although the actual figure was reported as much lower: 'They were covered in their comrade's blood, and the lydite shells had turned them into yellow [coloured] men.' However, the return fire from the enemy had been so intense that, as Churchill explained, 'the men got part of their packs shot off their backs'.

The general retreat continued and the Guardsmen's next halt came outside a large town, where trenches were prepared in readiness for a further German onslaught. Instead they were ordered to retire 'under cover of darkness, marching night and day up until 27th [August] making about 38–40 miles a day, the enemy constantly shelling to our rear'.

Then a halt was ordered; it was time to make a stand, and on 1 September Churchill's battalion dug-in ready to repel an attack, the men being relieved of their greatcoats and packs. Charles Churchill's No. 4 Company was detailed for the rear-guard action at a vital crossroad in a forest through which the enemy was expected to pass. Churchill's account went on to say that another section of British troops was ambushed by German machine-gunners and virtually annihilated: 'The forest was practically surrounded by the enemy and there was only a small open space at the rear through which they almost crawled until an opportunity arose to make a run for it.'

For Churchill's battalion the next few days of the retreat were largely uneventful. On Sunday, 6 September, the first day of the Battle of the Marne, they reached Fonteroy. Here they made a stand against the enemy, thus allowing a general British offensive to be launched along the whole front. Churchill and his comrades were entrenched with the enemy guns in front of them and the British artillery behind: 'Once the artillery duel began it was almost impossible to make oneself heard in the trench, but the shells were not dropping within fifty yards, although we lost an officer.' The Germans, who wasted much ammunition, then retired, pursued by the British troops. Despite this small victory, the general retreat continued, but in a more orderly fashion: 'You could judge what would have been the fate of anything or anyone that had stood in their path.'

In the meantime the tables were turning and Churchill remembered that during the morning of 9 September the British troops advanced from 6am until 9.30am. On reaching the crest of a large hill, however, they entered a more exposed position and enemy shells began to fall in among the Guardsman. A shrapnel shell exploded in the middle of Churchill's platoon, killing four men and wounding five others. Only the officer and four men were left standing. Seriously wounded by shrapnel, which passed through his right lung, Churchill was stretchered to a field hospital. From there he was evacuated back to England. While still convalescing, Churchill visited his home town, where he was interviewed by the press, who later reported his story.

Grenadier Guardsmen march to the front, 1914.

The 1st Battalion, Coldstream Guards was engaged at Neuve Chapelle on 26 September when the Germans took the village. Private Alphonso Bird fought during the bitter two-day battle to try to retake lost trenches. Following the general retreat, Private Bird's battalion found itself at Gheluvelt, south-east of Ypres. The battalion's *War Diary* recorded:

> On 29 October 1914, at Gheluvelt, the 1st Battalion suffered such casualties that it had no officers left and only 80 men.
>
> An attack by the Germans of which notice was received was beaten off at 5.30am in dense mist but was successful further south at [a] crossroads east-south-east of Gheluvelt: the result being that the battalion trenches were almost immediately afterwards attacked from the right rear. A retirement appears to have been ordered and a small portion of the battalion re-formed covering a battery of Royal Field Artillery. At night the battalion was withdrawn and bivouacked in woods west of Gheluvelt in Brigade Reserve.

Despite putting up a stiff resistance, the battalion was forced to retreat or risk being cut off: 'Four days later, after reinforcement, it had once more been reduced to no officers and 120 men only.' These reinforcements would have included a number of Staffordians, members of what the press had already dubbed the 'Stafford Pals'. One of these volunteers, a private in the 13th Company, Coldstream Guards, had earlier written from Caterham while still under training. His letter was dated 18 October:

I was lucky enough to get placed in the quarters formerly occupied by the Warrant Officers, and am far better off than some of the poor fellows who are still sleeping ten to fourteen in a tent. There are about 9,000 fellows here. [I] should say about half have left good jobs to come here. There are good recreation rooms and coffee bars, schoolrooms etc. They have finished giving khaki uniforms out, and are now distributing blue ones out, with a blue hat the same shape as they used in South Africa. I think we shall be sent to the Front in about four months. A lot of Stafford pals are being shifted to Windsor on Tuesday [including] George and Sidney Horne and Harry Venables.

We shall be here at least six weeks, then off to Windsor.

Mons/Marne inscriptions (from the County War Memorial).

With the high casualty rate among the 1st Coldstream Guards it was inevitable that local men would figure among the dead and wounded. The following appeared on 9 January 1915 in the *Staffordshire Chronicle*, under the heading 'Casualties among Staffordians':

During the week various rumours have been in circulation as to casualties among the men from Stafford who joined the Coldstream Guards. One of them, that concerning the death of Private Harold Maylott [1st Company, 1st Battalion, Coldstream Guards, killed in action on 27 December], baker and confectioner, Gaolgate Street. Having received an official notification that his son had been killed on active service, the sympathy of the town will be extended in a full measure to Mr. and Mrs. Maylott in their bereavement, the shock of which will be softened by the knowledge that their son died as a hero in the service of his country.

There is also information that Private Ritchie, also of the Coldstream Guards, has been wounded, and there is corroboration of this in a postcard which has been received in Stafford by a friend. On which Private Ritchie states that he is 'wounded and a prisoner of war in Germany'. It is one of the military postcards, and contains no information beyond the fact that he is wounded and a prisoner.

Postcards have been received from the Front on which statements were made that other Stafford young men have been wounded, including Private Tom Rudge, son of Mr. W.B. Rudge, and Private Bert Lamplugh, but no official information has as yet been published.

It is also reported that Corporal Blakemore is missing, but the report cannot be authenticated [Lance Corporal Robert Frank Blakemore was killed in action on 22 December 1914, and has no known grave]. We announced last week that Private Howarth had been wounded, and that he had been transferred to a hospital at Aberdeen.

The BEF suffered terrible losses during the first three months of the war, but through their bravery and devotion to duty the troops had helped save the day. Staffordians had shared in the valour and the losses. There were quiet moments on the front; time for reflection. Grenadier Guardsman Norman Cliff, although not from Stafford, summed up what must have been the thoughts of many of his comrades when he wrote: 'In solitary silence I mused. Behind the opposite parapet was a German sentry standing in mud, as I was; feeling cold, as I did; perhaps scanning the bright company of stars, as I was; thinking what a folly war was, as I thought; his mind hovering over the family at home, as mine did.'

CHAPTER 3

Christmas, 1914

The German advance was finally halted at Ypres. By December the war in France and Flanders had become entrenched. On a local scale the fighting fell into a pattern of attack followed by counter-attack during which any modest gains were quickly reversed. Meanwhile, as winter set in, mud became solid while water turned into ice.

Local man Corporal Taylor, 1st Battalion, North Staffordshire Regiment, wrote home on 21 December:

> I often lie in my trench at night and think of you all at home, especially being Christmas. I do not think you can realise how we look out here. It's hard to find a clean patch on my clothes. They are all mud and slush. There are four of us in our trench, and [we] generally pass the time at night singing hymns and songs, and trying to harmonise them.
>
> In some places here the German trenches are only about 40 yards away, and you can hear them speaking quite plainly.

Although there had already been occasional unofficial ceasefires to bury the dead (as reported in a letter home written by Lieutenant Geoffrey Heinekey, 2nd Battalion, Westminster Rifles on 19 December), the conflict continued in all of its ferocity, as Corporal Taylor went on to explain: 'We must not show our heads above the trench. We have to get everything at night, such as water, rations, and wood for the fires, and then we have to be careful, as the Germans have search-lights and rockets [i.e. flares].'

A few days later the mood had lightened. By the early hours of Christmas Eve a frost had enveloped the open ground of no man's land. The day's activities, however, initially followed what had already become the routine. There was the occasional shelling, sniper fire and exchange of grenades. But what happened next was to become an iconic moment of the war.

In Germany 24 December is celebrated over the 25th. Traditionally, it is the day when families share a special meal and when 'Father Christmas' delivers his gifts. And so on Christmas Eve, as dusk approached, on certain sections of the Western Front

German soldiers began to sing carols and place Christmas trees and lanterns on the parapets in front of their trenches.

The British High Command – stationed 27 miles behind the front line – had already taken measures to maintain the impetus of the war over the festive period. Brigadier General G.T. Forrester-Walker, Chief of Staff to Sir Horace Smith-Dorrien of II Group, had issued a directive giving the reasoning behind a ban on any form of informal Christmas truce or fraternization: 'It discourages initiative in commanders, and destroys the offensive spirit in all ranks', adding: 'Friendly intercourse with the enemy, unofficial armistices and exchanges of tobacco and other comforts, however tempting and occasionally amusing they may be, are absolutely prohibited.' In addition, a warning was sent out that intelligence led the High Command to believe there would be an attack by the enemy over the festive season: 'It is thought possible the enemy may be contemplating an attack during Christmas or New Year. Special vigilance will be maintained during this period.'

Captain William 'Billy' Congreve, of Chartley Hall, serving on the staff of the 3rd Division later reported how the Germans' overtures were thwarted in his section of the line: 'We have issued strict orders to the men not to on any account allow a truce, as we have heard rumours that they will probably try to. The Germans did. They came over towards us singing. So we opened rapid fire on them, which is the only truce they deserve.'

Also serving on the Army Staff was William Congreve's father, General Walter Congreve, VC. In a letter home Walter revealed that he might have participated in the truce had he not felt that his uniform would have been too tempting a target. His letter read:

Darling Dear – As I cannot be with you all, the next best thing is to write to you.

We have had a 'seasonable weather' day – which means sharp frost & fog. I went to church with two of my battalions in an enormous factory room and after lunch took [myself] down to the N. Staffords in my old trenches at Rue du Bois, [with] Mother's gifts of toffee, sweets, cigarettes, pencils, handkerchiefs and writing paper.

There I found an extraordinary state of affairs – this am a German shouted out that they wanted a day's truce and would one [of the North Staffordshire Regiment] come out [to parley]. So, very cautiously, one of our men lifted himself above the parapet and saw a German doing the same.

Both got out [of their trenches], then more [followed] and finally all day long . . . they have been walking about together giving each other cigars and singing songs. Officers as well as men were out and the German Colonel himself was talking to one of our Captains.

One of the men said he had had a fine day of it and had 'smoked a cigar with the best shot in the German army, then not more than eighteen. They say he's killed more of our men than any other twelve [snipers put] together, but I know now where he shoots from and I hope we down him tomorrow.'

I hope devoutly they will – next door the two battalions opposite each other were shooting away all day and so I hear it was [different again] further north [where] the 1st Rifle Brigade [were] playing football with the Germans opposite them – [while the] next Regiments [along the front continued] shooting [at] each other.

I was invited to go and see the Germans myself, but refrained as I thought they might not be able to resist a General.

General Walter Congreve had visited the men of the 1st Battalion, North Staffordshire Regiment whose section of the front lay on exposed open ground; one trench being christened 'Dead-Man's-Alley'. The battalion had rejoined the line on the 11th and was resigned to a miserable Christmas in the freezing cold and under combat conditions.

Occupying the opposite trenches was a Saxon Regiment. It was said that this shared heritage, Saxon and Anglo-Saxon, contributed towards the temporary cessation of hostilities. Here the ceasefire had developed after nightfall on Christmas Eve when the Saxons were heard singing carols, which earned them a ripple of applause and, in return, a British carol.

A senior NCO brought events to the attention of his officer, Captain Raymond Linay Armes. He described the scene in a letter to his wife, which he began on Christmas Eve:

I have just been through one of the most extraordinary scenes imaginable. Tonight is Christmas Eve and I came up into the trenches this evening for my tour of duty. Firing was going on all the time. Then [at] about seven the firing stopped. I was in my dugout reading a paper, and the mail was being dished out. It was reported that the Germans had lighted their trenches up all along our Front. We started calling to one another Christmas wishes. I went out and they shouted 'no shooting' and then somehow the scene became a peaceful one. All our men got out of the trenches and sat on the parapet, and the Germans did the same, and they talked to one another in English and broken English. I got on the top of the trench and talked German and asked them to sing, and they did. Then our men sang quite well and each side clapped and cheered the other.

Then Pope [Second Lieutenant Vyvyan Vasasour Pope, later Lieutenant General V.V. Pope CBE, DSO, MC] and I walked across and held a conversation with the German officer in command. One of his men introduced us properly; he asked my name and then presented me to his officer. I gave the latter permission to bury some German dead who were lying in between us, and we agreed to have no shooting until 12 midnight tomorrow. We talked together, ten or more Germans gathered around. I was almost in their lines within a yard or

British and German (Saxon) officers and other ranks observing the Christmas Truce.

so. We saluted each other, he thanked me for permission to bury his dead, and we fixed up how many men were to do it.

There was, however, a warning which Armes passed on to the troops in the trenches adjacent to the North Staffordshire Regiment. They were opposed by Prussians who remained hostile.

Then we wished one another good night and a good night's rest, and a happy Xmas and parted with a salute. I got back to the trench. The Germans sang '*Die Wacth am Rhein*', it sounded well. Then our men sang quite well '*Christians Awake*', and with a 'good night' we all got back to our trenches. It was a curious scene, a lovely moonlit (Christmas) night, the German trenches with small lights on them, and the men on both sides gathered in groups on the parapets.

At times we heard the guns in the distance and an occasional rifle shot. I can hear them now, but about us is absolute quiet. I allowed one or two men to go out and meet a German or two halfway. They exchanged cigars, a smoke and talked. The officer I spoke to hopes we shall do the same on New Year's Day. I said 'Yes, if I am here'.

Captain Armes finished that day's entry with the words:

I felt I must sit down and write the story of this Christmas Eve before I went to lie down. Of course no precautions are relaxed, but I feel they mean to play the game. All the same, I think I shall be awake all night so as to be on the safe side.

It is weird to think that tomorrow night we shall be at it again. If one gets through this show it will be a Xmas time to live in one's memory.

An artist's impression of the Christmas Truce, 1914.

Resuming his letter on Christmas morning, Armes added:

> All this morning we have been fraternizing, singing songs. I have been within a yard in front of their trenches, have spoken to and exchanged greetings with a colonel, staff officers and several company officers. All were very nice and friendly.
>
> We have just knocked off for dinner and have arranged to meet again afterwards. I left our friends, the Germans, on Christmas Day in a quiet mood.

Sadly, Captain Armes did not survive the war. He died on 9 April 1916, while serving with the 7th Battalion, North Staffordshire Regiment in Mesopotamia.

Sergeant C. Lightfoot, of Stafford, served in 'C' Company, 1st Battalion, North Staffordshire Regiment. His company held the line just to the west of Lille, between Frelinghien and Houplines. Lightfoot wrote home on 28 December, three days before his regiment was pulled out of the line:

> On Christmas Day we saw a sight past imagination. The Germans left their trenches and so did we. We met them half-way and you should have seen them shaking hands, exchanging addresses, and souvenirs &c. They brought us plenty of cigars and tobacco. There was not a shot fired between us all Christmas Day. One of our men played a melodeon and the Germans danced to it and gave us some very good singing.

On 3 January 1915, Lance Corporal H. Shufflebotham, also of the 1st Battalion, North Staffordshire Regiment, penned a letter to his parents at his home address at 27 Weston Road, Stafford:

We had a very good Christmas taking all things into consideration. You may not believe it but it is the truth. Our regiment and the Germans met halfway between the trenches (which are only forty to fifty yards apart) and shook hands and exchanged cigarettes, cigars &c. Not a shot was fired as it was arranged on both sides that there should not be. They (the Germans) seemed as though they were short of food as they even begged bully beef and we gave it to them freely. We had a fine Christmas box from Princess Mary and one from the *Staffordshire Sentinel* containing a pound box of chocolate and a New Year's gift from the same source of 20 packets of cigarettes and eight ounces of tobacco in addition to which we also had eight packets of cigarettes from 'B' Company, North Staffords at home.

Private Simnett, of the same battalion wrote: 'Several of the Germans were from London and were wishing the war was over. One of them even suggested that we should finish it off at football as we should not get hurt.'

Although not from Stafford, Corporal A.P. Oakes, also of the 1st Battalion, wrote a letter, which appeared in the *Evening Sentinel* of 13 January and adds further details to the general narrative:

Our chaps started to shout across good humouredly and the Germans replied in the same spirit. Then both sides got on the top of their respective trenches and one of each side met halfway. Then 'Peace on earth, goodwill towards men' was the order of the day or rather the night. A regular singing contest began our chaps giving *Tipperary, Thora, Way Down De Swannee River* and several other well-known songs.

The Germans reciprocated with:

The Austrian and German National Anthems and *The Watch on the Rhine*. A baritone singer gave *Sailor Beware* in English, and several other songs. We learned that he was a well-known opera singer. At 10 o'clock we sang *The King*, bade them good-night and turned in.

Christmas Day dawned at last but I found nothing in my socks but a pair of feet. If Santa Claus had not been round, Jack Frost had.

Today the carol perhaps most associated with the Christmas Truce is *Silent Night* (*Stille Nacht*), although it is rarely mentioned in first-hand accounts. One veteran, Rifleman Graham Williams, wrote in his memoirs that: 'This was actually the first time I heard this Carol'. The carols most commonly mentioned include *O Come All Ye Faithful* and *While Shepherds Watched Their Flocks*, *The First Nowell* and *O Tannenbaum*. Meanwhile, the Tommies gave their own renditions of *Home Sweet Home*, *It's A Long Way to Tipperary*, *Old Folks at Home* and *Auld Lang Syne*.

An anonymous letter from a British officer was published in the *Staffordshire Chronicle* of 6 January 1915, under the heading 'Friend and Foe and the Dead':

The previous night (Christmas Eve) their trenches were a blaze of Christmas trees, and our sentries were regaled for hours with the traditional Christmas songs of the Fatherland.

When I got out I found a large crowd of officers and men, English and German, grouped around the bodies, which had already been gathered together and laid out in rows. I went along those dreadful ranks and scanned the faces. They lay stiffly in contorted attitudes, dirty with frozen mud and powdered with grime. The digging parties were already busy on the two big common graves but the ground was hard and work slow and laborious.

Time drew on, and it was obvious that the burying would not be half finished with the expiration of armistice agreed upon, so we decided to renew it the following morning.

On Boxing Day at the agreed hour, on a prearranged signal being given, we turned out again. The output of officers of higher rank on their side was more marked, and the proceedings were more formal in consequence. They distributed cigars and cigarettes freely among our digging party who were much impressed by the cigars. Meanwhile the officers were amusing themselves by taking photographs of mixed groups. The Germans brought us copies to send to the English illustrated papers, as they received them regularly.

The digging completed, the shallow graves were filled in and the German officers remained to pay their tribute of respect while our chaplain read a short service. It was one of the most impressive sights I have ever witnessed. Friend and foe stood side by side, bare-headed, watching the full, grave figure of the padre outlined against the frosty landscape as he blessed the poor broken bodies at his feet. Then, with more formal salutes, we turned and made our way back to our respective ruts. Elsewhere along the line I hear our fellows played the Germans at football on Christmas Day.

The cigars mentioned may have derived from the boxes distributed to the German troops. The soldiers had the choice of a Meerschaum pipe bearing the image of the Crown Prince Friedrich Wilhelm or a box of cigars.

Of the many letters home to mention the truce, one, written by Coldstream Guardsman Private Oswald Johnson, of Stafford, was published in the *Staffordshire Chronicle* of 4 February 1915. Describing the nature of the trench system, Johnson revealed that the British front line was approached through a series of support trenches a quarter of a mile long and knee-deep in muddy water: 'We had to stand [with] the boot tops in mud and water for twenty-four hours, with the Germans about 200 yards in front of us. We could hear them singing quite plainly.' In Johnson's section of the line the truce did not go without incident: 'We had the misfortune to lose our Captain on Boxing Day. He was shot by a sniper about a yard from where I was standing and that made us feel a bit "down" for a time.'

When details of the Christmas Truce filtered back from the front the generals on both sides took immediate action. The German High Command moved the Saxon troops the following day. Meanwhile, the British officers involved were warned that they would be court-martialled should there be any repetition of events. Fearful that details of the truce might spread further afield and that a general cessation of hostilities could break out, the British High Command issued an official communiqué stating that the lull in the fighting was due to adverse weather.

Princess Mary's Christmas Tin

Private Oswald Johnson's letter mentioned: 'We had rather a good Christmas, with the usual pudding you get at home for dinner, and the King and Queen sent us a card. We also had a nice Christmas box from Princess Mary.' The 'Christmas box' to which Private Johnson referred was the Princess Mary Christmas tin which was issued to many front-line troops ahead of the 25th.

A 1914 Christmas tin.

When war was declared it was popularly believed that the conflict would be over by Christmas. Once it became apparent that hostilities might last months, if not years, the public got behind the idea of sending comforts to the troops in time for the festive season. In Stafford various local organizations and individuals supplied food, tobacco, warm clothing and other treats for the local Territorials still in Great Britain and members of the 1st Battalion, North Staffordshire Regiment then serving at the front.

Meanwhile, the 4 November edition of the *Tatler* ran an article launching a nationwide appeal. The magazine's front cover depicted a portrait of Princess Mary, while the feature heralded the creation of the Sailors and Soldiers Christmas Fund. The goal of the fund was to send 'every Sailor afloat and every Soldier at the Front' a 'gift from the nation' in time for Christmas. The article went on to explain: 'The Princess is providing boxes of smoking requisites as Christmas gifts for the troops at the Front, and we are sure that our readers will respond generously to this very excellent appeal.'

The response was overwhelming. Over 355,000 Christmas tins were distributed to those serving on Christmas Day 1914. The contents of the tin varied, depending on when and where they were issued, and the availability of supplies. The standard tin contained an ounce of pipe tobacco and twenty cigarettes, with a pipe issued separately (as it wouldn't fit into the tin). For the non-smokers there was a bag of acid-drop-type sweets and a writing kit, or a bar of chocolate. There were spices for the Indian troops, while nursing staff received a sewing kit. All of the tins included a monogrammed bullet with a silver or nickel top which concealed a pencil, while each box bore an embossed portrait of the princess as a part of the lid's design. A studio photograph was included along with a personal message: 'May God protect you and bring you home safe.' Those issued before Christmas included a Christmas card, wishing the soldiers 'A Happy Christmas and a Victorious New Year'. A different message was included in the tins presented just ahead of New Year's Day.

Due to the strong public support a total of £162,591. 12*s*. 5*d*. was raised. This meant that the gift was extended to all personnel 'wearing the King's uniform on Christmas Day 1914', raising the final figure to approximately 2,620,019 servicemen and women.

A shortage of brass, which was vital in the manufacture of munitions, meant that later issues were often made of plated alloy. As late as January 1919, a large number of the tins were yet to be distributed.

CHAPTER 4

The Guardsmen – The Cream of Kitchener's Volunteer Army, 1915

❖

Of the first recruits to answer the nation's call, the tallest, fittest and most highly educated were enlisted into the Coldstream and Grenadier Guards. These men were quickly put through training. Many were serving in the trenches by November 1914, replacing casualties. Their letters home from the front provide a valuable insight into daily life in the trenches during the first eighteen months of the hostilities.

Stafford Coldstream Guardsmen. Of the hundred or so to serve in the elite Guards regiments, these were the survivors.

One of the many Staffordians who enlisted at the Shire Hall during the first week of hostilities was Ernest W. Gisby, who served with No. 2 Company, 1st Battalion, Coldstream Guards. Private Gisby wrote from France on 18 January:

> I am getting on all right, and quite well. Now for a piece of news you will like to hear. I got my name and number taken by a Cameron Highlander officer for bringing in under fire one of his men, and our officer told me he would see that our commanding officer also got to hear of it. How's that? I did not know I had the pluck to do it, for the bullets did not half whiz round me those few eternal seconds, but thank God I was not hit.

Gisby's letter was unusually graphic when it came to details of the casualty, and what is all the more surprising was that his words were published in full: 'The poor chap I helped to carry in was shot clean through the forehead, and half his head was off. In fact I had to wipe his blood and brains off my trousers when we got him to the headquarters.'

Serving in the La Bassée region with the Army Service Corps (ASC), Private W. Hall, of Stafford, wrote home on 31 January. His letter described enemy activity that forced the Guardsmen he was fighting alongside to retreat under cover of night:

> This week has been a terrible one. Fighting has been terrific, and we have had hardly any sleep all the time. As sure as we have lain down for a few minutes we have been called out to stand by with loaded rifles, and get everything ready for a sudden move.
>
> The infantry regiments had it very hot the beginning of the week, and it took them all their time to hold the enemy back. The Germans gained a little ground, but we were driven back the day after. Thursday they again made a furious attack, but could not break through, although they were expected to do so. Now comes the worst part of all. Friday evening a very violent cannonade commenced, also a furious attack by the German infantry. [The] wounded were being brought along the roads in hundreds, and several shells went hissing over our heads, and fell in the town behind.
>
> At 11.15pm we were [called] out again. The guns were roaring, and the shells were falling like rain. Soon one of our batteries was silenced, but 'A' and 'Q' Batteries, belonging to our division, were sent into action, and they went with rousing cheers.
>
> We were all told to be ready to move at once, if necessary. Soon the order was given – this was at 1.30am, and our troops began to retire.
>
> Sections of German infantry had managed to get through our lines. This was serious, and we were ordered to retire beyond the town [of Bethune]. Several more German batteries commenced action and shells fell thicker than ever, but not near enough to us, although terrible were their effects on our retiring troops.

The situation looked bad and there might well have been a general retreat along his sector of the front:

Several thousand troops were hurried up to reinforce us. It was touch and go for quite half an hour, but by a piece of luck, we soon cut the enemy off, and surrounded them. They very soon surrendered, and the German reinforcements were seen [being] driven back by our artillery, which was mowing them down in hundreds. The fight lasted till about 3.30am.

Without perhaps realizing it, Hall had already accepted that the war would be one of attrition when he wrote: 'The same morning it was found we had suffered very heavily, two Scottish regiments had been three parts annihilated, but I still think we can claim it was a great victory, although no actual ground was gained by us.' In a more poignant note, he added:

On the roads that morning could be seen the traces of battle – for all the dead had not been picked up. There were still lots of them about, and the Field Ambulances were bringing in the wounded all day. This is the second great fight in which I have been. The casualty we suffered cast a cloud on our company.

In a letter to his father, former Inspector Templeton, of 92 Tixall Road, Private E. Templeton, 2nd Battalion, Coldstream Guards, wrote an account of the action at Cuinchy. This was later published in the *Staffordshire Chronicle* of 1 February 1915, under the heading 'Coldstreamer's experience':

We've had it hot and strong since last I wrote, and about the hottest I've ever been through. I've sent with this letter a bit of shell that went through my overcoat and jacket, and lodged in the bandage we all carry in the special pocket.

Our boys and the Irish Guards made a charge to take some brick kilns, from which the enemy was doing some awful damage amongst us. They were accounting for about twenty a day, and the cover was so good that we could not shift them out unless we made a bayonet charge. We were told of the charge, and you can guess most of us felt a bit 'nervy'.

Our artillery started bombarding their trenches, and of course theirs replied. The uproar was deafening, and we had one or two casualties before the charge.

At a quarter past two our CO gave the signal and over the trenches our lads and the Irish [Guards] scrambled. The charge they made was the finest sight I've seen, although we lost about twenty all told.

Well, you can bet your life the kilns were taken and the trench. We captured twenty prisoners.

I think the bit of shell [enclosed] struck me when I was bringing up the rations, and I was lucky to escape being buried, for my chum, who was helping me, had the side of the trench blown on top of him.

Private Templeton, who was described as being one of the 'Stafford Pals', added that he was in better health than he had ever been, and if he had no nearer shaves than 'that bit of shell' he would be quite satisfied.

Meanwhile, on 20 February 1915, an account from another Guardsman serving at Cuinchy appeared in the *Staffordshire Chronicle*. In his anonymous letter the local soldier provided an insight into the daily life on an active section of the front:

> Since writing last I have seen some rather lively scenes in the trenches not far from Bethune. The 'Allemandes' [Germans] were successful in taking a little of our ground and trenches, but our men successfully counter-attacked a couple of days later, and also took a trench or two from the Germans, as extras, I suppose, for the inconvenience.
>
> Two days later and word was passed up the trenches that part of the line was going to try and confiscate the German trenches in order to straighten our firing-line. At a fixed time the French and our artillery commenced to shell the enemy's trenches, and after a few minutes' grand work, the Germans began to retire. Our men then advanced, and with some splendid rifle fire from either side to aid them, gave the Germans a terrible time of it. When sufficient ground had been gained, our men quickly dug themselves in and made fresh trenches.

The writer then went on to describe an artillery bombardment in jovial terms. In reality this must have been an extremely traumatic experience:

> We were kept hard at work all night long, making preparations for a counter-attack. At about 3 o'clock [the following day], however, the Germans began to bombard us. Our guns were evidently just waiting for a chance to send a few more shells to the enemy, and for about a quarter of an hour we witnessed a great artillery duel. Everywhere shells, large and small, were bursting, and at times we could but see a few yards in front of us, the smoke from the shells being so dense.
>
> The Allies gradually gained the upper hand with their artillery fire, and instead of advancing the German lines were completely broken up. The officers in my company were highly pleased with this achievement, and expressed their appreciation of the deadly rifle fire from the Coldstreams. We lost very few men, but the 'Allemandes' must have had a large number of casualties, besides losing a good few men whom we took prisoners.

On a more sombre note, the letter contained details of local casualties: 'There were two or three Staffordians among our killed and wounded, among them being E. Crutchley [wounded] and J. Tavernor [Private John Tavernor, 3rd Battalion, Coldstream Guards, killed in action at Cuinchy on 6 February 1915].'

Another Staffordian serving with the division was Private Charles Robinson, 2nd

Battalion, Coldstream Guards. Robinson, of 3 Grey Friars, wrote home in February 1915, enclosing three buttons, which he cut off a German's uniform: 'I am quite well, and have come safely through three engagements.' The second engagement was a fierce hand-to-hand fight, which Private Robinson describes as 'very exciting', adding: 'We were up to our knees in mud.' His letter was tempered by a brief reference to an event that should have proved fatal, when a shell fell a few yards away from him but did not detonate.

Another of those who fought at Cuinchy was Private Lewis, 2nd Battalion, Grenadier Guards, formerly of Cramer Street. Lewis wrote home on 7 March. His letter, which was published in the *Staffordshire Chronicle* of 20 March 1915, read:

> I dare say you have read in the papers of that regiment of Huns who had the order 'not to take prisoners'. Well, we had the pleasure of meeting those 'gents' a few weeks ago.
>
> When we got up there we found them in possession of a brickfield. So what with bombers and snipers on the top of the stacks they made our trenches a very undesirable place to be in.
>
> Our brigade were not long before they made a few charges, in which one of the Irish Guards got a VC [Lance Corporal Michael O'Leary won the Victoria Cross on 1 February 1915]. Although the honour did not fall on our lot to do the actual charge. One day we caught them fairly on the hop. They left their grub and cigars. Everyone had a cigar that day, and sausages galore.
>
> In the finish we captured and held the whole of the brickstack, and 'that mob' were not long before they were relieved by another regiment. Judging by what they left lying there and what we captured, I don't think there were many of them to relieve. They tried many times to get back the ground they lost, but there was nothing doing. They did not mind spending a few shells over the deal.

The enemy laid down a terrific bombardment in the hope of driving the Guardsmen out of the brickstacks, as Lewis related:

> One day in particular they started from daylight . . . one of their hurricane bombardments. I slipped beneath a heap of bricks while it was on, and was smoking woodbines furiously to while away the time. I don't think any of us fancied our chances too much that day. However, our casualties were very slight, considering they say there was as many shells fired that day as what there was during the Boer War. So it will give you an idea what it was like. But I suppose it's all in the game.

Lewis recalled an incident that demonstrated that despite the carnage, chivalry was not dead:

A rather interesting incident occurred the other day. After they had been chased out of it [i.e. the brickstack] we occupied one of their trenches, and just in front of us lay one of their officers wounded. So after he had been laying there a while one of our chaps got up and waved [to] them (they were only 70 yards away) to come and get him and we were not going to shoot. They seemed a bit doubtful at first, but presently one of them got out of their trench followed by another one, and came running towards us. When they got to the officer they turned to us and saluted, and said: 'Very good Englishmen; we thought you'd shoot us.' As they went we gave them a good cheering, and they took it up on the other side. It was good for about five minutes – everyone with their heads above the parapet of the trench. As soon as they got him in it was heads down and business as usual – the souvenirs flying about us as usual.

In closing, Lewis expressed a sentiment already common in many letters home: 'I don't think it will last so very long now. What with this new army of ours and also the French Reserves in action there is bound to be a big move on. The sooner the better, and let us have it done with.'

Another of the 'Stafford Pals', Private A. Long, a journalist, was reported to be in the London General Hospital. In a letter to one of his colleagues on the *Staffordshire Chronicle*, Private Long wrote that 'what with "Jack Johnsons" [8.27, 15 or 17in shells], shrapnel grenades, and rifle bullets bursting all round them' they had a 'devil of a time' at the front.

Amid the death and destruction there were countless acts of gallantry and selflessness. What Long didn't mention was that he had earlier displayed exceptional gallantry in rescuing several of his comrades while under intense enemy fire, earning him the Distinguished Conduct Medal. Long's award was promulgated in the *London Gazette* of 18 February 1915, under the heading: 'The King has been graciously pleased to award the Distinguished Conduct Medal for acts of gallantry and devotion to duty'.

THE FIRST JOURNALIST-D.C.M.

STAFFORD COLDSTREAMER'S GALLANT DEED.

Among the honours awarded last week-end, the Distinguished Conduct Medal has been conferred upon Private Arthur Long (1st Coldstream Guards), who is at present lying in the first London General Hospital, Camberwell, S.E., recovering from frostbite and typhoid fever. Private Long, who is attached to The Staffordshire Advertiser reporting staff, is the first journalist to receive this coveted distinction, and members of the profession throughout the country will extend to him their congratulations.

The award was greeted with especial pleasure by Staffordshire journalists, among whom Private Long has worked for the last year or two. As soon as the news was received, his colleagues in the Stafford office of the Advertiser sent a congratulatory telegram, which was soon followed by a similar message from the North Staffordshire Branch of the National Union of Journalists. In addition, his own paper gave a photograph and a recital of the deed which won for him the medal, whilst other papers in the county editorially complimented the soldier-journalist.

Pte. Long, and a fellow-journalist from the Advertiser office, Lance-Corpl. J. Vernon Medley (who is at present in a Sunderland hospital suffering from frostbite), joined the 1st Battalion of Coldstream Guards with a number of their Stafford friends at the outbreak of the war.

Pte. Long is understood to have earned his coveted decoration by crawling out of the trenches and rescuing wounded comrades who were under fire. For this act of gallantry he was commended at the time by his own officer and the officer of a supporting regiment—the London Scottish—who called for his name and number. With characteristic modesty, Private Long did not reply. The request, however, became a command, and as a result Private Long's gallant conduct has been officially recognised.

We are glad to hear that Private Long is making considerable progress towards recovery, and is allowed out of bed for half-days.

Journalism claimed Private Long from a solicitor's office at his native town, Lyme Regis. He served his apprenticeship on The Bridport News (Dorset), and, before going to Staffordshire, was attached to The Sudbury Free Press (Suffolk).

Private A. Long DCM.

The citation for Long's award, published in the *London Gazette* of 1 April 1915, was brief: 'Private A. Long, of the Coldstream Guards. For conspicuous gallantry and devotion to duty on December 23rd, 1914, in rescuing a number of wounded men at great risk [while under heavy fire], the enemy being only fifty yards distant.' The story was later taken up by a number of local newspapers, including the *Stafford Newsletter*, which wrote on 17 July 1915:

> A pleasant gathering was held at the Swan Hotel on Wednesday morning when Private A. Long of the Coldstream Guards was presented with a silver cigarette case from his press colleges in Stafford as a mark of their admiration of the distinction conferred upon him. Mr. W.L. Bird presided and made the presentation, remarking that Private Long was the first journalist in the county to have the DCM.
>
> In reply, Long, who has recently been discharged from hospital after being there five months suffering from frost bite, enteric fever and blood poisoning, modestly related his experiences and described the act which won him the DCM.

Long, of Corporation Street, Stafford, was later granted a commission and ended the war as a lieutenant with the Coldstream Guards.

Among the guests at the informal ceremony was another local man, Sergeant G.W. Jackson, 1st Battalion, Coldstream Guards, who was at home enjoying a few days' leave following the unofficial news that he too had been awarded the DCM. The *London Gazette* of 23 June 1915 carried the official announcement of the award, along with the following citation: 'For conspicuous gallantry on 11 April 1915, at Rue du Bois, when he went out under a heavy fire, reconnoitred throughout the night, and brought back valuable information.'

The *Staffordshire Chronicle* of 26 June 1915 carried details of this and further gallantry awards to some of the 'Stafford Pals', in this instance, men of No. 8 Platoon, No. 2 Company, 1st Coldstream Guards: 'Honours to Siemens' Employees. Sergeant G.W. Jackson, Lance-Sergeant [Robert] Woollacott and Corporal W.E. Robinson, of the 1st Coldstream Guards, have been recommended for honours by Sir John French for gallant and distinguished service in the field. Jackson and Woollacott were both employed at Siemens' Works prior to their enlistment.' George Jackson had written home:

> I have been decorated with the DCM for gallantry in the field. The Colonel said he was proud to have such a man in his regiment – one who came out as a private, and was now a full sergeant with distinction. We are in the brickfields [at Cuinchy] now and when we come out again I will apply for leave on the strength of it.

As previously noted, Sergeant Jackson did get home leave, returning to Stafford, for what would be the last time. He was killed in action on 28 July 1915, not long after his return to the front. On 14 August the *Staffordshire Chronicle* reported the news:

Late Sergeant G.W. Jackson.
We announced last week that Sergeant G.W. Jackson, DCM, has been killed in action. It was in September that he enlisted in the 1st Coldstream Guards with a number of other young men who were at that time living in Stafford. He was made a corporal very early in his military career for clever reconnoitring and for carrying wounded under open fire. This was in January at La Bassee. He was afterwards promoted to the rank of sergeant and subsequently gained the Distinguished Conduct Medal.

The late sergeant who, only a few weeks ago was on a visit to Stafford, took an interest in various kinds of sports [he was a member of the Stafford Rugby Football team], and was a very popular young man in the town.

Since his lamented death, his father received a letter from Sergeant Woolacott, who has also won the DCM [downgraded to a Mention in Despatches, *London Gazette*, of 22 June 1915], as follows:

'As you are aware, George and I, being chums at Stafford, came to the Army together and have since been together. His death to me and a number of other fellows here from Stafford, as well as to a great number of friends whom he made by his good heart and nature, is a very great personal loss. We all express [to] you our very great sympathy. The men of his platoon wish me to express also their sympathy, and the universal respect he enjoyed for his gallantry and great personal qualities. The Colonel [Lieutenant Colonel Ponsonby] asked that I should leave the trenches to attend his funeral in Bethune to represent his family and friends. He is buried in the cemetery in that place, and when we are there again, No. 8 Platoon will place a wreath on his grave as also will a number of his personal friends. You may be sure his grave will be looked after and attended to whenever possible.'

In a postscript the writer says that 'the DCM ribbon is being sent home by the authorities [the medal not yet having been presented]'.

Corporal L. Hardy, 2nd Company, 1st Battalion, Coldstream Guards, wrote from France on 2 August 1915. In his letter he gave a little detail of the circumstances surrounding Sergeant Jackson's death:

We have been in the trenches for three days in one of the hottest parts of the line. We had not been up more than half-an-hour when two sergeants were killed, one being poor Jackson. You may guess how I felt. He had just been talking to me, and had got about twenty yards down the trench, where he stood talking to another sergeant, who was my platoon sergeant, when a bomb was thrown over. It dropped between them. Sergeant Jackson was hit in the back of the head. He was the first to be got away to the No. 1 Field Ambulance, and he died at 4.30 next morning.

A letter of condolence was addressed to the family by the officer commanding No. 2 Company of the 1st Battalion, Coldstream Guards (dated 29 July):

Dear Mr. Jackson, I am very grieved to have to inform you that Sergeant Jackson was killed-in-action last night. I am so very very sorry for you, as I know you are bound to feel his loss most sorely. I shall miss him very much indeed. He was a most gallant soldier, and was beloved by everyone who knew him. He suffered no pain, so the doctor informed me, as he was hit in the head by a shell and never regained consciousness.

Lieutenant Colonel Ponsonby, CO, 1st Battalion, Coldstream Guards, also wrote to express his sympathy. Referring to Sergeant Jackson's DCM, he added that his gallant conduct and devotion to duty had been 'frequently brought to his attention'. He concluded: 'Your son's name will always be remembered for his gallant deeds in the future history of the regiment.' Jackson's death, the first of a high-profile Staffordian, received considerable attention in the press. His family were reported as being 'inundated by, and are grateful for, the numerous expressions of sympathy which they have received'.

Death and serious injury was random in the trenches, as exemplified by the stories of other local servicemen.

Published in the *Staffordshire Chronicle* of 10 April 1915, Private G.H. Newman of 1st Battalion, Coldstream Guards wrote of a particularly lucky escape. He was struck in the chest by a piece of shrapnel. Newman explained that three bullet cartridges in his bandolier took the force of the impact; otherwise he would have received a serious wound. Newman's story was not untypical and most men who served at the front for any length of time had a tale of a 'near miss' from shrapnel or bullets.

Private S.J. Coates, also of the Coldstream Guards, a former Edwin Bostock & Co. employee, wrote of his experiences (on 29 May 1915):

I came out of the trenches yesterday after having had a rather hard three days. They were bombing us all the time. Naturally our boys retaliated, and gave them a warm time. It is the only way to quieten them. For every one they bang over we reply with two or three. We are very close to the Germans in this position, and you can hear them speaking quite distinctly, and occasionally hear English spoken very fluently.

Another former Bostock's employee, Private L. Booth, 1st Battalion, Coldstream Guards, wrote:

I am writing this letter in my dug-out. . . . In this position the trenches are very close to the Germans, so we have not had much peace, what with bombs, rifle grenades, trench mortars, and such like. There is one thing about the trench mortars, you can see their messages coming through the air, and are able to dodge them a little.

You will, perhaps be interested to know how the anniversary of the declaration of war was celebrated on the night of the 4th [August 1915]. At 12 o'clock midnight some of the lads in one of our companies in the reserve line started to play 'Rule Britannia' on the cornet and various other instruments . . . [we] joined the lads in the chorus. If the Germans were not able to hear all the words, they would not fail to catch the last line: 'Britons never shall be slaves.' It seemed to amuse them as they clapped their hands and shouted 'Hurrah', but I bet they soon changed their tune, for next we gave them a hail of bombs along the line, but we poor chaps in the front line didn't get much peace for the rest of the night. They tried to have their own back. Still we enjoyed the fun, for no one was hurt.

Private F. Coates, of the Grenadier Guards, had been serving in France since late 1914. He wrote a letter of thanks for a Christmas parcel (1915) from his former workmates at Edwin Bostock & Co.:

We spent our Christmas Day [1915] only a few yards from the Boche [sic], but things were pretty quiet. By next Christmas I hope we shall be back at the old [work] shop with everything settled up.

Very many thanks for the parcel of Woodbines etc, which I got just after coming out of the trenches where by the way we spent Christmas and Boxing Day.

Coates was one of three Guardsman brothers: there was also Private Robert Coates, 2nd Company, 1st Battalion, Coldstream Guards, who was killed in action on the Somme in 1916, then aged 19 years, and Private S.J. Coates, also of the Coldstream Guards.

Private A. Horobin, Coldstream Guards, another of the 'Stafford Pals' who had served in France for a year, wrote:

I am pleased to say that I am still keeping in the pink. Things are quiet where we are, but we are expecting it to be a bit warmer very soon. Our battalion has been out of the trenches for a short time but we expect go back shortly. Before long there will be some terrible fighting here, and I hope it will bring the war to an end, for one gets fed up with trench work.

Penned in the autumn of 1914 by an anonymous infantryman, a song lamenting the loss of his comrades on the Western Front soon became the anthem of a generation in uniform:

Private A. Horobin.

If you want the old battalion,
I know where they are, I know where they are,
If you want the old battalion,
I know where they are,
They're hanging on the old barbed wire.
I've seen 'em, I've seen 'em,
Hanging on the old barbed wire,
I've seen 'em,
Hanging on the old barbed wire.

CHAPTER 5

The Staffordshire Territorials and the Attack on the Hohenzollern Redoubt, 13 October 1915

❖

Stafford, like every major town and city, had its own Territorial units. These were mobilized on the outbreak of the war. The *Staffordshire Chronicle* of 8 August 1914 painted a vivid picture of the scene:

> England at war with Germany! Reservists called up and Territorials [the 6th (Stafford) Staffordshire Battery of the Royal Field Artillery and the 1/6th Battalion, North Staffordshire Regiment] ordered to mobilize!
>
> What other announcements could stir the emotions of English people to such a degree, and in common with other towns the streets of Stafford during the past week have presented a strange and animated appearance.

Another feature in the same edition elaborated:

> Large crowds have assembled outside the headquarters of the two companies of Territorials. Knots of people have gathered in the main thoroughfares anxiously awaiting the latest news.
>
> The 6th [1/6th] North Staffordshire Regiment and 6th [Stafford] Staffordshire Battery, RFA, were to have undergone their annual training at St Asaphs and Aldershot respectively, but on arrival they were immediately recalled. Both companies returned to the town on Monday [3 August] and their arrival was witnessed by a large and enthusiastic crowd.

The parents, wives and children of the men gathered round the [drill] halls in order to witness their departure, and bid them farewell. It was not until Wednesday afternoon [5 August], however, that the 1/6th North Staffs. left by road for Rugeley, en-route for Burton-on-Trent, which is to form the centre for mobilizing the whole Brigade. The Artillery have remained at the new Drill Hall throughout the week, with the exception of an ammunition party which left for Wolverhampton yesterday [Friday]; their camp will be on the Grammar School ground to-day.

The 1/5th and 1/6th Battalions of the South Staffordshire Regiment, the 1/5th and 1/6th Battalions of the North Staffordshire Regiment and the 6th (Stafford) Staffordshire Battery, RFA, formed part of the Staffordshire Brigade, North Midlands Division (later re-named 137th Brigade, 46th (North Midlands) Division), which had its Divisional HQ at Lichfield.

A South Staffordshire Regiment cap badge.

Meanwhile, a special meeting of the Staffordshire Territorial Forces Association was held on 5 August. Representatives of Edwin Bostock & Co. announced that the jobs of Reservists and Territorials would be held open. Furthermore, it pledged that two-thirds of the servicemen's wages would be paid to their dependants while they remained on active service.

The following months saw Stafford's Territorials undergo further training on home soil, frustrated at seeing other units being sent to France. The 46th Division was drafted overseas en masse in March 1915, the men of 'B' (Stafford) Company, 5th Platoon, 1/6th Battalion, North Staffordshire Regiment disembarking at Le Havre on 3 March. Initially the battalion was deployed to hold the Ypres Salient during a quiet time for that particular part of the front.

A slow trickle of letters from the front appeared in the *Staffordshire Chronicle*. Private G. Marshall, 'B' Company, 5th Platoon 1/6th Battalion, North Staffordshire Regiment, wrote home. His letter was published on 29 May 1915: 'As you know, we ("B" Company) have been in the fire trench from the first, which is about 80 yards from the Germans. On our way to the trenches, week after week, we pass through villages which are almost burned to the ground with the heavy fighting.'

However, in a letter home published in the *Staffordshire Chronicle* of 19 June, Private Jack Hill, of Mill Street, described a more idyllic scene in the reserve trenches:

As I am writing this in the trenches, I was just thinking that were I an artist, and able to depict the scene behind us, you would hardly credit its veracity, as for miles round the scenery is a picture to look upon, so peaceful, with the green fields and the avenues of trees (mountain ash), which seems peculiar to the country, and in the foreground the beautiful picture of rich green grass, with a large sprinkling of wild marguerites and bright red poppies, which forms a pleasing sight to the eyes.

Hill made only an oblique reference to his combat experiences when he added: 'We get plenty of hard work, but, we are the boys to do it.'

Corporal S. Taylor, 'D' Company, 1/6th Battalion, North Staffordshire Regiment wrote to his parents at 15 Crooked Bridge Street at about the same time. His letter was more 'gritty':

We have just had a very trying time – only 25 yards off the Germans, and every night it was a case of bombing one another, but we always seemed to come off best, as I think a Britisher can always beat the 'Boches' [sic] at throwing. We are out of the firing line, but still in the reserve trenches.

I had a nasty experience the other day. They gave us a very hot shelling, and 'D' Company had a few casualties. Well, I got the order to go and reinforce them with my section, and we did have some sport. We get relieved in a few days for a fortnight's rest, fourteen miles behind [the front]. We shall have plenty of football then.

Sergeant C. Underwood, 1/6th Battalion, North Staffordshire Regiment, a former Edwin Bostock & Co. employee, writing home in August 1915 recalled:

There has been a big battle raging for the past two days, and is still going on – shells bursting all over the place. The Germans used liquid fire [flamethrowers] on the Rifle Brigade and KRRR [King's Royal Rifle Regiment] yesterday morning, but they have paid for their temerity with very heavy losses for although ours have been bad enough, theirs were in the proportion to four or six to one.

A North Staffordshire Regiment cap badge.

In mid-September, Private G. Marshall, 1/6th Battalion, North Staffordshire Regiment wrote about a near miss in a letter home:

I had a warm time about a week ago, when I was on sentry repairing the parapet. A big flare came from my left ammunition pouch and shots and cartridges cases were flying about. A German sniper had seen me and hit my bayonet and pouches and exploded 20 rounds of ammunition. I was removed from the trench and escaped with only a slight cut on the left forefinger. But I am pleased to say that I am well again and ready for Fritz who are just over the parapet about 100 yards away.

The last few days have seemed like a huge thunderstorm. Bombardments have taken place and are still on our right and left, which I believe have been a great success to Lloyd George for the munitions he is getting us. There is no doubt that the Allies are playing a winning game. If only a few of the young fellows in England who are reading the papers could hear the noise and see the shrapnel bursting, perhaps they would realise what it means to win a war, and keep up an army.

By the time you get this I would not be surprised if we had been in a bayonet charge and if we do the boys won't half strafe 'em.

(signed) G. Marshall.

Despite the many fierce battles fought sporadically along the front when men advanced through heavy rifle and machine-gun fire, artillery shells would remain the biggest killer. This was highlighted by news which reached Stafford on 9 October 1915, when the deaths of six members of the 1/6th Battalion, North Staffordshire Regiment were reported; four of the casualties were Staffordians. During an artillery barrage on 30 September the men had been taking shelter in a shell-hole which was hit by a second round killing them instantly. The Stafford men were named as Corporal C.E. Collins, Privates L. Bond, R. Smith and H. Davies (Bond and Collins were former workmates at W.H. Dorman & Co. Ltd).

Although the Territorial Battalions of the North Staffordshire Regiment had been in France and Flanders since early spring, their first major action didn't come until early October, when they were transferred to the Loos Sector. Here the battalion was heavily involved in the attack on the Hohenzollern Redoubt, which took place on 13 October 1915.

The initial British attack on the Redoubt, a complex network of defensive works surrounding the pre-war mine known as Fosse 8, took place on the opening day of the Battle of Loos (25 September–13 October). The British were initially able to penetrate the Redoubt. However, stiff German resistance meant that by early October British forces only held the West Face. Whereas elsewhere the Loos battlefield had ceased to be the scene of major fighting after 28 September, a German counter-attack at Hohenzollern was launched on 8 October. The enemy was partly repulsed by the Guards Division.

On 13 October the 1/6th Battalion, North Staffordshire Regiment led a renewed assault. The key to holding the Redoubt was a former slag heap known as 'The Dump', or 'Big Willie', the capture of which was assigned to the Staffords. Having only recently been deployed in this sector, however, there had been no time to reconnoitre the enemy's positions; a factor that was to add to their high casualty rate.

At noon on the 13th the British artillery opened up with a barrage which was intended to cause heavy casualties and damage the enemy's defences. At 12.30pm the short-lived and relatively ineffective barrage gave way to gas and smoke shells. As the British guns fell silent the Germans emerged from the relative safety of their dug-outs

British troops advance through a smoke screen.

and set up their machine guns ready for the anticipated infantry attack. In the meantime the German artillery began a reciprocal barrage of the British trenches.

The command was given for troops to fix bayonets and mount the firing step ready for the signal to attack. At 2.00pm whistles blew all along the front as the 1/5th Battalions of the North and the South Staffordshire Regiments joined those of the Lincolnshire and the Leicester Regiments in the advance across open ground. The men of the 1/6th Battalion, North Staffordshire Regiment formed the third wave of the attack. Little progress had been achieved by the time they left their lines and the enemy was able to maintain a sweeping fire, cutting the Staffords down as they advanced in small rushes.

Some men did gain ground when their NCOs led them men in a headlong dash. The 1/6th Battalion, North Staffordshire Regiment managed to gain a 30yd stretch of the enemy's first-line trench, but they were surrounded on three fronts because of the failure of the rest of the attack. All that was left to do was to try to make it back to their own trenches, leaving the battlefield strewn with their dead and wounded.

Then came the expected German counter-attack. This time it was the enemy who paid the Grim Reaper. The Staffords then began bringing in their wounded under heavy fire. Those who were too far out to be reached had to wait until dark. Many died of their wounds or received further injuries from bullets or shrapnel as the ground continued to be raked by fire.

Meanwhile, the 1/6th Battalion, North Staffordshire (The Prince of Wales Own) Regiment were relieved by the Regiment's 1/5th Battalion, making their way down the communication trench to board trams which took them to a farm beyond Vermelles. Following a warm meal they were inspected by the Prince of Wales, the future King Edward VIII, who expressed his pride in the regiment that bore his name.

A first-hand account of the advance comes from a letter published on 6 November in the *Staffordshire Chronicle*. This was signed Sergeant C. Underhill, Lance Corporal H. Burgess and Lance Corporal L. Liddle, 1/6th Battalion, North Staffordshire Regiment on behalf of 'the boys':

We started for the trenches on the afternoon of the 12th, and arrived in them about 5 o'clock the next morning. After we had had about three hours' rest, we prepared to get some breakfast, and then for a couple of hours we were doing various sorts of jobs to enable us to get out of the trench when the time came.

At 12 o'clock prompt the guns started. While the bombardment was going on it was very hard work to keep the boys from going over [the top]. All at once there was a shout, 'The Lincolns are off,' and then, 'There go the Leicesters.' Then there was a much louder cry, 'Now the 1/5th North are off; get on the Staffords.'

Well, at 2.50pm came our turn. 'Over you go, boys, and the best of luck,' was the order, and away went the 1/6th, only to be met with a perfect hail of bullets and shrapnel from the Huns' side of the show. Before we could get going properly we lost Major Peach [of Stafford, who was wounded] and our platoon officer, who was one of the best officers who ever walked down a trench, for, like Major Peach, he would never send his men where he dare not go himself. What was left of us got across to the trench over the way.

The best part of the fun was when our bombers started to clear the Bosche [sic] out of the Redoubt. When that was cleared the boys said that while there was one of them who could stand there they were going to stick [there].

I can assure you that it was a sorry 'B' Company that answered the roll call, for all our officers had fallen, and there was only one sergeant and two lance-corporals [the signatories] left to take charge of a company that was one of the strongest in the battalion before the scrap.

Another account from the same battalion, this time anonymous, read:

Three or four were hit before we went over [the top] at two o'clock, and were buried alive [when the walls of their trench collapsed] . . . just before that time the Germans started to get the range of our parapet. We all waited there with fixed bayonets, and kept asking the time – the minutes didn't half drag.

Presently Colonel Ratcliff came along, and then the whistle blew, and over we all went. The Colonel led the way with a cigar in his mouth, a dog whip in one hand, and his revolver in the other, but as we went on the chaps fell in rows. The Grenadier Guards say they have never seen a more plucky charge.

Private G. Marshall, 1/6th Battalion, North Staffordshire Regiment wrote of his experiences. His letter appeared in the *Staffordshire Chronicle* of 6 November 1915:

I myself being attached to the Maxim machine gunners, and was able to get a good view of the bayonet charge, as we were kept in the reserve. After a heavy bombardment from artillery, the boys at a given time mounted the parapet and proceeded towards the enemy's trenches at a good pace. Although the ground was swept by the German machine guns, some of the lads gained a footing in the German trenches at several points.

The following is an extract from the *War Diary* of the 1/6th Battalion, North Staffordshire Regiment:

13 October
At 2pm Infantry of 137 Brigade advanced against Big Willie – Dump Trench & Fosse 8. A and B Companies [of the] 6th [Battalion,] North Staffordshire Regiment forming 3rd line; C and D Companies [were] in fourth line. [The] enemy's machine gun and rifle fire [were] very heavy on advancing infantry who were unable to proceed. Line established in old fire trench. Two bombing parties were found by this Battalion – one gaining 30 yards of Big Willie Trench but had to retire through heavy casualties and were relieved by the 1/5th South Staffordshire Regiment.

Enemy kept up a heavy fire on our trenches with their Artillery and Machine guns making the work of bringing in wounded a difficult one.

A total of 400 men from 137 Brigade (the 1/5th and the 1/6th Battalions of the North and South Staffordshire Regiments) died as a result of the assault on the Hohenzollern Redoubt on 13 October. The 1/6th Battalion, North Staffordshire Regiment lost 7 officers and 96 NCOs and other ranks killed, out of a total of 300 men wounded, killed or missing. Among their ranks were the following Staffordians, all from 'B' (Stafford) Company, 5th Platoon, 1/6th Battalion, North Staffordshire Regiment:

Private Alfred Clewlow
Private William Duffin
Private Fred Geohegan
Private John Shale
Private James Walters
Private William Worrall (DOW 16 October 1915)

On Saturday, 27 November 1915, the *Staffordshire Chronicle* published a poignant poem 'from one of your own town boys H.H., 1/6th Battalion, North Staffordshire Regiment'. This was most likely penned by Harry Houlding, who survived the assault only to die on 1 July 1916, the first day of the Somme:

And when this war is over,
God help the man who shirked,
While others fought the Germans,
Or on munitions worked.
Our Stafford Lads will shun him,
As some un-cleanly thing,
For playing the coward
When asked to be a soldier of the King.

On the ninety-first anniversary of the assault, a memorial was unveiled at Hohenzollern commemorating the officers and men of the 46th (North Midland) Division killed before the Redoubt. The inscription read: 'Their Country Found Them Ready', a line from the popular wartime song *Keep the Home Fires Burning*.

CHAPTER 6

The Stafford Battery

✣

On the morning of 14 August 1914, the 6th (Stafford) Staffordshire Battery, under the command of Major H.V.B. Satgé, left Stafford by road en route to Burton. Here they underwent daily drill with their 15-pounder field guns, practising limbering up, rapid deployment and 'firing' manoeuvres. With war fever at a high pitch, their training was closely followed by large crowds of onlookers.

Earlier in the week the battery's complement of horses had been supplemented, as reported in the *Staffordshire Chronicle* of 15 August: 'Horses collected by the military authorities in the district for the use of the Artillery, were branded with the Government stamp on the school field [King Edward VI Grammar School, Stafford], where they were being trained for the purpose of the Battery.'

A pre-war image of the Stafford Battery at training.

A field-battery crew at training.

The Stafford Battery, originally based at Bailey Street, had a complement of 4 15-pounder guns (later replaced by 18-pounder guns) and a peacetime strength of around 150 men. The Battery formed a part of the 46th Midland's Division, which embarked en masse for France in March 1915, initially serving on the Ypres Front. In early May 1915, as the Battle of Ypres (22 April–25 May) was drawing to a close, one member of the battery wrote home, giving a fascinating insight into their life at the front:

We have had a warm time this last fortnight, and after it all yesterday (May Day) and today has been as quiet as death all along the Front; it was impossible to tell that there is a war on, and yet the Germans are entrenched only a few yards from our Front, just waiting their chance which they won't get.

The battles have been fierce and long in our zone. At times it is like hell and then [it is] all quietens down.

It is a strange warfare, both sides practically living in the ground in the firing line. We have nice little dugouts in our position. All positions are practically obscured with woods, etc. from aeroplane scouts, of which there seem dozens. We get some big German shells over us which whistle and scream through the air; the only danger in them is where and when they are going to burst.

The ground around us is like a pepper-caster, with holes made by Jack Johnsons [heavy calibre shells] and shells from the Krupp guns; some of them make good places for a bathe when they fill with water. The 'Jackos' are not so plentiful now; either the Germans' stock is exhausted or they are saving them. They send us a lighter shell, Krupps 6-inch and weighing about 80lbs. The Germans fire at regular intervals, and we know almost the time and when the shells are coming.

While the writer was closing his letter the enemy opened up fine once again:

5pm another bombardment has just started; the din is incessant and deafening. Many nights we were called out in action; it is tiring, and I suppose, dangerous, but we're used to it now, and it is very exciting especially when we have some hot firing.

It's very impressive to see the infantry going to the forward trenches at night, marching along perhaps to death – no one knows until they come out again.

During the spring of 1915 the army faced a shortage of artillery shells, the rationing of which led to heavy casualties during advances. The scandal led to the bringing down of the Liberal government. Not long afterwards, and close to the first anniversary of the declaration of war, a number of former employees of Edwin Bostock & Co. (a factory by then devoted to the munitions work) who were serving in France with the Stafford Battery received parcels from the factory floor. These would have been shared out among their comrades.The men wrote 'thank you' letters back, a number of which were later published in the *Staffordshire Chronicle* of 14 August. Corporal Cyril Moore wrote:

We are still in action, and doing our bit to keep the Germans at bay until we make the final sweep.

No doubt it will interest you to know the 46th Division, to which the Stafford Artillery and Stafford Infantry belong, have been complimented for the way they repelled the enemy's attack on the nights of the 30th and 31st [July]. The fighting is still heavy round this quarter, and it is surprising the amount of shells the Germans are sending over. So we must have shells of all calibre to use against them. 'Shells – and more shells,' is the cry out here.

We are all eagerly waiting the order to advance. I must draw to a close and get back to the gun, as we are all expecting another artillery duel tonight.

Meanwhile a letter from Drivers C. Reynolds and E. Wood of the ASC further reinforced the call for local factories to increase their shell production. Forwarded to the press, their letter was printed in the *Staffordshire Chronicle* of 2 July 1915: 'Shells, Shells and More Shells. And now that they have organized the munitions trade we can look forward to the future with calm confidence, for it is shells, shells and more shells that we need.'

Driver S.C. Hughes was a telephonist. His letter contained details of the Battery's recent casualties:

Our battery has seen plenty of fighting, especially this last two months. So far we have been very lucky as regards casualties – two killed and one wounded, the two killed being telephonists, the last [(No. 1026) Harry Millward, killed in action 31 July 1915] by shrapnel on Saturday 31st [July], while out mending telephone wires. His loss is felt by his fellow telephonists, of whom I am one. He never knew what fear was and we can ill afford to lose such men. His people are to be sympathized with; this is the second son they have lost out here, and they still have two more [in uniform], one a gunner in our Battery, while the other has won the VC [an apparent recommendation for an award which came to nothing].

While on manoeuvres commands were relayed via two trumpeters. In France, however, a number of the Battery's drivers acted as signallers for officers liaising with HQ or manning forward observation posts. The telephones were used by spotters in order to pass on the co-ordinates of enemy positions to the battery commanders.

Another former Bostock's employee, Gunner William Cartwright, wrote:

We came out of the trenches last week for a rest for four days, but had to return after two. We should have been in the Battle of Neuve Chapelle [10 March–22 April], but they could not get us up quickly enough. We were kept in reserve for that, and have been in several bombardments. We have now moved further into the line, and it is rather hot at times.

Gunner E. Barratt added: 'We have had a bit of a 'bust-up' the last three days – "little Willie" [a reference to the German Kaiser Wilhelm II] was trying to break through, but he was caught napping. I think myself that it will be a long time before it all comes to an end unless something unusual happens.'

The Battery was fighting on the Ypres Salient where the war had settled into a deadly stalemate in which both sides continued to lose thousands of men, but neither making any gains. The Stafford Battery was transferred, with the rest of the division, to the Loos Front in time to take part in the fighting around the Hohenzollern Redoubt (13 October 1915). The action saw heavy casualties among the Territorial battalions of the North and South Staffordshire Regiments, but the Stafford Battery got off more lightly.

Close to Christmas of that year, Edwin Bostock & Co. sent their usual parcels augmented by over 100 mufflers and 200 mittens. Some of the packages were received by members of the Stafford Battery who were facing their first Christmas overseas, prompting further letters of thanks. Bombardier H. Birch wrote to his former workmates: 'All the Bostock boys in the Battery are in excellent health; in fact, taking the Battery as a whole, there is not much wrong. Although we were at the Front for Christmas, what with the good things from home and the good supply of dainties from the officers, we had a good time.'

On 23 May 1916, under a general reorganization, the Staffordshire Batteries were re-designated, forming elements of the 231st, 232nd and 233rd Brigades. This shake-up included the 6th (Stafford) Staffordshire Battery, which became 'C' Battery, 232nd Brigade. Under the revision the brigades' composition was thus:

231st Brigade
'A' Battery – formerly the 1st Staffordshire Battery
'B' Battery – formerly the 2nd Staffordshire Battery
'C' Battery – formerly the 3rd Staffordshire Battery
'D' Howitzer Battery – formerly 'R' Battery, 4th North Midland
   Brigade

232nd Brigade
'A' Battery – formerly the 4th Staffordshire Battery
'B' Battery – formerly the 5th Staffordshire Battery
'C' Battery – formerly the 6th Staffordshire Battery
'D' Howitzer Battery – formerly the 2nd Derbyshire Battery

233rd Brigade
'B' Battery – formerly 'D' Battery, 2nd North Midland Brigade
'C' Battery – formerly 'D' Battery, 3rd North Midland Brigade

The *Staffordshire Chronicle* of 19 August 1916 printed a letter home written a fortnight earlier by Corporal A. Horton, of 99 Lichfield Road, Stafford. Horton was formerly a member of St Paul's Choir. His letter reflects a change in the Battery's role, which brought them closer to the front line:

A beautiful Night scene:
We have done with the strongly-built gun-pits and dug-outs, and have got a little nearer to the real thing. All we have time to trouble about now when on the move is cover from the aeroplane, and disguising the guns so as to make it look from the outside nothing more than a mound in a field: and more times than not you would hardly tell it was a gun if you were on the ground less than twenty yards away.

Goodbye to the comfortable cosy dug-out with the improvised beds. What we have now is a narrow trench, as deep as ever you have time to dig, which serves as a bedroom or 'kip-house,' and a 'funk hole' [somewhere to retreat to during heavy bombardment].

At night it is absolutely a wonderful sight. As you stand at the gun and look round you would think that, if there were not such a terrible war raging, you were looking at some great carnival. Thousands upon thousands of different coloured rockets and several other strange lights, which fill you with wonder and amazement, while your ears are ringing and whistling with the deafening roar of the firing and bursting of shells.

Occasionally when there is a slight lull in the artillery firing you will hear the rattle of a machine gun and the crack, crack, crack, of the rifles.

By the time our day's work is done we are ready to drop off to sleep, so we retire to our sleeping compartment, and 'pack-down'.

We may be just getting off to sleep, or we may be well away, or it may be the early hours of the morning, when you hear a shout: 'Battery action!'

Further changes lay ahead for the Battery when, on 28 August 1916, 'C' (Stafford) Battery 232nd Brigade, RFA, was broken up with Right Section joining 'A' Battery, 232nd Brigade and Left Section going over to 'B' Battery, 232nd Brigade, thereby bringing these batteries up to six 18-pounder guns (the strength of a Regular Army battery). A further development came on 27 October, when the 512th Heavy Battery, RFA, was transferred over to the 232nd Brigade and, on 3 November 1916, was re-designated 'C' (Heavy) Battery, 232nd Brigade, RFA. This unit only existed until 2 January 1917.

The members of the former Stafford Battery, serving with either 'A' or 'B' Batteries of the 232nd Brigade, RFA, left the 46th Division on 3 January 1917, when the whole Brigade was re-named the 232nd Army Brigade, RFA, and became a part of the 56th Division. On the same day 'C' Battery 247 Brigade joined the 232nd Brigade and was given the Stafford Battery's former title ('C' Battery, 232nd Brigade, RFA), the third unit to be so designated.

Meanwhile, the Staffordians of 'A' and 'B' Batteries of the 232nd Army Brigade fought at the Battle of Arras (9 April–16 June 1917), remaining in action at the front with the 15th Division until the cessation of hostilities.

During the war great strides were made in the development of artillery and its deployment; the men of the Stafford Battery becoming familiar with the new tactics and innovations. These included the use of the creeping barrage, flash detection and ranging, and eventually sound ranging and identification.

The Stafford Battery's campaign in France and Flanders resulted in a number of gallantry awards. The first of these was to Driver Arthur Hawkins, awarded the Distinguished Conduct Medal, *London Gazette*, 14 January 1916. The initial announcement carried no citation, but this was subsequently rectified on 11 March 1916: 'For conspicuous gallantry. When repairing telephone wire he went to the assistance of a wounded comrade under heavy fire and successfully brought him to safety.' The man that Hawkins tried so valiantly to save was another member of the Battery, Signaller Harry Millward, a former workmate at W.H. Dorman & Co. The pair had been repairing their forward observer's telephone cables under heavy shellfire, when Millward was mortally wounded by a burst of shrapnel. Having carried Millward to a place of relative safety, Hawkins returned with a medic.

While on home leave Gunner Hawkins was invited to attend a concert at the

Borough Hall given for wounded soldiers from the Sandon Hall Red Cross Hospital. During a ceremony held at the interval the DCM was pinned onto his uniform by the mayor, T.S. Bailey.

The *Stafford Newsletter* reported that the mayor:

> Conveyed to the recipient his heartiest congratulations on the honour which had been conferred upon him. He congratulated him on the brave and heroic spirit in which he endeavoured to save his comrade. He hoped the honour conferred upon him, would stimulate him to other brave deeds, and that he would be spared to return to the town of his birth with all the honour and glory of a brave soldier.
>
> Those gathered then joined in singing *For He's a Jolly Good Fellow* followed by the *National Anthem*.

A second ceremony was also reported when: 'At Messers W.H. Dorman and Co.'s Works, Bombardier Hawkins, in the presence of the working staff, was presented with a gold watch and chain by [one of] the directors [Mr W. Barton] and employees of the firm in commemoration of his gallantry, for which he was awarded the DCM.' The watch was inscribed: 'Presented on 22nd September, 1916, to Bombardier Arthur Hawkins DMC, by his fellow employees at Messers W.H. Dorman & Co., Ltd., Stafford, to commemorate his winning the DCM at Ypres on 31st July, 1915.' Mr W. Barton commented that:

> Hawkins' action reflected gloriously not only upon the firm, but upon the town, of which Bombardier Hawkins was a native [*sic*]: He added the firm's appreciation of the gallant conduct and the service which Bombardier Hawkins had rendered to the country. He hoped that Bombardier Hawkins would come back in full health and vigour to settle down in civilian life, and become once more an employee of the company.

When it was learnt that the 19-year-old Hawkins was due to return to the front on Sunday, 24 September 1916, a civic parade was arranged to escort him from the Borough Hall to the railway station. It was later reported that 'the Band of the 13th Training Reserve Regiment, the Stafford Company of the Staffordshire Volunteer Regiment (under Colonel C.H. Wright) headed the parade, followed by the Volunteer Aid Detachment of the Red Cross, the Special Constables, the Fire Brigade (under Captain Espley), and the Cadets, were followed by the Boy Scouts'.

Hawkins walked alongside the mayor, taking the plaudits of the considerable crowds which lined the whole route:

> The procession, which was a considerable length and passed through thickly lined streets, spectators cheering and waving their handkerchiefs. The band played *See the Conquering Hero Come*.

The Station Square was occupied by one of the largest crowds that has ever assembled there. A temporary platform had been placed in front of the central lamp post and the Mayor with Sir Walter Essex, MP, Colonel Anson, and Bombardier Hawkins mounted it.

There were the obligatory speeches, while Hawkins was given three cheers before the band struck up the *National Anthem*. Following the formalities, the dignitaries shook Hawkins' hand before he was carried by the crowd shoulder-high to the station entrance. As Hawkins' train pulled away from the platform a volley of fog signals was set off in his honour.

A second award to a Stafford Battery member was announced in the *Staffordshire Chronicle* of 20 January 1917, with Bombardier B. Ashton receiving the Military Medal: 'Another Stafford Man Gets The M.M.'. The article read: 'Bombardier B. Ashton, son of Mrs. J. Ashton, 7, Common Road (formerly employed by Messers Simpson and Co., Rowley Street, Stafford), of the Stafford Battery RFA which went out in March 1915 has been awarded the Military Medal for rescuing a wounded comrade under heavy shell-fire, at a place called Bienvilliers, on the night of January 2nd [1917].'

While Bombardier Ashton had originally served with the Stafford Battery (which by then no longer existed as a unit), it was noted that he had been transferred to another unit (probably to either 'A' or 'B' Batteries of the 232nd Brigade, RFA) sometime before the action for which his award was made. In September 1917, Ashton was allowed home on leave, following treatment at Brook War Hospital for shrapnel wounds to the hand, knee, shoulder, chest and foot. Ashton was invited to his former workplace where a simple presentation took place. The ceremony was reported in the *Staffordshire Chronicle* of 22 September 1917:

On Saturday last [15th] the Mayor, on behalf of the firm and employees of Messers Simpson & Co. presented to Bombardier Ashton, a gold watch from the firm and a gold chain from the employees. The Mayor spoke in eloquent terms of the courage of the recipient:

'Whilst in charge of a convoy the Germans started shelling, and blew the leading team to pieces. At great personal risk he carried a wounded driver nearly a quarter of a mile to safety [into the cellar of an old house], and having rendered first aid fetched the RAMC men to his assistance. Gunned Ashton was complimented by the colonel of his regiment [*sic*] on his brave deed, as shells were dropping all round him whilst he was carrying his comrade in. Since then Gunner Ashton has been severely wounded [while in action prior to the Battle of Messines], and has just been discharged from hospital. In this instance a shell of high calibre dropped on his gun killing all the men except himself [two killed outright, and several badly wounded].

Following the presentation:

> Ashton spoke [and] said that words failed him, [and that he] should never forget the cordial reception and the handsome gift, which he valued most highly. If, when he recovered from his wounds, he [were to return to the front, then he assured those gathered that he] should do his duty with the same courage and determination as in the past.

The article continued, stating the Ashton 'had taken part in most of the big battles including on the Aisne and the Somme, and also at Messines and that he knew what it meant to face the enemy'. He had also been twice buried by exploding shells.

The initial press release had been somewhat premature, as Bombardier B. Ashton's award wasn't officially promulgated in the *London Gazette* until 12 March 1917. Although again wounded, Bertram Ashton survived the war and returned to his home town and his pre-war job.

A further gallantry medal was earned by another former Battery member when on 18 May 1917, the *London Gazette* announced that Acting Battery Sergeant Major A.J. Salter had been Mentioned in Despatches. Meanwhile, on 28 September 1917 the *London Gazette* announced the award of the Military Medal to Driver G.H. Downing.

STAFFORD ARTILLERYMAN HONOURED.

The name of Battery-Sergt.-Major A. J. (Bert) Salter, of the Royal Field Artillery, appears in the list of officers, N.C.O.s, and men mentioned in Sir Douglas Haig's despatches for conspicuous service on the Western front. He has proved himself an exceptionally smart N.C.O., and his promotion has been rapid and well earned.

Sergeant-Major Salter went out with the Stafford Territorial Battery in March, 1915. Prior to that time he was employed as a fitter at Messrs. W. H. Dorman and Co.'s works, Stafford, where his brother, Sergt. Wm. Salter, of the R.F.A., who was wounded last November, was engaged in the test-house.

Their father, Mr. Wm. Salter, formerly of Tillington-street, Stafford, SERGT.-MAJOR SALTER and now stationed at Pentonville Prison, served in the Coldstream Guards for several years, and on leaving the Army entered the prison service. He was principal warder at Stafford, and left the town about 12 months ago to take up his new duties in London.

News of Battery Sergeant Major A.J. Salter's Mention in Despatches.

The *Staffordshire Chronicle* picked up news of the medal via the War Office's regular press releases and published a feature on 20 October 1917:

After being several times recommended for distinction, Driver Dowding was awarded the Military Medal for carrying in [the] wounded and [for] repairing telephone cables under heavy fire. As a lad he attended the Christ Church (Rowley Street) Schools, and at the time of the outbreak of war was employed by Messers W.H. Dorman and Co Ltd. His Commanding Officer wrote a letter of congratulation which read:

'Dear Downing, very hearty congratulations. We have succeeded in getting you your well earned Military Medal. Good luck to you.'

The *Stafford Newsletter* of 3 November 1917 added: 'Sapper [*sic*] G.H. Downing won his medal for carrying wounded under severe shell fire when his staff H.Q. was being heavily shelled. He showed utter disregard of personal danger and had been recommended for the honour on four previous occasions. He went out with the original Stafford Battery and has been wounded twice.' Before the end of hostilities, Downing was wounded a further time and twice gassed.

Members of the Stafford Battery on a post-war parade.

Members of the Stafford Battery attending a post-war reunion.

In addition, the following awards are known to have been made to other former Stafford Battery members while serving with 'A' or 'B' Batteries of 232nd Brigade:

Sergeant A. Wooley, 'A' or 'B' Battery, 232nd Brigade, RFA (TF) – *London Gazette*, 12 June 1918, Military Medal

Corporal A.E. Dingley, 'A' Battery, 232nd Brigade, RFA (TF) – *London Gazette*, 11 December 1918, Military Medal

Driver W.B. Chilton, 'A' Battery, 232nd Brigade, RFA (TF) – *London Gazette*, 11 February 1919, Military Medal

Gunner Albert Robertson, 'A' Battery, 232nd Brigade (TF), RFA – *London Gazette*, 11 February 1919, Military Medal (Roberts was reported to be a fitter with the Stafford Battery and was twice wounded during the war)

Driver J. Ollier, 'B' Battery, 232nd Brigade, RFA (TF) – *London Gazette*, 14 May 1919, Military Medal (wounded in action)

Farrier Sergeant A.E. Frost, 'A' Battery, 232nd Brigade, RFA (TF) – *London Gazette*, 23 July 1919, Military Medal

Fitter Staff Sergeant R. Webb was Mentioned in Despatches, *London Gazette*, 18 May 1917 (Webb, a pre-war member of the Stafford Battery, died of wounds on 28 April 1917, when it was reported in the *Staffordshire Chronicle* that he 'was three times recommended for conspicuous bravery in the field. He was offered a commission but preferred to remain with his Battery.')

Battery Quartermaster Sergeant W.H.S. Cooper, RFA (Stafford) – *London Gazette*, 11 October 1916, Meritorious Service Medal (*Staffordshire Chronicle*, 23 October 1916: 'Battery Quartermaster-Sergeant W.H.S. Cooper, of Stafford, who is attached to the RFA, has been the recipient of a signal honour, in being presented with the MSM following upon two years' arduous service in France. Before the war Cooper was a police clerk in the Chief Constable's office at Stafford.' In the article Cooper was described as 'formerly of the Stafford Battery'.)

CHAPTER 7

The 1/1st Battalion, Staffordshire Yeomanry

Among the local units to see active service overseas was the Stafford Troop, 1/1st Battalion, Staffordshire Yeomanry. The Yeomanry was mobilized on 4 August 1914. Its Stafford depot on Bailey Street very soon became inundated with new recruits. Both new recruits and existing members were asked to sign the 'Imperial Service Undertaking', volunteering for active service anywhere the Empire was threatened. This was the first step towards an overseas deployment.

Initially the new recruits did not have horses, while modern rifles, standard uniform and equipment were in short supply and reserved for men bound for France and Flanders. The troopers' fitness levels needed improving and there followed an intense period of seemingly endless drill, including route marches to Newport or Milford. Many Staffordians later recalled seeing the men march by giving renditions of *It's a Long Way to Tipperary*, *A Soldiers Man* and *Who's Your Lady Friend*.

Members of the Stafford Troop on manouevres on Milford Common, 1914.

Members of the Staffordshire Yeomanry outside the Station Hotel prior to embarking for Diss, 1914.

As a part of their training a series of lectures and instruction on weaponry and combat techniques were given by Sergeant Watson, drafted in from the Hanley depot. Then came a long spell at Tixall, where the men were billeted in local cottages for several months.

In early November, the 1/1st Battalion, Staffordshire Yeomanry marched to Stafford railway station, where they entrained for Diss, Norfolk, making their temporary base at the training camp at Billingford, where they were stationed for the best part of a year. The Regimental HQ was located at the Scole Inn, the rank and file being billeted at nearby farms. The new recruits were issued with proper uniforms and received riding instruction – despite the number of men drawn from the countryside around Stafford few had actually ridden before enlisting.

While many at the War Office realized that the cavalry had had its day, there were still some who held onto the idea that there might be a big breakthrough on the Western Front. However, at the beginning of August 1915, while stationed at Langley Park, the 1/1st Battalion was ordered to hand over its horses to their 2/1st Battalion. The 1/1st Battalion was issued with rifles and bayonets, replacing their shorter carbines, and undertook instruction in hand-to-hand combat in preparation for trench warfare on the Western Front.

No sooner was their training near completion, than the orders were revoked, and in September their horses were returned – it had been decided that the 1/1st Battalion was bound for action in the Gallipoli Campaign. On 25 October orders reached the HQ of the North Midland Mounted Brigade; the unit was to embark en masse for the Mediterranean. In preparation for their deployment, a detachment of the 1/1st Battalion's officers were sent to a conference at Mudros (the operational HQ for the Gallipoli and Salonika operations) the day before the regiment entrained for Southampton.

The 1/1st Battalion, Staffordshire Yeomanry set sail for Gallipoli on the 27th. The voyage was hazardous with the threat of mines, attack from surface vessels and German U-boats to contend with. Seasickness was rampant, but the woes of the Stafford men's journey were eclipsed by news that 150 men of the Lincolnshire Yeomanry had been killed when a U-boat surfaced alongside their troop ship, pounding it with their deck guns. During the Staffordshire Yeomanry's voyage their orders were rescinded and they were re-directed to Alexandria. Here the men disembarked, bound for service in Egypt in the fight against the Senussi tribe who were allied to the Turkish Army.

A Staffordshire Yeomanry cap badge.

Landing on 9 November, the troops were sent to the Mena House camp in Cairo. While there they enjoyed a few days' leave, buying souvenirs in the bazaars or taking advantage of the opportunity for adventure and scaling the Pyramids. Towards the end of the month the troops entrained for Fayoum where they saw out the year, making occasional forays while on outpost duty.

In 1916 the Staffordshire Yeomanry was sent to El Azzab before transferring to northern Sinai. Here their role became one of mounting patrols to defend the railway and a water pipeline which ran from Egypt towards enemy occupied Palestine. While the men served periods on outpost duty, there was little real action. The time spent in the desert was not wasted, however, the men learning survival skills that were to prove invaluable in the campaign that lay ahead.

Serving as a part of the Yeomanry Mounted Division, the Staffordshire Yeomanry was present during the protracted struggle for Gaza. It was vitally important that the city be captured if the Allies were to advance northwards on Jerusalem, for centuries regarded as the heart of the territory. The First Battle of Gaza, which began on 26 March 1917, soon developed from promising beginnings into a farce through a combination of poor intelligence and a serious breakdown in operational communications. The battle on the ground went far better than could have been planned and, although the troops faced stiff opposition, this soon gave way and the infantry made considerable gains in the suburbs of the city.

The Staffordshire Yeomanry's role was to hold a position to the north-east, ready to cut off the enemy's retreat and head off an anticipated Turkish relief column from Beersheba.

The generals, miles to the rear of the battle, received information that was 2 or 3 hours old, and therefore believed British troops were still experiencing difficulties in taking the first-line defences. Furthermore, two erroneous reports of enemy relief columns came in from the RFC – the map references were wrong and therefore convinced the Staff that the enemy was close to hand, while their numbers were grossly exaggerated – and as a result the attack was called off almost at the moment of victory. A second attack was made nearly a month later, but faced strengthened defences. Almost inevitably the Second Battle of Gaza (17 April) was a very costly defeat, the Staffordshire Yeomanry suffering a number of casualties.

The Staffordshire Yeomanry made reconnaissance patrols near Beersheba in late August during which they clashed with the enemy and were forced to retire through an enemy artillery barrage.

The final victory at Gaza came on 31 October 1917. The Stafford Troop held an observation post from where the generals received more reliable updates, allowing them to direct the unfolding battle.

A Staffordshire Yeomanry shoulder title.

Beersheba fell on 5 November, the troops picking their way between shell holes and enemy barbed wire entanglements in order to breach the enemy's defences. The men had orders not to touch anything for fear of booby traps. Moving northwards the following day, the Staffordshire Yeomanry came under heavy and accurate shellfire and suffered further casualties. There then followed a period of re-grouping before the next planned advance.

Far from home, and suffering from the heat and humidity of the desert, the Stafford men looked forward to post from home, while current copies of the local papers were regularly passed around. Sometimes, though, the news from home made them feel they were almost forgotten. It was at about this time that local man Private C. Biddulph, of 'C' Squadron, wrote home. His letter, which was published in the *Staffordshire Chronicle* of 10 November 1917, noted that although he had heard of the Stafford Soldiers' Comfort Fund, 'I am sorry to say that neither I nor any other Stafford man in this regiment has received any benefit from this fund.' Biddulph reminisced: 'We Stafford lads often talk of the good times we used to have at the Welcome Club [at Stafford's Carnegie Free Lending Library]. Of course, that is two and a half years ago. I am sure it would do our eyes good if we could cast them upon those nice cups of tea and cakes we used to get there.' Biddulph signed off: 'Hoping some kind friends will remember we Stafford lads in Palestine.'

As the advance continued the Staffordshire Yeomanry covered ground quickly, often riding for days without finding water. On 8 November they lost contact with the enemy overnight: 'riding past dead horses and dead Turks'. One squadron, acting as advanced guard, had a nasty fright: 'We came over the crest of a hill, we were looking down the muzzles of four enemy mountain guns.' The troopers quickly turned away from the immediate danger as the gunners fired their first rounds.

The scarcity of fresh water remained the greatest danger and on the 12th the troopers walked for 3 hours under cover of darkness to fill their bottles, all the time under the sights of enemy artillery. With their kit dulled to prevent the moonlight's reflection from giving away their position, they made it safely back to camp without being detected.

During the following day (13th) the Staffordshire Yeomanry was back on the move, joining the general advance of the 22nd Mounted Brigade. While progressing along a dried riverbed about a mile across, however, they came under heavy machine-gun and rifle fire. The men were in an exposed position and so the order was given to draw their swords and 'Charge!'. The Yeomanry galloped head-long into the mass of enemy forces, which was easily routed. By the end of the day 2 field guns, a dozen machine guns and 1,000 Turkish troops had been captured in an unprecedented route in the campaign. In reply Staffordshire Yeomanry's 'D' Squadron suffered one killed and a handful with minor wounds.

On 14 November the Stafford Troop was detached to act as an escort to Royal Engineer sappers whose job it was to set charges on the railway lines into Jerusalem. This was to prevent the possible resupply of the enemy garrison. They carried off their mission without a hitch, taking a number of prisoners along the way. The Stafford Troop was in action again on the following day. The order was given to dismount for close-quarter combat, the men acting as close support to a section of machine-gunners, with the Royal Horse Artillery (RHA) providing the main firepower. One trooper described the Yeomanry's attack: 'The RHA did wonderful work, driving Johnny [the Turkish troops] from one point, then another, our dismounted fellows sending leaden messengers as he scuttled about. When our fellows fixed bayonets for the final assault it was too much for Johnny and he bolted.'

Advancing slowly across mountainous terrain to relive the Middlesex Yeomanry, the troopers were forced to leave their mounts behind. Then, on 23 November, 'C' Squadron was ordered to relieve the Lincolnshire Yeomanry which had suffered a number of casualties while holding a ridge commanding a position over the enemy's position. Local man, Private J.W. Dick, wrote:

'C' Squadron got the brunt of it and suffered pretty heavily. We held on all afternoon, a battery of artillery coming up from 'goodness knows where', and quite saving a nasty situation. Our Troop was sent out to look for, and bring in 'C' Squadron's wounded and some of our fellows did marvellously cool work under heavy rifle and machine-gun fire.

The 6th Mounted Brigade continued in their advance on 28 November. Elements of the Staffordshire Yeomanry attacked a Turkish machine-gun post on the summit of a hill, which commanded the intended route of the advance. Facing heavy fire, the assault soon broke down, with a number of wounded men being caught out in the open. Once again, Private J.W. Dick was among the men who went out under fire to bring in the wounded:

Early on the Colonel was hit and the MO sent for me. Together we crawled out under fire and succeeded in getting him. Then others began to come in and I had, I think, the hardest day of my life. We were under fire all the time but somehow the men had to be dressed and carried to safety. It was well into the afternoon before we got them all in. Never before was I so completely exhausted; limbs and brain alike refused to work and for the first time I began to feel my nerves.

The retreat continued under heavy fire until the Troop reached its original position. Elsewhere, however, the advance had been more successful and the way was now open to Jerusalem, which fell on 9 December 1917.

Following the capture of Jerusalem, the Yeomanry Mounted Division was withdrawn and rested at Deir el Belah near Gaza. The 1/1st Battalion, Staffordshire Yeomanry was ordered to cross Palestine and deploy in the Jordan Valley in March 1918. In July, the Division was reformed as the Fourth Cavalry Division, under the command of General Allenby. In September 1918, the Staffordshire Yeomanry began an advance across the coastal plain of Sharon to El Affule, covering 60 miles in two days. Over the following few days some 5,800 prisoners were taken, the Corps making a triumphal entry into Damascus in Syria on 2 October.

The remnants of the 1/1st Battalion, Staffordshire Yeomanry, now numbering only seventy-five of all ranks due largely to the ravages of malaria, began a 200-mile trek to Aleppo, which was captured on 25 October 1918. Turkey surrendered five days later, bringing an end to the campaign.

Home Leave was very rare for the troops serving in the Middle East. Even following victory, the Yeomanry was forced to remain in a policing role. This meant that there would be no early homecoming for these men, many of whom did not see our shores until 1919.

CHAPTER 8

Taking the King's Shilling

❖

The Regular Army

Like any town, Stafford had its fair share of Regular servicemen, men who had enlisted (for a minimum of seven years) in the pre-war army or navy. Once these men left the service they were subject to a further five years as Reservists. There were also Special Reservists who were part-time servicemen who enlisted for six years. They were liable to call-up in the event of a war. On the declaration of war these men formed a part of the National Reserve and were mobilized and recalled to their units, supplementing the standing army.

The Territorial Army

The local militias and companies of volunteers were disbanded in 1907/8 on the formation of the Reservists and the Territorials (the latter under the Territorial Forces Act of 1907). Under the new system, most of the county infantry regiments formed two Territorial battalions and the North and South Staffordshire Regiments were no exceptions. These units were recruited locally due to transport restrictions, with volunteers generally joining at their nearest depot.

Training was at weekends, evenings and at summer camps, which were arranged to coincide with the local staple industry's annual holiday. The Territorials were formed as home defence units, but men and boys (boys could enlist in the Territorials at under 18 years old) enlisted on the basis that in the event of war they could be called upon for full-time service. On the declaration of war most battalions signed their overseas papers en masse.

The British Regular Army, and to some extent the Territorial Army, was decimated during the first five months of conflict. The generals did not have to look far for eager replacements. On his appointment as Secretary of State for War on 5 August 1914, Field Marshal Lord Kitchener issued a call for an army of 100,000 volunteers, which was initially intended to be the first of 5 similar appeals. In fact, his overall goal of 500,000 was quickly exceeded and doubled before the end of the year.

After the form-filling and a medical examination, when potential recruits had to meet requirements of height, weight and chest expansion, the process concluded with the 'taking the King's Shilling'.

The volunteers attested in front of a commissioned officer or a Justice of the Peace. Holding a copy of the Bible, the recruits swore to 'honestly and faithfully defend His Majesty King George the Fifth in Person, Crown and Dignity against all enemies' and to 'observe and obey the orders of all generals and officers' over him.

Recruits were then given their instructions and travel warrant a day or two later (there was traditionally always a 24-hour 'cooling off period', when a recruit could change his mind).

The atmosphere in the town remained 'electric', with the war being the main topic of conversation. A recruiting depot had been opened at the Shire Hall to accept recruits for what had already been dubbed 'Kitchener's Army'. In the great clamour to volunteer, many boys were able to enlist under-age, something that was condoned by some recruiting sergeants, who received a bonus for each man they enlisted. When boys looked too young they were often told to 'come back tomorrow when you are two years older!'. The *Staffordshire Chronicle* of Saturday 15 August reported: 'A station had been opened in the town to accept recruits for the second army the War Secretary is raising.' By 29 August the *Staffordshire Chronicle* could boast that the borough was doing very well in response to Kitchener's call. Between 11 and 27 August no less than 246 men had come forward, only 10 of these being rejected on medical grounds.

On 2 September a meeting of Siemens Brothers' employees was held at the Carnegie Free Library with a view to forming a 'company of chums' from volunteers. Following other local factories' leads, the firm announced that they would look after the families of members of its workforce who enlisted.

Recruiting was in full swing and the regular 'Stafford in War Times' column in the *Staffordshire Chronicle* carried the following article on 5 September:

Remarkable Rally of Recruits
Enthusiastic Scenes

We are living in memorable times, and Stafford is playing to the full its part in the great struggle in which England is now engaged. A 'call to arms' has been made, and, as in the past, the loyalty and patriotism of Stafford men have not been found wanting.

Naturally there had been a strong response to Lord Kitchener's appeal which, it was reported:

has gone straight to the hearts of the men of Stafford. Over 500 men have joined the Army in less than a week [while a rate of around 250 volunteers per week would be maintained for some time to come].

The Shire Hall has been the centre of a busy scene during the past week and the military officials, doctors, and recruiting sergeants have had their hands full in dealing with the steady stream of recruits anxious to serve their country.

Early on Monday morning a large crowd gathered at the station [including the mayor, Mr J.C. Mycock] to see off a number of Siemens' youths and a couple of local journalists who had enlisted in the 1st Battalion, Coldstream Guards. Each evening a party of men were escorted from the Shire Hall to the station by family and friends, leaving the town in good spirits.

The same issue of the *Staffordshire Chronicle* reported:

Recruiting Fever Still High

Recruiting has been vigorously carried on during the week at Stafford, as the Roll of Honour on another page testifies. The rush of recruits has been so great during the last two or three weeks that it has been found impossible to deal with the masses of men satisfactorily at the various HQs.

The recruitment campaign would soon feature the now famous poster image of Lord Kitchener of Khartoum, whose sombre gaze and waxed handlebar moustache confronted the viewer, his outstretched index finger pointing directly out of the poster: 'Your Country Needs YOU.' The poster was first seen on the streets on 6 September, although the image had appeared in an earlier issue of *London Opinion*, while the slogan 'Your Country Needs You!' had been the strapline for an article in the *Daily Mail* on 28 August 1914. By this date volunteers already numbered close to 300,000, the final figure for the end of the year standing at 1,186,357 volunteers.

Field Marshal Lord Kitchener appealed for a 100,000-strong Volunteer Army.

On 7 September a recruiting meeting was held in the Shire Hall. The following report appeared in the *Staffordshire Chronicle* of the 12th:

Stafford has witnessed many memorable scenes during its long and eventful history, and the great recruiting meeting held in the Shire Hall on Monday [7th] was worthy of the best tradition of the town. It was an appeal to the loyalty and patriotism of the men and women of the borough, for sacrifices are demanded of both, and the appeal was not made in vain. The meeting gave an impetus to the rally of recruits which began earlier in the day, and Stafford responded nobly to the country's call. Long before eight o'clock a steady stream of men gathered in the Shire Hall, and the Market Square was thronged with unbounded enthusiasm – the wave of patriotism had left no one untouched – and the scene was an inspiring one.

An early recruitment gathering in the Market Square, August 1914.

Among the speakers were the mayor, Mr J.C. Mycock, Lord Dartmouth, Lord Lieutenant of the County, Lord Lichfield, Lord Hatherton and Sir Walter Essex MP. It was reported that Mr Mycock rejoiced to see that so many had rallied to the Colours. He said that he hoped that as a result of the meeting the army would have a great influx of recruits. Meanwhile, Lord Dartmouth emphasized that Britons were not fighting for Serbia or to defend French or Belgian soil, but for the Empire, for the country's trade and independence. Calling for volunteers, he explained: 'If we are defeated it will mean the extinction of England as we have always known it; it means the loss of our trade and the loss of our liberty.' Appealing directly for further recruits, Lord Dartmouth made reference to the exploits of the BEF in France:

> You will be in time to back up the Expeditionary Force, and to show the world that the men of Stafford are ready and willing to help England to hold her own. Already 70 units of the Territorial Forces have volunteered for active service at the front. Are you going to shelter yourself behind the sacrifices they have made and live at home in ease?

Among the early volunteers were many of the town's young elite, including scholars and sportsmen. Stafford Rugby Club lost most of its team to the army, while Stafford Rangers soon had thirteen players and four members of its coaching staff serving in the Colours. Many of the young volunteers who enlisted into the Guards Division were rushed through their basic training in a matter of weeks and were fighting in France by the winter.

Enlistment

In 1914–15 the enlistment process followed a set procedure. On acceptance a new recruit was initially sent to his regimental depot. Here he received his kit and was introduced to army discipline and training. Next he was posted to a main training camp where his batch of recruits joined a battalion. Because of the massive expansion of the army, few regiments had the required stocks of equipment or the manpower to train the flood of recruits.

The initial influx inevitably slowed down to an average of 100,000 a month into early 1915. Many of the new recruits had to wear their own clothes, or old-style red jackets from the Boer War era, while others wore blue uniforms (known as 'Kitchener Blue') or those purchased by public subscription. Weapons continued to be in short supply. Often new recruits were put through their initial training with obsolete weapons, wooden rifles or even broomsticks.

Finding officers to train the men was also difficult: most of the Regular officers and NCOs were serving overseas. Officers on the Reserve List were called upon to carry out the work, assisted by NCOs.

Early recruits outside the Station Hotel, August 1914.

Underage Recruits

On the outbreak of the war the country was caught up in a wave of patriotic euphoria. In their eagerness to serve their King and Country, many enlisted underage. Not untypical was the story of Alan E.H. Smith, a 16-year-old pupil of King Edward VI Grammar School, Stafford. Smith was one of those who flocked to the Shire Hall where he tried to enlist. He was recognized and told to 'go back to school'. Unperturbed, Smith went by rail to Stone where he lied about his age and enlisted. Alan Smith passed through basic training and was posted to the 4th Battalion, Royal Fusiliers, which formed a part of the 3rd Division's 9th Brigade. Private Smith's regiment was sent to France in February 1915, taking part in the fighting at Zillebeke, St Eloi and Hill 60.

Private Smith was severely wounded at Ypres on 20 April 1915, and spent the next six months in hospital followed by a similar period of convalescence before being sent back to the front. In late July 1916, Smith's gallantry while bringing in the wounded under shellfire during the Battle of Somme was recognized with his promotion to lance corporal. He was wounded for a second time in September that year. This time, Smith's wounds were severe enough for him to be evacuated home and he spent several months in Northampton Hospital. Alan had by this time completed two tours of the front while still underage.

Another of the many under aged recruits was George Crewe, who was initially assigned to the 1/6th Battalion, North Staffordshire Regiment, a Territorial battalion brought up to full strength with new volunteers. George's battalion sailed for France in March 1915 and was soon to relieve battle-weary troops already in the front line on the Ypres Salient. Transferred to the Loos Sector, they fought at the Hohenzollern Redoubt (13 October) before being withdrawn to bring on new recruits to fill their depleted ranks. George found himself once more in France, engaged in bitter trench warfare, from 16 February 1916.

Through a letter home his parents were able to discover his battalion and immediately wrote to his CO, giving his correct date of birth and asking that he be taken off the regimental strength; George was duly transferred. He did not, however, return home, as the army had a special battalion stationed in France for under-aged soldiers – there the boys could continue under military training and be filtered back into front line units as soon as they attained the age of 19. Although he didn't initially appreciate being removed from his comrades, George was probably saved from an early grave, as only a few weeks later, on 1 July 1916, the 1/6th Battalion, North Staffordshire Regiment suffered heavy casualties at Gommecourt (on the first day of the Battle of the Somme).

Following a period of further training and a posting to Ireland on policing duties, George returned to France, this time serving with the 13th (Service) Battalion, Royal Scots. He was to spend another year in the trenches fighting at the Third Battle of Ypres (known as Passchaendale, 31 July–10 November 1917), the Second Battle of the Somme (21 March–4 July 1918) and throughout the advance to victory, beginning in August 1918.

National Registration and Conscription

By spring 1915 the stalemate of trench warfare had set in, and with growing casualties on both sides it became apparent that in this war of attrition the side with the greater resources in terms of men and munitions would win. By the spring recruitment figures were beginning to dwindle. To complicate matters many men from heavy industry and agriculture had left their jobs to enlist, thus inadvertently hampering war production and the country's ability to feed its population. The government needed more service-age men in uniform, but had to fill the places of essential workers before they left their positions. To this end a national survey, or mini census, was needed to give a better idea of the pool of men available.

The National Registration Act was passed on 15 July 1915, as the first step towards conscription. The *Stafford Newsletter* of 24 July carried an appeal for assistance with the distribution and collection of completed National Registration forms which was to

This Certificate must be signed and care-fully preserved by the person to whom it is issued.

If the place of residence of the holder of the Certificate is changed otherwise than temporarily, the Certificate must within 28 days be handed in at a Post Office or sent or delivered to the Clerk of the Council of the Borough, Urban or Rural District in which the new residence is situate (or, in Scotland, the Town or County Clerk), with the new address written in the space below. A fresh Certificate will be supplied in due course.

Space for new address.

NATIONAL

REGISTRATION

ACT, 1915.

The cover of a National Registration ID card.

This is to Certify that

(a) Albert Perry

(b) Miller, engineering

(26) (647)

(c) of 10 Bellasis Street

STAFFORD

has been Registered under the NATIONAL REGISTRATION ACT, 1915.

BOROUGH OF STAFFORD

Signature of Holder.

GOD SAVE THE KING.

(a) Name. (b) Occupation. (c) Postal Address.

A National Registration ID card.

take place between 7 and 21 August. Men aged between 15 and 65 were required to register, providing details of their age, occupation and address (the information later being used to assist with conscription). The results revealed that 3,400,000 men between the ages of 18 and 41 were theoretically available for military service.

Lord Derby was appointed Director General of Recruiting on 11 October 1915, and five days later he introduced a new recruitment drive focusing on 'white collar' workers. This became known as the Derby Scheme, a halfway measure towards conscription, whereby men of service age could enlist but remain in employment until called up for active duty. On 11 October, King George V made a rallying speech in which he outlined the need for resurgence in volunteers:

At this grave moment in the struggle between my people and a highly-organized enemy, who has transgressed the laws of nations and changed the ordinance that binds civilized Europe together, I appeal to you.

I rejoice in my Empire's effort, and I feel pride in the voluntary response from my subjects all over the world who have sacrificed home, fortune, and life itself, in order that another may not inherit the free Empire which their ancestors and mine have built.

I ask you to make good these sacrifices.

The end is not in sight. More men and yet more are wanted to keep my armies in the field, and through them to secure victory and enduring peace.

I ask you, men of all classes, to come forward voluntarily, and take your share in the fight.

It was later reported in the *Staffordshire Chronicle* of 30 October 1915 that 'fifty recruits have been sent from Stafford during the past week, and compared with previous weeks the figures show that the [King's] appeal has been met with a satisfactory response in the borough'. The Derby scheme had also made its mark and continued to reap rewards and during November the foreman of W.H. Dorman & Co. Ltd marched to the recruiting office with a total of twenty-five volunteers. This scene was repeated until all those fitting the requirements of the services had completed their attestation papers and finally enlisted. Under the scheme, volunteers were allowed to return to their normal jobs until called up. This staggered process allowed for women, invalided servicemen and non-service-age men to be trained up ready to step into the volunteers' roles without noticeable loss of production.

Consequently, the *Staffordshire Chronicle* of 20 November was able to report: 'Recently at Stafford during the previous week has been reminiscent of the early days of the war, and the figures again show a marked improvement on previous weeks, while a reasonable number of recruits have been secured for the coming week.' The article went on to acknowledge the results of the King's appeal: 'Over 100 have enlisted during the past 7 days and of this number only half have joined under the Lord Derby group scheme.'

The momentum had to be maintained, and the *Staffordshire Chronicle* of 27 November 1915 urged men to come forward under the Derby Scheme, thus avoiding the need to introduce conscription.

Despite the renewed influx of volunteers, it remained apparent that the losses at the front were by far outstripping recruitment. As the Derby Scheme drew to a close, and on the eve of the introduction of conscription, the *Staffordshire Chronicle* carried the following:

> The Mayor of Stafford (Mr. T.S. Bailey) has received a telegram from Lord Derby inviting him to do all in his power to induce single men to join the Army under the group system, which is still open for voluntary enlistment. The Mayor appeals to all the young men in the district who are eligible and have not yet come forward before the Military Service Bill becomes operative, to do so at once, and help Stafford to be amongst the districts who have only a negligible number who have not responded to the call.

The wave of patriotism that had swept through the country meant that a staggering 2,466,719 men had enlisted by December 1915. Conscription, however, would bring Great Britain in line with the other combatant nations and give the services the additional fighting strength required to compete in the war of attrition.

A Snapshot of Stafford's Recruitment Drives

All of Stafford's industries played their part in the recruitment drives, including the boot and shoe factories. An insight into the town's war effort may be gleaned from a study of a single factory's contribution. By January 1916, the eve of conscription, Edwin Bostock & Co. had 280 former workers in the armed services, including 3 of the owner's sons. A further 240 had attested under Lord Derby's recruiting scheme and were awaiting call-up. While many of their former employees were still under military training, others had been wounded or were serving in units that were being rested. Nearly 120 were then reckoned to be on active service at the front; 12 had been killed in action. The factory's efforts were mirrored across the town.

The First of the Derby Scheme Volunteers Depart and the Introduction of Conscription

The *Staffordshire Chronicle* of 22 January announced the departure of Staffordians under the Derby Scheme: 'The first company of men from Stafford called up under the group system departed for Lichfield on Thursday [20th], they having a cordial "send off" at the railway station.'

With the recruitment drives over and the war still taking a heavy toll, there remained only the conscription option. The Military Service Act of 27 January 1916 brought conscription into effect. Along with the Defence of the Realm Act, it was possibly the most important piece of legislation in placing Britain onto a 'total war' footing. Under the terms of the Act, every British male subject who, on 15 August 1915, was ordinarily resident in Great Britain and who had attained the age of 19 but was not yet 41 and, on 2 November 1915, was unmarried or a widower without dependent children, was deemed to have enlisted.

From September 1916, men called up were first assigned to a unit of the Training Reserve. Meanwhile, further Acts were passed, extending the range of men deemed to have enlisted, and at the same time the exemptions were tightened. The necessity to revert to conscription was clear, if controversial, as by the end of the war the British Army was largely composed of conscripts, with half of the soldiers serving in France and Flanders aged 18 years.

Military Tribunals
Following the introduction of conscription, a military tribunal sat regularly at Stafford's Guildhall, ruling on cases where conscripts were in reserved occupations, a family's sole means of income, too ill to undertake military training or had other reasons for needing to remain in the town. When it came to reserved occupations, there were strict guidelines laid down by the War Office, stating which workers could legitimately be regarded as being exempt. Those who claimed to be conscientious objectors might be enlisted into the RAMC, for work as stretcher-bearers.

Men medically unfit for military service had to go before a board of doctors before they were given a certificate of proof, which they presented at their hearing. Among those whose cases were rejected by the committee was that of Mr Percy Spronston, hosier, of Bridge Street. Spronston's appeal was put before the military tribunal on three occasions, but having been passed fit by the Military Board, he was drafted into the 'motor transport'. No doubt the ASC was considered less physically arduous than the role of infantryman, an acknowledgement of sorts that Spronston was not A1 fit.

Those who knew Percy Spronston, however, were fully aware that his health was not up to the rigours of any form of military service. While on an early morning route march during his initial military training on Salisbury Plain, no place for a man of a sickly disposition, Spronston caught a chill. His health went into a rapid decline and he was admitted to hospital, where he died from pneumonia. Spronston's body was sent by rail to the county town, where he was buried at St Mary's, Castle Church.

The tragedy did not end there. Among the mourners was his friend Sapper Bernard Grattidge, RE. He had served nearly two years at the front before being hospitilized due to 'shell shock'. On his return to Stafford, Bernard was informed that he had been re-classified as medically unfit for further service in the trenches. His uniform was duly taken away from him. Following Sponston's internment, Grattidge returned to his lodgings, where he committed suicide, leaving a note in which he asked of his mother: 'Forgive me; it is all for the best. I shall never get better or fit for duty.'

Bernard Grattidge had been a telegraphist at Stafford post office prior to the war and had only recently returned to the town to resume his job. Tragically, he was unable to cope with the effects of post-traumatic stress disorder and the fact that he would not be allowed back to serve alongside his former comrades. Sadly, his name does not appear on the post office memorial, although he was clearly a casualty of war.

Conscription ceased on 11 November 1918, and all conscripts were discharged, if they had not already been so, on 31 March 1920.

CHAPTER 9

Training for the Front

✦

The training facilities of the Regular Army were soon overwhelmed by the numbers of men that enlisted in 1914. The hundreds of thousands of raw recruits had to be rushed through a massively over stretched training system before they could be sent overseas to reinforce the BEF. Training for ordinary servicemen began with building up their physical fitness; other ranks had to be able to route-march with 61lb of basic kit on their backs. This was done in conjunction with an introduction to the rudiments of squad drill and marching discipline, supplemented by essential field craft and the use of weaponry, including the .303 Short Lee–Enfield rifle and 1907 Pattern bayonet. Later, if the soldier was selected for special duties such as a machine-gunner, signaller or stretcher-bearer, he would attend a course of instruction relevant to his role.

Military life helped broaden men's minds and vision as they found themselves training alongside a cross-section of society. Staffordian, Reginald Wilkes, enlisted into the 16th (Birmingham Pals) Battalion, Warwickshire Regiment. In a letter home, published in the *Staffordshire Chronicle*, he described his experiences during his initial training: 'The small faults in fellows, which often were much exaggerated by our narrow-minded society and social convention, one now more easily condoned and lost sight of, in the face of new qualities, many of which have before been dormant.'

Private Thomas Emberton of the Royal Engineers in full kit, c. 1916.

New training camps were constructed. Some of them were vast affairs, with their own canteens, hospitals, post offices, clubs and so on. Many such camps were developed, with principal concentrations at Salisbury Plain, Clipstone in

Brocton Training Camp with training trenches in the foreground.

Nottinghamshire, East Anglia and the North Wales coast. There were two camps locally on Cannock Chase, one near Hednesford and the other at Brocton.

Cannock Chase Camps

On 12 December 1914, the *Staffordshire Chronicle* announced: 'A military camp for the accommodation of about 20,000 troops is about to be built on Cannock Chase, between Hednesford and Rugeley, and in order to facilitate the work, a special railway is to be laid down connecting the site of the camp with the West Cannock Colliery railway siding at Hednesford, a distance of about two miles.' To put the scale of the camps into perspective, the town's population at the time was around 24,000 (although at any one time, up to 5,000 men might have been in uniform and therefore away from home).

The *Staffordshire Advertiser* of 16 January 1915 carried the news that work had already begun on Hednesford Camp at Penkridge Bank, while the Brocton Camp was less well advanced. Meanwhile, there were plans for a railway line to be laid from Milford to the Camp, with a new siding at Milford station. The *Staffordshire Advertiser* of 27 February recorded marked progress on the Brocton Camp, with a team of carpenters expected the following week to build prefabricated huts for 20,000 troops. The Church of England Temperance Society established a coffee house and rest room at neighbouring Milford for soldiers travelling to and from Brocton Camp. Here there was room for 200 men to enjoy games, read newspapers or write home. There were weekly concerts and Sunday services.

Many different regiments passed through the camps over the years. In late 1917 the New Zealand Rifle Brigade arrived at Brocton Camp, and was subsequently responsible for the construction of the Messine Model. A number of larger scale models were created in France as aids to officers involved in set-piece battles, and the Brocton example served a similar purpose. Before the New Zealanders left the camp in May 1919, they gifted the model to the people of Stafford. Their departure was marked by a parade in the Market Square, the events being filmed and a copy presented to the Corporation.

The logistics of essentially building two temporary towns on the Chase were immense. There was a sewage disposal unit constructed in Sherbrook Valley erected by the War Office, water coming from the reservoir at Milford, which also served Stafford. The Hednesford Camp had its own hospital, while a 1,000-seat cinema and a recreational venue were provided by the Lichfield Diocese and Union of Church of England's Men's Society, with concert and recreation rooms, a YMCA hut, a NAAFI shop and sports facilities, while Brookfield department store of Stafford had a branch here too. The camp hospital treated shell-shock and gas cases until 1924, while a few of the huts that weren't sold or demolished were used by the Reservists and local Territorials well into the 1960s.

Early in the development of the Hednesford Camp the Earl of Lichfield sanctioned the consecration of a parcel of land adjacent to the site which was to be used as a cemetery. Training was always dangerous, especially when using live ammunition, and there were always fatalities due to natural causes. Tragically, the majority of the burials relate to the influenza epidemic which swept through Europe in1918–19. The adjacent German Cemetery, it should be noted, dates from the 1960s when fatalities from both wars were re-interred at a central location.

Training Camps in France

As active service drew closer, the troops were given a refresher course in first aid, and later trained in gas defence. Once posted overseas and closer to the front, the men picked up front-line skills at unit level. Life expectancy depended on which sector of the front a man's unit was posted to, as some could remain fairly quiet for months on end, with losses through routine shelling, sniping and trench raids. In more active areas

Bayonet practice.

Recruits practice an advance with fixed bayonets.

there was a high turnover of men. Often the shocking experience of combat conditions meant that a man either adapted or died – any mistake could be fatal.

Technological innovations meant that weaponry and tactics developed throughout the war. Officers and NCOs were often taken out of the line for additional training in camps established in France. These were also giant holding areas housing thousands of men on their way from basic training in England to the front, or 'resting' between deployments. Men who were still recovering from wounds might be sent to holding battalions, where they were put through training in preparation for a return to combat.

These camps included the notorious 'Bull Ring' at Étaples, where discipline was so harsh that men found a return to a quieter section of the front line to be preferable. These camps meant that while units were being 'rested' they could be retrained but remain close enough to the front should there be a need to call them back into action.

Unit Composition
An infantry battalion (1,000 men, of whom 30 were officers) was composed of 4 companies: each company was divided into 4 platoons, each made up of 4 sections.

CHAPTER 10

Serving in the Trenches

The stalemate of trench warfare on the Western Front developed within months of the outbreak of the war. The German offensive of 1914 failed to strike a decisive blow. Following initial German gains, their logistical support became over stretched, while the BEF's last stand halted their advance and eventually pushed the enemy back. With neither side able to make ground and winter closing in, the troops began to 'dig-in' and construct trench systems. From these they could fire upon the opposite line, while receiving some degree of shelter from return fire and enemy artillery. Two opposing lines of trench systems quickly developed running from the border with neutral Switzerland to the Channel coast, a distance of some 440 miles.

The Germans fell back to a strong defensive line on the Aisne. They controlled the high ground, which they intended to hold. The Allies, on the other hand, regarded their lines as temporary from which they would advance to reclaim lost territory. The opposing trenches were constructed in line with these mindsets: the Germans dug deep and elaborate trench systems, often extending several miles to the rear; the Allies constructed shallow dug-outs, with communication trenches reaching back to the rear.

A typical British trench system consisted of three main fire or support trenches. These were connected by communication trenches alongside medical and command posts and saps. By 1916 the Germans, however, had developed a network of trench systems three or four layers deep, extending for several miles behind the front line. By 1917, this had deepened even further so that the assaults of 1918 faced defensive systems several miles deep.

Each sector of the front was different due to the variety of terrain, soil types, drainage etc. At Ypres, for instance, the water table is very high. Shelling quickly destroyed the farmers' ditches, flooding the trenches. Here raised defences or breastworks had to be built up using timber and sandbags. Elsewhere trench systems were excavated. Along the River Somme, the soil is chalky and easily dug, but the trench sides degraded in heavy rain or under shellfire. Here the sides of trenches had to be strengthened with timber or sandbag revetments. The front line was never straight.

A bayonet charge with minimal kit.

Instead it followed the contours and natural features. The Germans generally held the higher ground, allowing them good defence and a commanding view over the Allies' lines.

The front-line trenches were constructed in small sections or bays (viewed from above, they represented a Grecian key pattern), so that if a shell exploded inside one bay, or if the enemy captured it, then only that section was immediately lost. If the next bay held out long enough then a counter-attack might be made to regain control of that section of the front line. A little to the rear were trenches with dug-outs cut into their walls. These were often very small with room for only three or four men to squeeze in for shelter from the elements and from shell splinters.

Private G. Marshall, 'B' Company, 5th Platoon, 1/6th Battalion, North Staffordshire wrote home from Belgium. His letter was published in the *Staffordshire Chronicle* of 29 May 1915:

While we are in the trench we are kept busy either with a rifle or spade, sometimes almost day and night. The French mortar is used often now, which is most dangerous, as it accounts for about ten lives when well ranged. A few minutes ago one came over, but luckily it missed the mark. We have had several casualties, but considering the position we hold it would be impossible for all our [sic] shots to miss the mark.

In each trench is made a dug-out large enough for about three men to be down in and rest wherever time allows.

If you could take a walk down here you would see signs like this Leicester Square, Tottenham Corner, Swan Hotel (proprietor J. Winstone), etc.

We eat very little biscuit, but occasionally we have to do so, as the bread is not sufficient always. A nice parcel from home makes us smile at these times.

Communication trenches zigzagged to the rear. These were vital for bringing up reinforcements, equipment and supplies. Extending out beyond the front line into no man's land were saps. These were used as listening or observation posts. Corporal S. Taylor, 'D' Company, 1/6th Battalion, North Staffordshire Regiment wrote to his parents at 15 Crooked Bridge Street, in mid-June 1915: 'The same night we had to go out in front of our lines about 20 yards and do listening post – a very unpleasant job, especially when there are thousands of rats running about and over you. You are afraid to move or cough as the Germans are just in front.'

No man's land, which lay between the two opposing front lines, varied from as little as 50ft to several hundred yards. Both sides left gaps in their wire in preparation for a speedy advance or the retirement of a friendly patrol. Both sides trained their machine guns and artillery on these narrow corridors in the event of an enemy attack.

It was difficult to consolidate a captured enemy trench, as they were designed to be heavily protected from the front and were comparatively weakly protected from the rear. On capture, an enemy trench had to be 'turned around'.

Living conditions at the front were, by the very nature of trench warfare, rudimentary and for much of the time the men were exposed to the elements. The winter of 1916–17 in France and Flanders was the coldest in living memory. The bottom of the trench was raised by wooden duckboards, but still flooded in the wet, sometimes to waist height, whenever it rained. Men suffered from exposure, frostbite and respiratory illnesses.

There was little spare water for washing, something that the men found hard to deal with, as Corporal S. Taylor, 1/6th Battalion, North Staffordshire Regiment explained in a letter home penned in mid-1915: 'I haven't had a wash or shave [in] over a week. I have been wet through three or four times, and am covered in mud.' A latrine comprised a deep hole over which was set a plank as a seat. If its location was observed by the enemy, then it was often targeted by enemy snipers and shellfire.

Regimental Diaries

While on active service every battalion maintained an official *War Diary* in which daily entries were maintained. These were written at the battalion HQ and gave details of the unit's disposition, events of the day, casualties (by numbers of officers, NCOs and other rank, rather than by name) and intelligence reports. The records were occasionally supplemented by hand-drawn maps, aerial photographs and copies of official orders. The names of prominent officers and NCOs were only occasionally mentioned, while the names of ordinary soldiers rarely appear, unless recording a remarkable event, such as an act of gallantry, news of an award etc.

The Trench Cycle

There was no hard and fast rule on the rotation of troops as soldiers might be expected to spend longer stints at the front if they were on a quiet sector, while it might not be possible to relieve them during the middle of an attack. Troops could expect to be two weeks at the frontline and a week in the support trenches. The first stop when leaving the support trenches was the bathhouse, where a whole company would clean up while their clothes were washed and treated for lice. In a year only seventy days were spent at rest or in training camps.

Private A. Horobin, 3rd Battalion, Coldstream Guards, another Edwin Bostock & Co. employee, wrote home in August 1915, providing an idea of the routine of trench life in his sector:

> We have had a busy time lately in the trenches. The enemy keep letting us have a few shells and bombs, though we seem to be very lucky, as we haven't had many hit. The other week a 'Jack Johnson' burst on the road and blew two of our men into a dyke; they only got wet through. The Germans lay in wait for us when we are leaving the trenches and drop some across then. We are doing sixteen days in the trenches and eight out. Spending my holiday 'Somewhere in France.' And still smiling.

Sentry Duty

Every man took his turn on sentry duty for up to 2 hours a day with 4 hours off, the remaining troops occupying the fire or support trench, in sections. Sentries kept their rifles with 'one up the spout' (a round in the chamber), but with the safety catch on. An extract from *Notes on Trench Routine and Discipline, 1916* provides more detail: 'Sentries should always have one hours' rest before posting. Bear in mind any physical weakness of a man before putting on sentry, eg bad hearing, natural tendency to sleepiness, disability, nerves etc.' The penalty for being caught asleep on sentry duty was death, although most found guilty by a court martial had their sentences commuted, and were ordered to serve anything from ten years' hard labour to a one-year suspended sentence.

Sentry duty on the Somme.

Trench Raids and Night-life in the Trenches

At night troops might be sent out to bring in the wounded. Soldiers could also be assigned to occupy the sap in front of the trenches from where they could monitor signs of enemy activity. The most dangerous of all was going on raiding parties to search the enemy dead for papers or bring in prisoners for interrogation.

Sometimes enemy patrols would meet in no man's land, engaging in silent hand-to-hand fighting. If either side's sentries heard the struggle, then they might illuminate the scene with a Verey pistol, artillery 'star shells' or parachute flares. All hell would then be let loose with artillery and machine-gun fire directed at the opposing raiding party and their trenches. The following extract is taken from a British instructional manual.

Officers in-charge of parties will be held personally responsible that all under their command are stripped of all identifying marks [i.e. regimental badges]. Particular attention will be paid to ensure that the following articles are taken from the men and deposited in sandbags to be left at the regimental transport lines: cap badges, sleeve patches, pay books, regimental buttons, numerals, identity discs [this meant that a fatality would be denied a named grave], shoulder badges, roll books etc.

A member of the Stafford Battery wrote in early May 1915:

Troops wearing full-face respirators fix bayonets in preparation for an attack.

The trenches in front of us are only about 80 yards between our infantry and the German infantry, and at night it is one continual crack of rifles. The Germans practically light up the whole Front at night by constant stream of star shell or flares, which are fired from pistols and make a light as big as a large street arc lamp for a few seconds; they float down 20 or 30ft into the air from the enemy trenches to ours.

General Assaults

Dawn and dusk were the most likely time for a general assault to be made. Both sides of the line were ordered to 'Stand To!'. This meant manning the trenches in preparation for an enemy attack, which could be mounted in order to gain strategically important positions (the Germans generally fell back to higher ground) or to straighten the front lines and prevent a possible out-flanking manoeuvre.

Attacks might be heralded by short barrages, designed to destroy enemy positions and barbed wire entanglements. These were often in two sections, each 40yd deep. The enemy's front-line trenches would be damaged and troops killed, while no man's land was left pockmarked with craters which could be used for cover during an assault. Smoke and gas shells provided cover and sent waves of panic through the defending forces.

If the attacking force reached the enemy lines in any number, then bombing parties and bayonet teams got to work with close-quarter fighting clearing the trenches bay by bay. In the melee there was little opportunity to take prisoners. Company sergeants would impress upon their troops that in the heat of battle there was 'nothing more dangerous than a wounded enemy soldier'. As one veteran later put it: 'No artist or poet can depict a trench after fighting in its stark hellishness.'

The men on the front line kept their bayonets fixed during hours of darkness or whenever there was an alert of enemy activity. No one could leave their posts without permission of their immediate superior, while an officer had to approve him leaving the trench. This was only permissible to collect rations or other supplies. Even the wounded had to have permission to make their way to the First Aid Post.

Rations and other supplies were brought up under cover of darkness, the carriers often returning with the wounded and dead. Aerial reconnaissance, however, meant that the enemy was aware of the location of communication trenches and their snipers and artillery would be trained on these routes if troop movements were detected.

Snipers

Between offensives the front could be relatively quiet, although complacency might be equally as fatal as 'going over the top'. Both sides used snipers whose role it was to pick off any men who showed themselves above the parapet. One of many fatalities was Private W. Harris, who served with 'C' Company, 2nd Battalion, Northumberland Fusiliers. The following is an extract from a letter received by his next of kin, published in the *Staffordshire Chronicle* of 11 September 1915:

> I am to give you a few details about Private W. Harris, of the Northumberland Fusiliers, who was killed on the morning of 29 August 1915:
>
> Private Harris was in my company, and was one of the best and most soldier-like men I had. He was always steady and to be relied upon; in fact, he will be a great loss to me and the company. A few days before he was killed I had been asked for some good men as regimental snipers by our commanding officer, and Private Harris was a good shot, and a thoroughly reliable man. I asked him if I should send his name in, and he agreed to it.
>
> He was shot through the head, being killed immediately, whilst carrying out his duty as a sniper. I am sorry to say he was killed by over-eagerness and putting his head over the trench.
>
> His duty as a sniper was to fire from loopholes in the trench and try to kill enemy snipers, or any of the enemy who put their heads over their trench.

Private Harris had killed three men in the morning he was himself shot. As soon as his accident was reported to me I proceeded along the trench to him, but he had died immediately, suffering no pain. I have had a cross made and placed it over his grave, which is in a special burial ground for British soldiers at Kemmel, in Belgium. If all men did their duty as well as Private Harris this war would end very soon. He died as only a good Englishman can die, 'doing his duty.'

(signed) Lieutenant B.H. Hoffman

While some meals were brought up to the front line, the troops would also cook – especially breakfast – using make-shift braziers in their dug-outs. It was important that smoke from fires was masked so as not to give away their position to snipers and artillery spotters. Collecting supplies or water could be equally dangerous, as any regular movement by day attracted the enemy's attention.

The death of Private Grimes was as a result of sniper fire. His story was recorded in the *Staffordshire Chronicle* of 13 November 1915:

Killed While Fetching Water

Mr. J. Grimes, 16, Izaak Walton Street, Tillington, has received the following letter from Captain S.F. Thomas, commanding 'B' company, [6th (Service) Battalion] King's Shropshire Light Infantry:

It is with very great regret that I have to inform you of the death of your son, Pte F. Grimes, which took place yesterday morning. He had gone to fetch some water from a spring just behind the front-line, and was hit by a bullet in the knee, apparently not seriously. Another of my men saw him fall, and went to his assistance, and your son was again hit through the shoulder, and he expired after a few minutes. The same shot also killed Pte. Broomfield, who had gone to assist him . . . I trust you will find some slight consolation in the fact that your son fell while doing his duty.

Private Grimes was 18 years old, too young for overseas service and had lied about his age.

Daily Death in the Trenches

Even in less active sectors there was a daily routine of shelling which brought with it random death or injury; artillery shrapnel caused 60 per cent of all casualties on the Western Front. The high percentage of head wounds suffered during the early months of the war led to the production of the tin helmet. The British wide-brimmed helmet (designed by J.L. Brodie) came into use from August 1915, but could only stop spent bullets or shrapnel.

A letter front featuring the censor's stamp.

Shell-fire

A letter home from the A.E. Hanam of the Royal Army Medical Corps, written in mid-September 1915 gave a rare impression of what it must have been like to be under shell fire. Nothing, however, could truly prepare a soldier for the sight of the terrible wounds caused by a close burst. Hanam's letter was published under the headline: 'We Have Been Subjected to Shell Fire':

> You may have an idea as to what an awfully uncomfortable feeling it is to be shelled. We are ready to crawl up any hole and corner to avoid the flying fragments. Their advent is only too well known. In our work, alas we have only too often seen the results of these hellish instruments of war. The courage and patience of our fellows are beyond words.
>
> The desolation and ruin of the villages here is pitiable. In one village I passed through a short time ago, the church attracted me and on going into the grave yard I noticed the graves had been blown open and the dead exposed. But amid all the ruin stood a crucifix, untouched save for bits of shrapnel which had struck the bottom of the cross.

Despite all that he had witnessed, and as a medic Hanam would have seen terrible wounds and suffering, he still felt it his patriotic duty to encourage those at home to enlist: 'If only some of the good folk who sit happy and comfortable at home could see the horrors which innocent people out here had had to undergo at the hands of the Satanic host, I feel sure that they would feel no sacrifice would be too great in order to accomplish the object we have in view.'

The Burial of the Dead

The disposal of the dead caught in no man's land or half-buried in the sides of trenches was a constant problem. The following extract comes from an instructional manual dated 1917:

Treatment of Bodies Exposed in the Open which
cannot be Buried or Cremated.

Bodies in a state of putrefaction lying out in advance of the trenches which cannot be buried or cremated owing to hostile fire, or bodies uncovered in parapets of trenches where they have been hastily buried often give rise to considerable nuisance. They should be dealt with in the following manner:

i) Bodies in the Open

Deodorants will be found useful. The bodies may be sprayed with solution C, and if sufficient time is available the clothes should be ripped up so that the solution may be applied to the whole body, particularly in the region of the abdomen, or the bodies can be covered with quick-lime, powered sulphate of iron, or a mixture of 80lbs lime freshly slaked, 11lbs sulphate of iron, ½lb salt.

Spraying with 5 per cent cresol [sic] or with petrol is also useful in allaying putrefaction and preventing smell.

Corpses in front of the trenches out of reach can be sprayed by means of No. 7 spray or can be drawn in by means of a grappling iron.

ii) Bodies in Walls of Trenches, &c.

Dead bodies and remains of animals in the sides and walls of trenches, mine craters, & where removal is impossible should be treated with chlorine of lime, quick-lime or sprayed with cresol or solution C and then isolated either by means of boarding filled in with earth and chlorine of lime or by sandbags soaked in heavy petroleum oil.

Vermin Including Rats and Lice

Millions of rats infested the trenches, spreading disease. They fed off the carcasses of dead animals and the unburied victims of war and grew to the size of cats.

Another plague that infested the trenches was the problem of lice. These creatures carried trench fever, relapsing fever and typhus. They laid their eggs in the seams of clothing; within a few hours of the clothes being reworn the body heat generated would cause the eggs to hatch. Soldiers often killed lice by holding the seams of their clothing over a candle flame. Fumigation and the other control methods could not prevent the spread of lice and the diseases they carried.

And the Smell

The first thing that hit men on their arrival at the front was the appalling reek created by rotting bodies, animal and human, which lay unburied in their thousands. Open latrines would similarly give off a most offensive stench, while many of the troops had not been able to bathe in weeks. There was also the overpowering odour of creosol or chloride of lime, used to stave off the constant threat of disease and infection. Added to this was the smell of cordite and lingering poison gases, rotting sandbags, stagnant water, cigarette smoke, stale sweat and cooking.

Daily Chores

Following 'Stand To!', troops attended to their daily chores. These included general repairs to their trenches and the bailing out of rainwater. Once this was completed the men cleaned their rifle and kit, prior to inspection. Next breakfast was cooked.

Driver Charles Glover sent a letter home to his mother, dated 26 May 1915, which described how self-catering at the front might not be to everyone's taste:

> I must tell you I made a bread pudding last Sunday. It was a treat. I put the bread into a sack, and placed it in the brook to soak. When the pudding was made it was full of hairs, wire, nails, dirt and other useful things. Never mind it went down.

At dusk the morning ritual of 'Stand To!' was repeated to guard against a surprise attack launched as night fell and the mist descended. The troops were stood to and manned the firing step.

Relief

At the end of their stint, the men in the trenches were relieved by fresh troops in the dead of night when there was less chance of detection. However, German spotter planes might locate troop build-ups to the rear during the day and call up an artillery bombardment to catch the men in more exposed positions as they made their way up from the reserve trenches. The handover meant that the trenches themselves were more vulnerable to attack as men would be out of position.

Leave

Leave varied, with perhaps ten days being granted during the year. Home Leave was rarer still, with officers returning to Great Britain every five to seven months, while the other ranks might have to wait eighteen months or more. For those granted Home Leave, their journey began with a march back to the nearest railway station from where they made their way to Boulogne and then via a troopship to Folkestone. From here they took a train to Victoria station, where they could exchange their French currency.

There were restrictions on what could be brought home, as outlined in an official leaflet entitled 'Instructions for Officers and Men Proceeding on Leave':

1) Rifles will be taken but no ammunition. This is to be left with unit.
2) It is strictly forbidden to take on leave any of the following:

A Bainsfather cartoon '"Somewhere" the sun is shining'.

Service stripes; each stripe represents a year's overseas' service.

Bombs, Shells, Shell Cases.

Trophies captured from the Enemy (with the exception of German helmets, caps, badges, numerals, and buttons).

Uncensored letters.

No bottles of liquor are to be taken on the train or boat either going or on returning.

If any of the above articles are found to be in possession of men, their leave will be cancelled and they will be sent back to their Units.

A written report of any infringement of this order will be made by the Base Commandant through GOCL of C Area.

Men only returned to Stafford once or twice during the whole period of their service overseas. And many found that while everything in the town had remained familiar, their perspective on everything had changed, shaped by their experiences in France and Flanders.

CHAPTER 11

The Officers' Sacrifice

❖

The characteristics of good leadership were instilled in the boys who attended public schools and universities, most particularly those members of the military academies, and, later, the OTCs. Successful cadets earned a 'Certificate A', which was the first step towards a commission in the Regular Army, while a 'Certificate B' qualified them for a Territorial commission.

As a result of the reorganization of the army in 1908 more OTCs were set up and eventually there were 23 university and 166 public school OTCs. The OTCs were staffed by a combination of civilians and servicemen. Their purpose was to attract well-educated young men into the army. They operated on a set curriculum, which included field training as well as a written exam. A pass guaranteed a second lieutenancy should the cadet decide to join the army. Where a cadet studied had an influence on the regiments he might be eligible to serve with. For instance, Oxford and Cambridge universities, along with Harrow and Eton schools, provided the greater proportion of Guards officers. Between them the OTCs produced 20,577 second lieutenants, many of whom went on to become the backbone of the British Army during the First World War.

The early months of the war took a particularly heavy toll of officers and senior NCOs. Meanwhile, Lord Kitchener's New Volunteer Army required junior officers. With many university educated men having volunteered for military service in 1914–15, there was a gradual but fairly ad hoc process which resulted in many of these men being promoted through the ranks, eventually making officer status.

The following announcement appeared in *The Times* of 19 August 1914, as the search began for officers to command the Volunteer Army:

Temporary Commissions in His Majesty's Army.
2,000 Junior Officers (un-married) are immediately required in consequence of the increase of the Regular Army.
'How to obtain His Majesty's Commission.
Cadets or ex Cadets of the University Training Corps or members of the

Stafford Grammar School Cadets, 1915.

University should apply to their Commanding Officer, or to the Authorities of the University.

Otherwise young men of good education should apply in person to the Officer Commanding their nearest depot. Full information can be obtained by written application to the War Office.

'God Save the King.'

By January 1915 King Edward VI Grammar School, Stafford, had a fifty-strong Cadet Corps, 'with uniforms similar to army wear'. A sergeant and two platoon commanders were promoted from within their own ranks. Meanwhile, the school's former pupils had not been slow to heed the call to arms, and by the end of the following month a hundred were reckoned to be serving under the Colours. A number would become junior officer or NCOs.

In February 1916, a new system was introduced for the selection of applicants for temporary or wartime commissions. Potential officers who hadn't attended an OTC had to have already served in the rank and file and to have graduated on an officer cadet course. Of the twenty-six officer cadet battalions, the 8th Battalion was based at Lichfield's Whittington Barracks. Out of necessity, the officer training course was shorter than the pre-war version, lasting four-and-a-half months, after which successful cadets passed-out as second lieutenants. Once awarded their commission, the men were posted to a unit, often going straight to the front.

Officers and senior NCOs undertook courses throughout their service, learning about the new weapons, such as poison gas, tanks and the use of the creeping barrage.

STAFFORD OFFICERS ON ACTIVE SERVICE.

CAPT. RIDGE'S COMMAND OF A MANCHESTER BATTALION.

CAPT. W. H. RIDGE.   CECIL S. RIDGE,   LIEUT. D. H. RIDGE,   LIEUT. W. LAWS.

The spirit of patriotism runs high in the family of Mr. and Mrs. W. H. Ridge, of White House, Foregate, Stafford, and formerly of Eastgate in that town, who have three sons and a son-in-law serving with distinction in the Army. The portraits of the four are reproduced above. Mr. and Mr. Ridge's three sons, all athletic young fellows, each six feet in height, were educated at Stafford Grammar School and Dunstone College. They relinquished good positions to join the colours.

The eldest, Lieut. Douglas Harcourt Ridge, is with the Army Service Corps, and recently returned from his home in Northampton to the front after a short leave of absence. An experienced campaigner, he, like his younger brother, went through the South African War, being attached to the 17th Lancers (" Death or Glory Boys "). The conditions of that campaign were, he says, infinitely more picturesque than the present war. When hostilities began last year, he at once offered his services and accepted a commission in the A.S.C. Within nine days he was in France, where he has been rendering useful service ever since.

The second son of Mr. and Mrs. Ridge—Cecil Stafford—was resident in British Columbia when the war broke out, and, having joined the Colours to fight for Empire, he came to England with the second Canadian contingent as a member of the 1st Canadians. He is now attached as non-commissioned officer to the 7th Battalion, British Columbia Regiment, and has been recommended for a commission, having been at the front since May 1.

Capt. William Hughes Ridge, the youngest son, held a commission as lieutenant in the old Stafford Volunteers, and took out a company to the Boer War. The members of this detachment were presented with the honorary freedom of the borough on their return. Subsequently, he served as a lieutenant in the Imperial Yeomanry during the same campaign. As soon as war broke out, he offered his services to the War Office, and was attached to the Army Service Corps as lieutenant. June 14 last he was gazetted captain, and since

then has been commanding officer of the 5th Manchester Regiment at Southport. At the recent military sports held there in aid of the Infirmary, a Wigan team belonging to the regiment beat the 3rd-6th Manchester Regiment and 3rd-8th Lancashire Fusiliers in the inter-regimental Swedish drill competition, whilst another Wigan squad won the premier prize in the marching order competition. These successes bear ample testimony to the physical fitness of the men under Capt. Ridge's command.

In an appreciative notice of the local teams' performances, the *Wigan Examiner* says :—" The 5th Manchesters have been exceptionally fortunate in the choice of commanding and other officers, and in Capt. Ridge they have one whose sole interest is to turn out a soldier who can and will maintain the highest traditions of the British Army. Capt. Ridge sets the example of manliness, combined with the strictest discipline. He concerns himself with the personal well-being of the men as regards billeting and feeding, clothing, and healthy recreation, and under him the men are thoroughly happy and contented. That is the reason he is developing and getting the best out of them on lines which encourage sympathetic action and working in cohesion, and that is the reason the 5th Manchesters are held up as an example of what soldiers of the British Army ought to be." Capt. Ridge, it may be added, is now appealing for another 400 men for his regiment, to take the place of drafts sent to the Dardanelles, and a big recruiting rally is to be inaugurated to-day (Saturday).

Lieut. William Laws, B.Sc., son-in-law of Mr. and Mrs. Ridge, held a commission in the General Reserve of Officers when the war began, having been a member of the O.T.C. at Durham University, and he was called to duty immediately. He has been in the firing line in France since Jan. 1, with the 2nd South Lancashire Regiment, and after spending four months in the trenches, he was invalided home for three months, and is now performing light duty at headquarters, near Liverpool. The photo of Lieut. Laws is by Mr. A. J. Guy, of Stafford.

The Ridge brothers and Lieutenant Laws.

Some became specialists in communications or intelligence gathering. Leading their men in the field, junior officers were easy targets for enemy machine-gunners and snipers. Casualty rates remained disproportionately high, despite the order in April of 1915 that officers should no longer carry their swords into battle. Other changes included the removal of sleeve rank badges, while many officers wore other rank webbing and carried a rifle to make them less of a target.

There were a number of local businessmen who held pre-war commissions in the county's Territorial battalions. Among these men was Second Lieutenant Humphrey Thomas Bostock, son or Mr Edwin Bostock, proprietor of Edwin Bostock & Co. Lieutenant H.T. Bostock, who was attached to the Tamworth Company, 1/6th Battalion, North Staffordshire Regiment, was seriously wounded at Messines in 1915, when a howitzer shell detonated in his trench. Several of his men were killed and others wounded.

Lieutenant Bostock was Mentioned in Despatches on 1 January 1916, and later awarded the Military Cross (*London Gazette*, 14 January 1916). Lieutenant Bostock, of 'Sunnyside', Deans Hill, Stafford, had two siblings who also fought as junior officers in France. Captain Guy Edwin Bostock, 8th Battalion, Royal Munster Fusiliers was killed in action on 30 January 1916. Humphrey's other brother, Lieutenant John Kenneth Bostock, served with 'C' Company, 1st Battalion, North Staffordshire Regiment. He was awarded the Military Cross for gallantry at Delville Wood during the Battle of the Somme, in circumstances not untypical of those facing so many junior officers thrown in at the deep end.

The 1st Battalion, North Staffordshire Regiment, a part of the 72nd Brigade, took over the line at Delville Wood on 31 August 1916. The wood had been the site of numerous attacks and counter-attacks since the beginning of the Somme Offensive and as a result was littered with bodies in varying stages of decomposition – anyone who ventured into 'Devil's Wood', as it became known, had to have a strong stomach and great courage.

The 1st Battalion was deployed in a section of the line previously held by the 9th Battalion, Rifle Brigade. As the troops were in the process of relieving the trenches, they were caught in an artillery barrage. Minutes later the enemy attacked across no man's land. After bitter fighting, the assault was successfully repulsed. However, a second enemy push began at around 7.00pm, just after dusk. The Germans had gathered intelligence and made for the weakest section of the line which at that time was held by a company of the 1st Battalion, South Staffordshire Regiment. The enemy managed to capture a number of trenches and a Lewis gun position thus exposing the right flank of the 1st Battalion, North Staffordshire Regiment.

Lieutenant John Bostock quickly established a line of his own men who put down a suppressing fire which kept the enemy's head down and prevented them from gaining any further ground or from sending reinforcements up to their new forward position. At the same time Lieutenant Bostock was able to organize the men from the 1st Battalion, South Staffordshire Regiment who, without an officer, had been pushed back

LEEK OFFICER KILLED IN ACTION.

FORMERLY ASSISTANT MASTER AT STAFFORD.

Official intimation was received at the week-end by his parents, who reside at Park Vale, Leek, that Lieut. J. Carlton Wagstaffe, of the South Staffordshire Regiment, was killed in action on Oct. 12. He met his death at the hands of an enemy sniper on the afternoon of that day.

He was a member of the Stafford Pals party who enlisted in the Coldstream Guards shortly

THE LATE LIEUT. J. C. WAGSTAFFE.

after the outbreak of war, prior to which time he was an assistant master on the staff of St. Mary's School (mixed department), under the Head-master (Mr. W. Tomlinson). He was educated at Leek High School and was formerly a teacher at St. Luke's School, Leek. Lieut. Wagstaffe was a fine, manly young fellow, fond of healthy recreation and sport, and was a great favourite with the boys he used to teach. In May, 1915, he was invalided home with muscular rheumatism and frost bite. He quickly rose to the rank of sergeant in the Army, and received his commission as 2nd-lieutenant in January, 1916, being gazetted to the South Staffordshire Regiment.

He took a prominent part in the Stafford Millenary Pageant of 1913, and gave a capital impersonation of the part of Monckton, a fellow-candidate with Sheridan, in an 18th century election scene. Lieut. Wagstaffe was an enthusiastic playing member of the Stafford Rugby Club, and also took great interest in swimming.

General sympathy is felt with Mr. and Mrs. Wagstaffe in their sad bereavement. The Commanding Officer of the regiment, in a letter to Mrs. Wagstaffe, says :—" You will doubtless have heard from the War Office of your very sad loss in the death of your son. He was killed by an enemy sniper about 4 p.m. on the 12th inst. in the very front of the battle, after having gallantly led his men right up to their final objective. Lieut. Wagstaffe was one of the bravest and most capable officers in the battalion, and he died giving his best for his men, his regiment, and his country. Many of the N.C.O.s and men have expressed to me in glowing terms their admiration for his perfect fearlessness and devotion to duty. This afternoon General Robertson, who received his report on the capture of the enemy position, expressed his deep regret at the death of such a gallant officer. His loss will be most seriously felt in the battalion, and his place one that will be hard to fill. Personally, I cannot speak too highly of his many splendid qualities as a soldier and a gentleman. There is little I can say that will ease your pain and grief, but I beg that you will accept this assurance of my deepest sympathy and this letter as a little tribute to the memory of one of the finest men I have ever had the good fortune to know."

in some disorder. During the melee, Lieutenant Bostock was wounded, but continued to ensure that the line held at what was a vital time. As the battle continued, however, he was wounded again, this time severely. He was forced to leave his trench in order to report back his situation.

Lieutenant John Kenneth Bostock was evacuated down the line and sent, via a Hospital Ship, to 1st Southern General Hospital, Edgbaston, Birmingham. Here he made a good recovery. For gallantry in saving his men from being outflanked and possibly overrun, Lieutenant Bostock was award the Military Cross, which was promulgated in the *London Gazette* of 14 November 1916: 'For conspicuous gallantry in action. Although wounded, he rallied his own men and men of another unit under very heavy fire, with great courage and determination. He was again severely wounded, but managed to return with information before fainting.'

In mid-October 1917 news reached Stafford of the death of Lieutenant John Carleton Wagstaffe while serving with the 8th Battalion, South Staffordshire Regiment. John Wagstaffe, a former assistant master at St Mary's School, had taken a prominent part in Stafford's Millenary Pageant celebrations of 1913, playing the part of Colonel Monckton, a candidate in the eighteenth-century election tableaux. Wagstaffe had been a member of the Stafford Rugby Club and, along with his fellow players, had enlisted soon after the declaration of war. He initially served in the ranks in the 'Stafford Pals' Company of the Coldstream Guards.

Lieutenant Wagstaffe went to France with one of the early batches of reinforcements, but was wounded and invalided home in May 1915. On returning to the front, Wagstaffe was singled out for promotion and was given his sergeant's stripes before being recommended for a commission. Having completed his course, John Wagstaffe was commissioned as a second lieutenant in January

The announcement of the death of Lieutenant Wagstaffe.

1916. It was considered bad for discipline for a man from the rank and file to continue to serve alongside his friends once he became an officer. Consequently, Wagstaffe was transferred to the 8th Battalion, South Staffordshire Regiment. He was serving with his battalion in France when he was killed in action on 12 October. His company commander wrote a letter of condolence to Wagstaffe's parents:

> You will doubtless have heard from the War Office of your very sad loss in the death of your son. He was killed by an enemy sniper at about 4pm on the 12th inst. in the very front of the battle, after gallantly leading his men right up to their final objective.
>
> Lieutenant Wagstaffe was one of the bravest and most capable officers in the battalion, and he died giving his best for his men, his regiment, and his country.
>
> Many of the NCOs and men have expressed to me in glowing terms their admiration for his perfect fearlessness and devotion to duty. This afternoon, General Robertson, who received his report on the capture of the enemy position, expressed his deep regret at the death of such a gallant officer. His loss will be most seriously felt in the battalion, and his place one that will be hard to fill. Personally, I cannot speak too highly of his many splendid qualities as a soldier and a gentleman. There is little I can say that will ease your pain and grief, but I beg that you will accept this assurance of my deepest sympathy and this letter as a little tribute to the memory of one of the finest men I have ever had the good fortune to know.

On 13 October 1917, the *Staffordshire Chronicle* announced the death of another local officer, Second Lieutenant Kenneth Francis Amies, 2/6th Battalion, North Staffordshire Regiment: 'Stafford Officer Killed In Action. Mr. Frank Amies, JP, of Inglewood, Rowley Park, Stafford, received information on Sunday that his only son, Lieutenant Kenneth F. Amies, had been killed in action during an enemy counter-attack on Sunday, 23 September 1917.' Amies' story was not untypical of so many former pupils of King Edward VI Grammar School. He was an athlete of some renown and back at home his parents were guardians of a number of medals won during his sporting days. Amies was formerly the captain of the Stafford Rugby Club and was one of a number of players who joined the Colours in September 1914.

Following his initial training, Amies served in France from early 1915. He was singled out for promotion and was for some time his unit's Chief NCO instructor in the use of gas in the trenches, for which he was highly commended by his officers. Kenneth Amies was recommended for a commission. In January 1917, he joined the 8th Battalion, Officer Cadets based at Whittington Barracks, Lichfield, passing out with distinction. Amies was commissioned as a second lieutenant in the 2/6th Battalion, North Staffordshire Regiment in July 1917.

During his time undergoing officer training, Amies was able to visit his long-term sweetheart, Miss Gertrude Brown, of Stafford, the couple later becoming engaged.

Second-Lieutenant Amies returned to France on 26 August 1917 and saw considerable action during the following three weeks. Amies' company commander, Captain W.H. Clay, wrote to his family on 3 October:

> It is with real grief that I write to offer my most sincere sympathy to you in the loss of you son. As his Company Commander, I had formed the highest opinion of him, and though he had only been with me a short time, I miss him very much personally. He would have made a first rate officer, as he could be on good terms with his men without losing discipline, and every one, officer and men, grieve sincerely for his loss. It may be of some slight consolation to you to know that he probably suffered very little pain. He was hit by a shell, and I think never was conscious afterwards, and died very shortly after he was put on the stretcher.

The following letter, dated 4 October, was received from Amies' battalion commander, Major Oscar Keating, who added his condolences to the family:

> Although he had been with us such a short time, we had all grown to love and respect him. I had quite early on in my acquaintance with him made a mental note to the effect that he was one of our up and coming officers, and hoped shortly to be able to place him in a better position which better fitted his great ability.

Major Keating's letter went on to provide a little more information surrounding Amies' death:

> During a counter attack he went along the line encouraging his men, in spite of the fact that heavy shelling was in progress. He was killed instantaneously by shrapnel. I am quite sure that he felt no pain. I had his body sent down and he was buried at the Quartermaster's Base, all his men being present.

Another officer fatality was Richard Birkenhead 'Dick' Wilton who, prior to the war, had worked in the same office as his father, who was Clerk to the Board of Guardians on the Rural District Council. Wilton had enlisted in November 1914. Following his basic training he was posted to the Argyll and Sutherland Highlanders and went to France at the end of April 1915. He was gassed at Festubert on 12 May 1915. Following a short period of recuperation in Chepstow, Wilton was posted to the regimental headquarters.

Wilton volunteered to go out with the next draft to help reinforce another battalion of his regiment, then holding the line around Albert. But the pressing need for good junior officers meant that Wilton's name was put forward for a commission and he was sent home. Following a brief period at an OTU establishment, he was granted a temporary commission as second-lieutenant with the 9th (Service) Battalion, Yorkshire Regiment (Princess Alexandra's Own) in November 1915.

In July 1916, Wilton transferred into another battalion of the same regiment then serving in France, and fought throughout the Battle of the Somme. He was present at the capture of Contalmaison and Le Sars. During October 1916, his battalion transferred to the Ypres Sector, where Wilton remained throughout the winter, acting as his unit's intelligence officer. He was on more than one occasion complimented on his good work by his company commander.

In April 1917, Richard Wilton was invalided home owing to ill health. After leaving hospital he was sent to West Hartlepool for three months' convalescence, but had been there only two weeks when he and two other officers volunteered for service in France. Wilton's request was turned down and he was sent to a training camp in the Midlands, where he passed on his combat knowledge to recruits under training. Unperturbed, he wrote to his former Commanding Officer in France, asking to be sent back overseas, returning to the Western Front on 8 September.

In what turned out to be his last letter home, written on 27 September, Richard said that he expected to be going 'over the top again', commenting how he and his brother officers were looking forward to the next advance.

Lieutenant Wilton was known as a young man of quiet demeanour, with a cheerful disposition, and was popular with all who knew him. Before leaving home Wilton had said: 'I shall make good.' Like so many officers and men, he had felt guilty for the time he had been forced to leave his men at the front. Sadly, Second Lieutenant Wilton led his new platoon for only a few weeks before he was killed in action. On Sunday, 7 October Mr C.B. Wilton received a telegram from the War Office in which it was said: 'Deeply regret to inform you that Second-Lieutenant Wilton, attached to 9th Battalion, Yorkshire Regiment (Alexandra Princess of Wales's Own), was killed in action on October 1st. Army Council express their sympathy to next-of-kin on register.' In mid-October 1917, Mr Wilton received a letter of condolence from Second Lieutenant Wilton's battalion commander, Lieutenant Colonel R.A.S. Hart:

A few words to offer you my deepest sympathy on the loss of your son, who was killed-in-action south of Polygon Wood on 1 October 1917, gallantly defending a post of which he was in command. Your son's company was in a part of the line against which the Germans launched a desperate counter-attack and it was thanks to their gallantry and devotion to duty that the enemy did not gain a footing. There were four officers in the company, all of whom died at their posts sooner than be driven back. Their names will be forever remembered by the Yorkshire Regiment.

The *Staffordshire Chronicle* of 3 November 1917 reported the contents of a letter to Mr C.B. Wilton penned by Private J.T. Collins, 9th Battalion, Yorkshire Regiment, giving details of his death:

He says that Lieutenant Wilton was killed instantly, that he did not suffer one second.

'On the day he was killed,' he adds, 'I was not with him. I was on another duty not far away. If I had been with him he would not have been dead now. It would have been me, and God knows, I would rather have died than Dick. He was worth any man's life. On this morning we were holding a very hard position, and it had to be held at all costs. Lieutenant Wilton was in command, and it meant a lot to him. We were fighting like mad dogs all along the Front; we were losing very heavily, and if it had not been for our hero, God knows what would have happened. He came along saying "Stick it, boys," and every man was always ready to serve him. One man had said (which I learned later) that we were running short of ammunition. Lieutenant Wilton sprang out of the bit of trenches we had, and walked over No-Man's-Land for ammunition. He got it across with the aid of some carriers, but did not reach the trench with it. He was hit and killed instantly. The boys said it was the quickest they ever saw. He was smiling when he got hit.'

Private Collins says that every man in his Company, especially No. 10 Platoon, which was his platoon, loved him, and he goes on to say: 'If ever a man earned a VC, your son did that day, and he has been always the same. Last winter he was intelligence officer. He and I used to go in No-Man's-Land to find out anything about the Boche [sic]. We used to lie for hours on the Boche [sic] lines in all the mud. He only used to laugh, no matter what danger he was in. He got recommended for his good work last winter by the General, and he was pleased: so was I.'

Private Collin added the touching words: 'Please don't take the hardest blow of your lives too hard. You must say your boy was one of the bravest that put a soldier's coat on, and was loved by every Tommy in his regiment.'

A mystery surrounded the death of another Staffordian, Second Lieutenant Thomas Victor Wheeldon, 16th Battalion, Northumberland Fusiliers. Wheeldon was reported wounded and missing on Thursday, 12 July 1917, having been hit in the leg and left behind while the remainder of his battalion continued their advance – soldiers were under strict orders not to stop to attend to their wounded as this risked the success of the general advance. Nothing further was heard of Wheeldon, whose death was presumed a year later, when his parents, Mr and Mrs John Wheeldon, of Corporation Street, Stafford, received an impersonal official notification from the War Office:

Army Form B 104-82A

Sir

It is my painful duty to inform you that no further news having been received relative to 2nd Lieutenant Thomas Victor Wheeldon, 16th Battalion, Northumberland Fusiliers.

Who has been missing since 12 July 1917, the Army Council have been regrettably constrained to conclude that he is dead, and that his death took place on the 12 July 1917 (or since).

I am to express to you the sympathy of the Army Council with you in your loss.

Wheeldon had earlier been wounded by a gunshot to the hand on the Somme in April 1917, when he was sent to Bristol Hospital, before enjoying three weeks' leave in Stafford. Further information regarding the circumstances surrounding Thomas Wheeldon's death came in a letter from Sergeant J. Smith, 16th Battalion, Northumberland Fusiliers:

He was in charge of 'C' Company when we went over [the top] at Nieuport, and I was just on his right when he called out 'I'm hit' and dropped. I carried him to a shell hole, made a splint of a rifle, and bound his leg to it. I then had to carry on but saw stretcher bearers about an hour later and gave them the information and the locality. As the fighting and shelling were very severe and the weather foggy, I am afraid he never got back.

His Commanding Officer wrote: 'Your son took part in an attack on the 11th July, which was only partially successful and was last seen in the darkness in No-Man's-Land, but still carrying on. We were all extremely sorry, for your son was a fine soldier, and was popular with his men.' Thomas Wheeldon, who was 20 years old, was educated at Corporation Street School, where his father, Mr John Wheeldon (after whom the school was later re-named), was headmaster.

Another fatality was Second Lieutenant Maurice McFerran, Royal Irish Rifles, MC, of Rickerscote Hall. McFerran was sent to No. 7 Officer Cadet Battalion, at Furge Camp, Curragh, Ireland on 29 May 1916. He passed out of his course and was commissioned in September 1916. McFerran fought through the Battle of Messines, the 3rd Battle of Ypres and the Battle of Cambrai before being killed in action at Pozières on 21 March 1918, during the German Spring Offensive.

Second Lieutenant Maurice McFerran was awarded the Military Cross, *London Gazette*, 5 July 1918: 'For conspicuous gallantry and devotion to duty. During three days fighting he maintained touch between the leading companies and Battalion HQ. He went four times to the front through a heavy barrage and brought back valuable information.' Following McFerran's death his battalion's colonel wrote:

He has been working as my intelligence officer for some time and during the recent battle [of Cambrai] he has done great work for me: this young lad was indefatigable in running about under all sort of fire and maintaining touch between me and the companies. I owe the success of the battalion in great measure to his energy and bravery.

CHAPTER 12

Local Gentry at the Front

❖

Traditionally members of the local aristocracy had served as senior officers in the local Militia and Volunteer units. This continued, to a lesser extent, with the Territorial Army. Members of the local gentry, including Captain L. Meynell and Lieutenant F. Wrottesley, served with the 6th (Stafford) Staffordshire Battery in 1914. Meanwhile, from mid-1915, Second Lieutenant Dudley Ryder, Lord Sandon, son and heir of the Earl of Harrowby, of Sandon Hall, saw active service on the Western Front as a junior officer with the Battery. He was seriously wounded in Northern France in late September 1915, receiving treatment in King's Hospital, London.

In 1913 the Fitzherbert family of Swynnerton Hall, near Stafford, inherited the baronetcy of Stafford. Francis Edward Fitzherbert-Stafford, JP, DL, DSO, 12th Baron of Stafford, had earlier served with the Queen's Own Imperial Yeomanry in the Boer

An RFA battery in action.

War. He was Mentioned in Despatches and made a Companion of the Distinguished Service Order (1900). Considered too old for command in France, he became the figurehead for a number of home-based units. Meanwhile, Francis' younger brother, Edward Stafford Fitzherbert (later 13th Baron of Stafford), served with distinction in the Royal Navy. He was made a Companion of the Order of the Bath (CB) in 1918, and a Knight Commander, Order of the Bath (KCB) in 1920. Another brother of the 12th Baron was Captain the Honourable Thomas Fitzherbert. He had served with the Lancashire Hussars in the Boer War and on 10 July 1916 was acting as Brigade Bombing Officer to the 14th Cyclist Brigade, Cupar, Fife, Scotland, when he saved the life of a soldier in a grenade incident. He was duly awarded the Albert Medal in bronze (Land). The citation to the award was promulgated in the *London Gazette*, 1 January 1918:

The Albert Medal (Second Class – Bronze).

On the 10th July, 1916, an instructional party was throwing live bombs from separate pits. A volley was ordered. All the bombs were thrown successfully except one, which hit the parapet and stuck in the mud. For three or four seconds the accident was unnoticed, as everyone was watching the bombs in the air and the man who threw the bomb was too frightened to call out or to move. Suddenly Captain Fitzherbert noticed smoke issuing from the parapet and saw the bomb. He might have placed himself in safety by throwing himself on the bottom of his pit, but seeing that the man would be exposed to the full force of the explosion, he picked the bomb out of the mud and threw it clear just as it exploded.

By his courage and presence of mind he undoubtedly saved the man's life, while risking his own.

The Levett family of Milford Hall, near Stafford lost their only son to the war. Captain William Levett's son, Richard Levett was educated at St Peter's Court, before attending Eton. While Richard came from a privileged background, he and his fellow pupils were aware of their duty to Country and Empire, summed up in a pre-war address to the College by His Majesty King George V: 'The British Empire requires at the present time hard service from all her sons. It requires the hardest service from those to whom most has been given.'

Richard was a member of the Eton Volunteer Corps, passing out on 4 June 1913. He matriculated at Magdalen College, Oxford, on 19/20 March 1915, before earning a place at the Royal Military Academy, Sandhurst, later the same year. Many of Richard Levett's near contemporaries, friends from school, Eton, Oxford and Sandhurst, were a year or so older and had progressed one or two steps ahead of him. Many were serving at the front while he was still under training, something he remarked upon in his diary: 'The casualty lists are so awful they rather depress one – in yesterday's list I knew four killed and one missing, two of whom were at Broadstairs with me and three killed the day before one also knew very well.'

Commissioned in July 1916, Second Lieutenant Richard William Byrd Levett served in France, commanding No. 8 Platoon, 'B' Company, 2nd Battalion, King's Royal Rifle Corps, from 28 December. Tragically, he was killed by a shell splinter on the night of 10 March 1917, while leading the advance on the Grévillers trench before the village of Irles, near Bapaume; it was his first advance. Of the assault, Richard Levett's commanding officer, Captain Smith, later wrote:

> The attack was an enormous success and we advanced over half a mile, took no prisoners, three machine guns and three trench mortars, and the whole loss in the Battalion was only 43 killed and wounded, which is wonderful in these days.
>
> There is no doubt that Dick was killed by our own barrage, in fact nearly all the casualties were caused by our own barrage, but it is impossible to avoid that in this modern warfare and the modern method of attacking, the troops have to follow so closely that the Boche [sic] have not time to come out of their dug-out. There is no doubt that following up the barrage so closely was the reason of there being so little machine gun fire to contend with.

Richard Levett's batman, Rifleman Farndon, wrote to the Levett family to express his sorrow at losing his officer:

> Our artillery barrage opened at 05.15 sharp and Mr. Richard who went over with the first wave was out of the trench and calling his men on. Before we had gone 200 yards we were being peppered by our own artillery. We laid down just in front of the enemy's wire for a bit, and then when the barrage lifted . . .
>
> Mr. Richard was off like a shot, his orderly and I after him, the barbed wire which I got hung up in was my undoing . . . the mist made everything so confused . . . no one seems to have seen Mr. Richard fall.
>
> Mr. Richard's body was found between the German wire and the trench. He had been hit on the head by a piece of shell.

The official pamphlet *SS 135 Instructions for the Training of Infantry Divisions for Offensive Actions* outlined the 'Importance of creeping barrage and the primary role of artillery to fire the infantry onto the enemy objective, supported by mortars and Vickers machine-gun barrages. Thereafter resistance would be broken using a combination of snipers, Stokes mortar, Lewis guns, rifle-grenades and smoke barrages. Infantry and bombers (Mills bombs) to mop-up resistance.' Richard Levett had obeyed his orders to the letter by following the creeping barrage as it swept over the enemy's positions. Sadly, his bravery cost him his life.

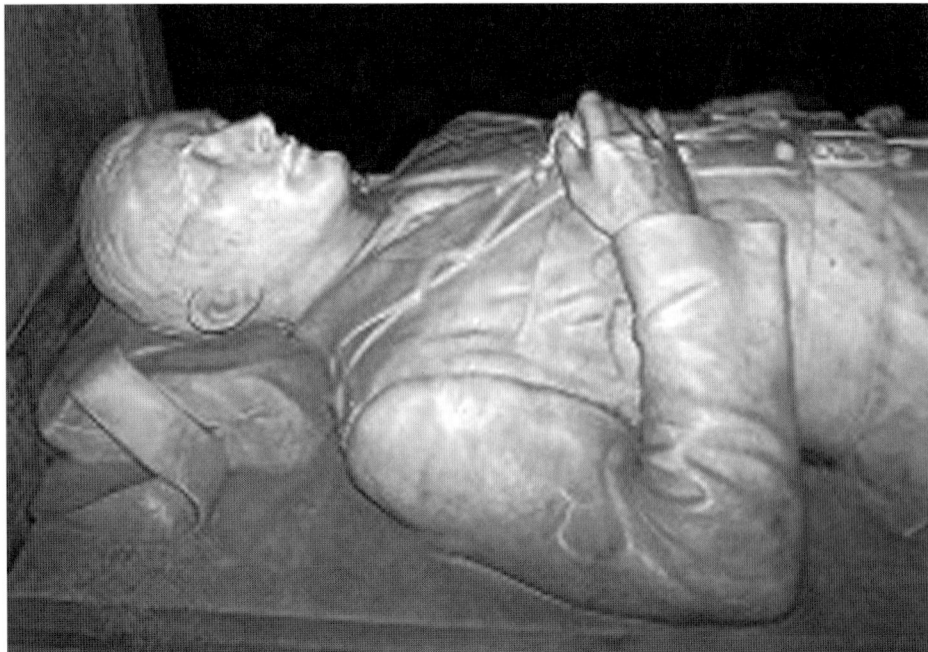

Richard Levett's Memorial.

A memorial service for Richard Levett was held at St Thomas' Church, Walton-on-the-Hill on 20 March 1917. Determined that their son's sacrifice would be remembered, Richard's grieving parents took the almost unprecedented step of erecting a magnificent full-length alabaster altar tomb of a recumbent effigy of their son in the medieval style in the church's St George's Chapel. The central design takes the form of a faithful likeness of Second Lieutenant Richard Levett, wearing his officer's uniform and insignia, a cap at his feet. The memorial bears the inscription 'Lost leading his men in a brilliantly successful attack', and the personal epitaph 'So passed a brave soldier a gallant gentleman and a radiant soul'.

William Congreve.

Of all the local gentry, perhaps the most significant contribution was made by the Congreve family of Congreve Manor, near Stafford. Although geographically a little beyond the scope of this book, the Congreves were highly influential in the county town and their story is worthy of a mention. The most decorated member of the family was Brevet Major William La Touche Congreve, VC, DSO, MC, MiD and *Légion d'honneur*.

William Congreve was born on 22 March 1891. His father, Walter N. Congreve, VC, was a career soldier and so William's early years were spent with his family in India prior to his father's posting back to England. The old castle ruins at Chartley, near Stafford, became his playground. Congreve attended Eton, serving in the college's

Cadet Corps, before gaining a place at the Royal Military Academy, Sandhurst. There he was the model Officer Cadet, coming second to his best friend and rival for the Sword of Honour when he passed out in 1911. William's first posting was to the 3rd Battalion, Rifle Brigade, his father's old regiment, then stationed in Tipperary.

His father, Walter Congreve, had earlier won the Victoria Cross while serving in the Boer War. In 1909, while Commander of the School of Musketry at Hythe, Walter had pushed for the army to increase their firepower at battalion level, from two Vickers machine guns to six. Sir Douglas Haig, however, was of the opinion that two was 'more than sufficient'. Conscious of the need for greater firepower, Congreve introduced a new intensive musketry programme. This produced riflemen who could fire fifteen aimed rounds per minute using the 1906 Short Lee–Enfield; some achieved as many as thirty rounds. The significance of Congreve's contribution cannot be over-estimated – in 1914 many German commanders reported that they were facing British troops armed with machine guns.

In 1914, Lieutenant William Congreve served as Aide-de-Camp to Major General Hubert Hamilton, CB, CVO, DSO, MiD, Commander of the 3rd Division. Hamilton's division was in the forefront of the action at Mons, Le Cateau, the Marne and at the Aisne.

Among the other General Staff Officers then serving at the Army HQ were William's father, Brigadier General W.N. Congreve, VC (later CB and Commander of the 18th Infantry Brigade), his uncle, Captain F.L. Congreve (later Lieutenant Colonel F.L. Congreve, DSO, MC) and his cousin, Lieutenant C.R. Congreve (later DSO, OBE).

On the death of Major General Hamilton, who was killed in action on 14 October 1914, William Congreve served under his successor, acting as a General Staff officer. The young Lieutenant Congreve won the admiration of the men in the field and Staff officers alike as a result of his willingness to reconnoitre the situation at the front, dashing out to any trouble spot where he served alongside the other ranks. Congreve was able to boost the men's morale at a time when all of their officers had been killed. For his actions William was Mentioned in Despatches for gallantry and initiative at the front during the retreat from Mons, as were his father, uncle and cousin.

During 1915, Lieutenant William Congreve was in action at the Hooge, which saw bitter hand-to-hand combat, with frequent trench raids and fierce fighting along the whole sector. He personally led numerous raids and was partly responsible for the capture of sections of the line towards the end of the battle, which nevertheless ended in stalemate. The battle cost the lives of 360 officers and 9,000 other ranks. For his part in the operations at the Hooge, William Congreve received a second Mentioned in Despatches and was later awarded the Military Cross for gallantry (*London Gazette* of 11 January 1916). Further recognition came on 6 November 1915 with the announcement of the award of the French *Legion d'honneur* (permission to wear the award was announced in the *London Gazette*, 24 February 1916), which his father saw pinned on the young William's tunic at a ceremony presided over by General de Boiselle, Commander of the French XXX Corps.

On 1 March 1916, the by now Captain William Congreve helped to plan and later led the successful assault by the 2nd Suffolk Regiment at the Bluff. An earlier attack had seen sixty men go out under cover of darkness and none return, but Congreve's daring daylight strike caught the enemy off-guard and was carried out with minimal casualties.

A few weeks later, on 27 March, an advance was launched in the St Elio Sector. Captain Congreve was again instrumental in making good ground almost without loss. On 3 April, he led an attack under cover of thick fog. However, with the objective almost within his grasp, his troops came under crossfire from both the enemy's front line and a detachment of Germans occupying a huge crater in no man's land. In the full view of the enemy, Congreve ventured out alone and on reaching the edge of the crater he pointed his Webley revolver at the nearest German and demanded that he throw down his weapon and surrender. Caught totally off-guard, he obeyed the command, rapidly followed by five officers and seventy-six other ranks.

For this act of gallantry William Congreve was recommended for the Victoria Cross, which was downgraded to an immediate Distinguished Service Order. The award was announced in the *London Gazette*, 16 May 1916: 'For conspicuous gallantry. He consolidated a newly-won position under very difficult conditions at a critical moment, and by personal courage brought about the surrender of a considerable body of enemy officers and men.' Promoted to Brevet Major, William Congreve had shown consistent gallantry over a long period while at the front. His disregard for danger had become almost legendary among his regiment. He inspired his men by calmly moving among them while under sniper fire. On occasions he left the trenches armed with a rifle and his shooting spectacles in order to hunt German snipers, which he did with some success.

A further acknowledgement of William Congreve's bravery came when he was once again Mentioned in Despatches on 15 June 1916. Earlier, on 1 June 1916, during a brief period of Home Leave, William had married his sweetheart, Pamela Cynthia, second daughter of Mr Cyril Maude. Returning to the front, Brevet Major William Congreve remained as fearless as ever in carrying out his duties. His luck finally ran out, however, when he was targeted by a sniper on 20 July 1916, while leading his men back to the relative safety of their trench following an unsuccessful attack.

William's father was informed of his death and was able to pay his final respects to William before his body was taken for burial. Walter later wrote: '[I] was struck by his beauty and strength of face. I never felt so proud of him as I did when I said goodbye to him. I myself put in his hands a posy of poppies, cornflowers and daisies and with a kiss I left him.' William Congreve's gallantry had been noted at the highest levels in France and Brigadier-General Kentish, Commander of Congreve's 76th Brigade, recommended him for a posthumous award of the Victoria Cross, which was approved by His Majesty King George V. The award was promulgated in the *London Gazette*, 26 October 1916:

Brevet Major Congreve's grave.

William Congreve's wedding photograph.

For most conspicuous bravery during a period of fourteen days preceding his death in action.

This officer constantly performed acts of gallantry and showed the greatest devotion to duty, and by his personal example inspired all those around him with confidence at critical periods of the operations. During preliminary preparations for the attack he carried out personal reconnaissances of the enemy lines, taking out parties of officers and non-commissioned officers for over 1,000 yards in front of our line, in order to acquaint them with the ground. All these preparations were made under fire.

Later, by night, Major Congreve conducted a battalion to its position of employment, afterwards returning to it to ascertain the situation after assault. He established himself in an exposed forward position from whence he successfully observed the enemy, and gave orders necessary to drive them from their positions. Two days later, when Brigade Headquarters were heavily shelled and many casualties resulted, he went out and assisted the medical officer to remove the wounded to places of safety, although he himself was suffering severely from gas and other shell effects, He again on a subsequent occasion showed supreme courage in tending wounded under heavy shell fire.

He finally returned to the front line to ascertain the situation after an unsuccessful attack, and whilst in the act of writing his report was shot and killed instantly.

Brevet Major William Congreve was only 25 when he died, leaving his wife of eight weeks and never knowing that he was to be a father. He was buried at Corbie Cemetery.

William's Divisional Commander, under whom he served for over eighteen months, wrote of him:

His loss to me is irreparable, and the Army in him loses one of its very best soldiers. He possessed qualities which are generally to be found only in men of much riper years and of far greater experience. He was distinguished by the highest standards of duty which guided him. Had he lived but a few months longer he must inevitably have attained to the command of a brigade. Under his modesty and gentleness he possessed great strength of character. The whole Division mourns his loss, for he was beloved by all ranks, and the fine example he set of duty well done will for long keep him alive in their memories.

The Victoria Cross 'For Valour'.

A quiet presentation ceremony took place at Buckingham Palace on 1 November 1916. Among the next of kin receiving decorations was William Congreve's widow. His Majesty King George V presented her first with the VC, the DSO and finally with the MC. William Congreve received one further accolade when he was posthumously Mentioned in Despatches, in the *London Gazette* of 4 January 1917. The same issue included a Mention in Despatches for his father, Major General (temporary Lieutenant Colonel) Walter N. Congreve, VC, CB, MVO.

Walter Congreve was later knighted and as Lieutenant General Sir W.N. Congreve, VC, KCB, MVO he was again Mentioned in Despatches in the *London Gazette* of 20 May 1918. Meanwhile, William's sister, Miss Congreve, had led a party of ladies to assist in a Belgian Field Hospital. His mother, Lady Congreve, had turned the family home over as a Red Cross hospital and also served in France in a nursing role. She was awarded the French *Croix de Guerre* for gallantry. The *Staffordshire Chronicle* of 31 August 1918 announced the award, which was 'In recognition of her courage and coolness when the Hospital area of Nancy, where she was nursing, was under shell fire, and attacks from bombing aeroplanes.'

The Emblem of the Victoria Cross from the grave of Brevet Major William Congreve.

CHAPTER 13

Gallipoli

❖

The Gallipoli Peninsula's strategic position lay in the fact that its coastal batteries controlled the Dardenelles Straits between the Aegean and Sea of Marmara, and the Black Sea and beyond. The plan behind the campaign was to control the Straits, thus allowing the British to make landings via the Black Sea and develop their own Second Front against the Central Powers, with the ultimate goal of capturing Constantinople. The conquest of Turkey would have provided a supply route to Russia, whose army was then in full retreat. The campaign against Turkish troops was fought between 25 April 1915 and 9 January 1916, and resulted in 265,000 Allied casualties. Of these, 213,000 were British, with 145,000 due to dysentery, diarrhoea and enteric fever.

The Gallipoli Peninsula is 10 miles wide and 45 miles long and lies on the western edge of Turkey, forming one land side of the Dardanelles Straits. The terrain is very inhospitable, with steep-sided hills cut into by deep ravines. Several small beaches along the western limits of the Peninsula were selected as landing grounds. The element of surprise was essential as these beaches are overlooked by cliffs or by hills further inland. One of the beaches, at Cape Helles, was dominated by the Turkish troops on Achi Baba, while Sari Bair overshadows the whole of what became known as ANZAC beach (named after the combined Australian and New Zealand forces that landed and were decimated there).

The campaign was doomed from the outset. The Turkish troops had early warning of a potential invasion when the Straits' Forts were bombarded (9 February–16 March). This failed to silence the shore batteries and was followed by an abandoned attempt to force the Straits (18 March). Finally, it was decided to capture the guns with a land assault.

The first landings were made on 25 April. Navigational errors meant that some of the boats headed for the wrong beaches, resulting in heavy losses. Such was the intensity of the enemy fire and the desperate nature of the efforts to forge a bridgehead that the men of the Lancashire Fusiliers won 'five VCs before breakfast'.

The media was fed ambitious rhetoric, leading to the *Daily Telegraph* printing (26 April): 'Great attack on the Dardanelles, Fleet and armies. Allied troops land in

Troops go 'over the top' at Gallipoli.

The Gallipoli beaches, showing the domination of the cliffs.

Gallipoli. Success of operations. Large Forces Advance.' Two days later the same paper went on to claim that that Allied troops had advanced 20 miles inland, when the reality was that most were still trapped on the cliff edges.

Despite the gallantry of the troops, they could not achieve anything more than a foothold, pinned down by the enemy who held all of the high ground. There then followed a series of bloody battles as the invading forces tried to push inland, paying a high price for every inch of ground. Company Sergeant Major Horsfall, 2nd Battalion, Royal Fusiliers, formerly of Tillington Avenue, wrote an account of life under fire on the bridgehead:

I have really not been able to find much time for writing since we landed, as we have been kept going both night and day. My word, the times and trials we have gone through will for ever be in my mind.

We landed at daybreak on Sunday, the 25th of April, having to wade through the water for about fifty yards up to the chest, just where it catches your breath, and I don't think we had more than two hours rest for about a week.

The Turks used to keep us worried by a few snipers during the day, and roll up against us at night time in thousands. Oh! it has at times been murder.

The climate here is very hot by day and gets very cold at nights, and all we have for a bed is a hole in the ground, when there is time to dig one, and the sky for a blanket.

Rations have been rather good, consisting of bacon, cheese, jam, corned beef, and biscuits. Just lately we have managed to get a little bread, which has been quite a luxury. For water we sometimes had to dig wells for it, so we very seldom get it clear. Often it would be just like soup.

I received your postcard on Saturday, the 22 May, and the same night I got wounded. In fact, I think I was exceedingly lucky to get back alive that night; we were out under heavy fire. Two bullets passed through my cap and never touched my head. Then a bomb burst in front of me, and I was blinded for about half an hour, but I kept on firing as well as I could, as it seemed like life or death for us as we were about 100 strong up against thousands of Turks.

Later on I was sent back to the trenches with a message and to get more ammunition. The trenches were 200 yards away, and I thought I was never going to reach there, feeling my way on my hands and knees.

Well, I'm on one of the hospital ships going to Alexandria. My right eye is now all right, and the doctor tells me my left one may get all right again. It has been a treat to get back to a bed again and I am making up for lost time as regards sleep.

Company Sergeant Major Horsfall was a Regular, having served in the army since 1903. He was evacuated home and sent to a Manchester hospital where he made a good recovery from his wounds.

Another first-hand account came from RE Motor Despatch Cyclist Corporal G.B. Cross, formerly of Stafford, and of the staff of the L&NWR. Cross witnessed the initial bombardment from a destroyer that was at anchor about 2 miles off the Gallipoli Peninsula. Writing home on 25 May 1915, some time after the initial landings, Cross recalled: 'There has been quite a number of battleships in action, stationed at intervals round the foot of the Peninsula, and it has been possible to see, after hearing the explosion, where the shots have landed.' He wrote of the men who formed the bridgehead:

Both Turkish and German snipers were right up to the landing places. We landed on the Gallipoli Peninsula in the Dardanelles on Monday, 3 May, at 11 o'clock, and immediately experienced what it felt like to be under shell fire. In fact we had not landed more than two hours before three of our party had been wounded, including our Major.

At the present moment we are having a shell once a minute. But most of it has been bursting to the right of me. We instantly set about digging our dugouts.

I met Rifleman Leonard Peach, son of Mr. W. Peach, JP, of Stafford. Last Saturday evening he came and had a meal with us in our dug-out. It went off most successfully, and we spent quite a pleasant evening together.

[We experience] the greatest difficulty in getting drinking water, all having to be brought by beast, and we cook all our own meals.

It is a terrible sight seeing the wounded being brought from the firing line.

The terrain beyond the ANZAC Beach.

ANZAC Cove, August 1915.

The terrain was very rough, the troops essentially living on an open hillside pockmarked by dug-outs and lined by trenches. There were no paths, only routes that men scrambled along. The Allies' positions were overlooked by the enemy who occupied the higher ground and there was the ever-present danger of sniper fire. Corporal Cross continued: 'We are taking the dispatches on foot at present, as motor cycling is out of the question. I enclose for you a Turkish bullet, which I picked up outside my dug-out.'

Attempts were made to make further landings in the hope of outflanking the enemy and providing some relief for the troops pinned down in their hillside positions. Stafford's Colour Sergeant J. Wright, 1/4th Battalion, Royal Sussex Regiment, landed at Suvla Bay on 6 August. His party's role was to get off the beach quickly and head for the high ground from where they could attack the Turkish troops. Around 750 men made the landing, and initial casualties were relatively low. However, once ashore the operation quickly deteriorated and they were unable to reach their objective. Before they were evacuated in December, they had lost over 500 men. It was later reported that Wright, a former Coldstream Guardsman and Regular soldier, was 'commissioned for gallantry during the Gallipoli Campaign. He went on to serve as an officer with the Worcestershire Regiment, before returning to England suffering from dysentery'.

A number of gallantry awards were made to Staffordians who fought during the campaign. These included the Belgian *Croix de Guerre* which was awarded to Sapper William Rupert Machin, RE, *London Gazette*, 15 April 1918. The *Staffordshire Chronicle* of 16 February 1918 recorded: 'He joined the army in August 1914. In 1915 he went to Egypt, and was with his company in Gallipoli where he was slightly wounded. He went to France in the latter part of 1916, where he is still on active service.'

The main battles during the campaign included the First Battle of Krithia (28 April), the Turkish night counter-attack (2 May), the Second Battle of Krithia (6 May), the Third Battle of Krithia (4 June), the Battle of Gully Ravine (28 June), the landings at Suvla Bay (6 August), the ANZAC attack on Chunuk Bair (6–9 August), and the Battle of Scimitar Hill and attack on Hill 60 (21 August). Further skirmishes continued on a daily basis, but it was clear that there would be no breakthrough, in what would only have been the first stage in the struggle for the control of the Straits, itself only the initial phase of a longer campaign. The evacuation of the ANZAC bridgehead and Suvla Bay began on 10 December and lasted for nine days, while the last troops at Cape Helles were not evacuated until 9 January 1916.

The 'Dardanelles' inscription (from the County War Memorial).

CHAPTER 14

The Gardeners of Salonika

In October 1915 the British and French dispatched expeditionary forces to Salonika (Thessalonika) on the request of the Greek Prime Minister. The initial plan was to support the Serbs in their armed struggle with Bulgaria. The appeal, however, came too late as the Serbian Army had capitulated before the Allies landed. Despite the pressing need for reinforcements in France and Flanders, and the stagnation of the Dardenelles Campaign, it was decided to keep the troops in the region, while awaiting redeployment.

Initially welcomed, the Allies soon faced opposition from pro-German factions. In December 1915, following their withdrawal from Serbia, the British fought at the Battle of Kosturino. During early 1916, the British Salonika Force was largely employed in constructing a defensive line which became known as the 'Birdcage'. In turn, the Bulgarians and Austrians fortified their positions in the hills surrounding Salonika, making any break-out potentially very costly. Rather than withdraw, however, the British contingent was reinforced to four divisions.

In January 1916 Private F.W. Perry, of Stafford, who was serving in Greece with the 2nd Battalion, King's Shropshire Light Infantry, wrote to his former workmates at Edwin Bostock & Co.:

Just a few lines to let you know I received your [Christmas] parcel which came in very handy. The fags are just what I wanted, for we cannot get English fags out here. Of course one gets the weekly allowance but they are not like the good Woodbines. The muffler is grand, and it, with the mittens, will keep me warm at nights.

The country is very different from France – nothing but a lot of uncultivated land which doesn't seem worth fighting for.

With the coming of spring, things looked rosier. On 29 April 1916, a letter written by former *Staffordshire Chronicle* staff member Sapper C.H. Spronston appeared in the newspaper: 'There are vineyards and orchards and wild flowers bloom in profusion.

The sweet violet, poppy, primrose, daisy, buttercup, Star of Bethlehem, and many other varieties of flowers make a walk very interesting.'

The Salonika force dug-in until the summer of 1916, by which time the international element had been reinforced by Serbian, Russian and Italian units. Consequently, the Bulgarian attempted invasion of Greece in July of that year was repulsed. At the beginning of October the British, in co-operation with her allies along other sections of the front, began operations on the River Struma, capturing the Rupell Pass and advancing to within a few miles of Serres.

A further letter by Sapper C.H. Spronston, written on 1 January 1917, but published on 3 March, read: 'We are in dugout, and are having wretched weather, snow, rain, and occasional frost, but it is surprising how one can adapt one self to almost any conditions.' The worst killers in the campaign were dysentery and fever. Not untypical was the story of Stafford's Gunner A.H. Robinson, RFA, who, it was reported, was admitted to hospital for the second time on 5 May 1917, suffering from a fever. Many of the troops who served in Greece endured several bouts of sickness. Some troops became so ill that they had to be evacuated to Malta, Alexandria, Gibraltar or back home.

During 1917 there was comparatively little activity on the British section of the front. There was, however, fighting around Lake Doiran, where the line was adjusted several times by each side. In April a British attack gained a considerable amount of ground, resisting strong counter-attacks. During the following month a Bulgarian counter-attack on the British positions failed, but triggered a series of engagements elsewhere, known collectively as the Battle of Vardar.

In July the following year (1918), the Allied troops in Salonika began a major offensive intended to end the war in the Balkans. The British contingent did not play a significant role until early September, when an assault was made in the Lake Doiran area on the 18th and 19th. Here they met with stiff opposition and were pushed back, while an advance against 'Pip Ridge' and Grand Couronne resulted in very heavy casualties.

It was reported that Private George Bruce, 1st Battalion, South Wales Borderers who served in Salonika was a POW in Bulgaria between 29 March 1917 and 28 October 1918. He was three times Mentioned in Despatches for gallantry.

There were few other gallantry and other awards bestowed for service in the campaign, although the *Staffordshire Chronicle* of 9 April 1918 reported:

Quarter-Master-Sergeant Hawkins 31st Field Ambulance, Royal Army Medical Corps, only son of Mr. and Mrs. R.T. Hawkins, Tithe Barn Road, Stafford, has been awarded the Meritorious Service Medal [for devotion to duty].

Quarter-Master-Sergeant Hawkins has been on continuous active service since July 1915. He took part in the Suvla Bay landings. At the end of September following, the 10th Division, to which the 31st Field Ambulance was attached, was moved from the Dardanelles to Salonika, being the first British troops to land at that port.

The Meritorious Service Medal.

The Greek Military Cross, 3rd Class.

Quarter-Master-Sergeant Hawkins took part in the thrilling attempt to relieve Serbia, and narrowly escaped capture by the Bulgars. He served on the Salonika Front for nearly two years, but left last September [1917] for Egypt, here he later took part in the recent campaign.

The award was officially announced in the *London Gazette* of 12 December 1917.

A further award came after the end of the war with Private C. Devonhill, 68th Field Ambulance, RAMC, who fought in the Salonika Campaign, being awarded the Military Medal for 'bravery in the field'. Unfortunately, the medal was announced in the *London Gazette* of 13 March 1919, without a citation.

Another Staffordian who was honoured for his role in the Salonika Campaign was Corporal (acting Sergeant) Percy Rowell, RAMC, who was awarded the Greek Military Cross 3rd Class. Permission to wear the award was granted to Rowell and officially announced in the *London Gazette* of 23 July 1919.

The main actions (many of which were awarded as Battle Honours to the engaged regiments) during the Salonika Campaign included: the occupation of Mazirko (2 October 1916), the capture of Karajakois (30 September–2 October 1916), the capture of Yenikoi (3–4 October 1916), the First Battle of Doiran (22 April–8 May 1917), the capture of Ferdie and Essex Trenches (15 May 1917), the capture of Bairaki and Kumli (16 May 1917), the capture of Homonodos (14 October 1917), the Battle of Tumbitza Farm (17 November–7 December 1917), the capture of the Roche

Acting Sergeant P. Rowell, RAMC.

Noir Salient (1–2 September 1918), the Second Battle of Doiran (18–19 September 1918), the passage of the Vardar and the pursuit to the Strumica Valley (20–30 September 1918). The Armistice was agreed on 30 September 1918.

CHAPTER 15

Stafford's Naval Heroes

❖

Great Britain ruled her Empire through the Royal Navy, which truly did 'rule the waves'. The army, too small to defend against a European threat, acted largely as a policing force, strong enough to be strategically deployed in greater numbers as and when required.

A number of Stafford's earliest casualties were in the Senior Service. On 1 November 1914, the Royal Navy met with a major setback at the Battle of Coronel, fought off the coast of Chile. During the engagement HMS *Good Hope* and HMS *Monmouth* were sunk by the SMS *Scharnhorst* and SMS *Gneisenau*, under the overall command of Graf Maximiliam von Spee. The battle was hopelessly one-sided and Admiral Sir Christopher Cradock, who died on the *Good Hope*, has been roundly criticized for taking his vessels into action when they were so heavily out-gunned.

With the loss of HMS *Good Hope* three Staffordians went to the bottom of the ocean: Harry Pearce Ancill, of 29 Rowley Street, Arthur Birch, of 34 Mynors Street, and Frank Reynolds, of 14 Castle Street. Ancill and Birch were stokers and probably killed when the ship's boilers exploded as she sank.

The German battleships *Scharnhorst* and *Gneisenau* were in action again a month later at the Battle of the Falklands. Here they clashed with the battlecruisers HMS *Invincible* and HMS *Inflexible*, both armed with eight 12in and sixteen 4in guns. The two British battlecruisers had been detached from the Grand Fleet and sailed from Devonport on 8 November with the newly appointed Commander-in-Chief in the South Atlantic and Pacific, Vice Admiral Sir Frederick C. Doveton Sturdee, KCB, CVO, CMG. The Battle of the Falklands was an important victory for the Royal Navy, the British Squadron routing the Germans under Vice Admiral von Spee. HMS *Invincible*, Vice Admiral Sturdee's flagship, played an important part in the battle. Her arrival in the flotilla on 26 November raised morale after the shock of the loss of the *Good Hope* and *Monmouth*, along with their crews. Unknown to the enemy, the Royal Navy had two vessels in the vicinity of the Falklands that were capable of taking on their battleships.

Prior to the battle the British maintained the element of surprise; the *Invincible* and

SMS Scharnhorst.

Inflexible concealing themselves in the 'shadow' of the Falklands while the lighter British cruisers acted as the 'bait' – the trap was sprung early on 8 December 1914. Von Spee, flying his flag from the *Scharnhorst*, headed towards Port William with the *Gneisenau* and the *Nuremberg* in advance and at a distance of some 6 miles. Reports that two battlecruisers and five cruisers lay ahead were dismissed. As the enemy approached, the *Gneisenau* was straddled by a 12in shell from HMS *Canopus*, which was hiding the other side of the island behind hills, her batteries skilfully directed by land-based range-finders. The Germans, caught off-guard, turned and ran – and so began a chase that was to see their fleet partly dispersed, placing the Royal Navy in the command of the direction of the unfolding battle.

At 1300 hours HMS *Invincible* engaged the *Leipzig* at a range of 15,000yd. Outgunned, the enemy turned away, along with the *Nuremberg* and *Dresden*. The German light cruisers were pursued and sunk by the combined fire of the *Glasgow*, *Kent* and *Cornwall*. In a separate engagement the *Invincible* and her sister ship stalked the *Scharnhorst* and *Gneisenau*, forcing them to join battle at 1330 hours when the *Invincible* drew alongside the *Scharnhorst* and on a parallel course at a range of 16,000yd.

Von Spee attempted to break off the engagement but the Royal Navy vessels had the advantage of superior speed. By 1445 hours the battle was raging once again. Accurate gunnery led to hits on the *Scharnhorst*, which caught fire forward. Return fire diminished with every salvo that hit her. The *Scharnhorst's* third salvo registered several hits on the *Invincible*. Suddenly a direct hit on one of the *Scharnhorst's* giant funnels led to its collapse across the decks, debris disabling more of her guns. The doomed *Scharnhorst* turned, bringing her others guns to bear. The odds were, however, too great and they were silenced one by one. At 1604 hours, the *Scharnhorst* was seen

SMS Gneisenau.

to be listing heavily to port, and within a matter of a minute began to roll, disappearing beneath the waves at 1617 hours.

With the destruction of the *Scharnhorst*, all attention was focused on the *Gneisenau* which had already sustained damage from the guns of HMS *Inflexible*, reducing its speed and rate of fire. She was at the mercy of *Inflexible* and *Invincible*, which by then had been joined by HMS *Carnarvon*. The German sailors maintained a dogged defence for 2 hours until, at around 1710 hours, one of *Gneisenau's* funnels and her main gun turrets were seen to collapse, debris falling across the decks and into the sea. In order to save the crew of the *Gneisenau* from further losses, 20 minutes later Vice-Admiral Sturdee ordered his battle cruisers to 'cease fire!'. The German gunners manning the only remaining operational turret, however, continued their fire and so, reluctantly, the exchange continued for a further half an hour until the German gunners ran out of ammunition and the *Invincible* and *Inflexible* ceased fire.

But the gunners' futile gesture had a terrible consequence. Had they stopped firing earlier and the order been given to 'abandon ship', the ship's crew might have launched the lifeboats and escaped the *Gneisenau's* inevitable fate before she too rolled onto her side. Only around 200 or so survivors were seen clinging to her hull. Those who were wounded or temporarily stunned by the icy waters quickly drowned. The crew of HMS *Invincible* pulled just over 100 men out of the sea, 14 of whom died shortly afterwards. Another eighty men were picked up by *Inflexible* and *Canarvon*. Among those taken POW were fifteen officers and the ship's captain. Despite being hit about twenty-two times, twice below the water line, not a single man on board HMS *Invincible* was killed.

A further dramatic incident occurred during the engagements that took place off the Falkland Islands. It exposed a major flaw in the ammunition chain between the gun batteries and the magazines deep in the heart of the vessels. One of the 6in gun turrets on HMS *Kent* was damaged, killing six of its crew. As a result, flaming cordite charges descended the ammunition hoist into the magazine. A Royal Marine averted disaster, fighting the fire and preventing the magazine from igniting. The details of the action reached the highest authorities and the Marine was recommended for the Victoria Cross, although the award was downgraded to the Conspicuous Gallantry Medal.

Remarkably, no lessons were learned at the Admiralty when it came to the design and operation of anti-flashback doors along the ammunition chain. Less than six months later, on 31 May 1916, the Royal Navy was to pay a terrible price with the loss of four of her premier battlecruisers: HMS *Queen Mary*, HMS *Indefatigable* and her sister ship, HMS *Invincible,* and HMS *Defence.* All of these vessels suffered the same fate; 4 enemy shells causing the deaths of nearly 4,000 men. Each was destroyed during the Battle of Jutland, hit by a single salvo.

Admiral J.R. Jellicoe.

HMS *Invincible* was completed in 1908 and the design of her gunnery systems was influenced by John Rushworth Jellicoe, then the Director of Naval Ordnance. By 1916, John Jellicoe had been knighted and was Commander-in-Chief of the British Grand Fleet – to him fell the glory of the victory off Jutland and at his door may be laid at least part of the blame for the disproportionately high casualty rate suffered by the Royal Navy.

The Battle of Jutland was the only major fleet action of the war. It was fought in a thick mist and so in the pre-radio and radar days of naval warfare the exact deployment of forces and progress of the action was unknown to either Commander-in-Chief. In one sector of the battle the only narrative came from a handful of survivors, these out of crews of over a thousand men. Included on the list of the dead was Stoker 1st Class Alfred T. Plant, of Tenterbanks, Stafford, who served on HMS *Invincible*.

Rear Admiral The Honourable Horace Hood's flagship, HMS *Invincible*, was captained by A.L. Cay, a seasoned naval officer with over twenty years' experience, and to whom no blame may be attached for the loss of the vessel and crew. Captain Cay took his ship into battle to aid HMS *Chester,* which was then under sustained attack from the German battlecruisers *Frankfurt, Wiesbaden* and *Pilla.* As the sea battle developed the *Invincible* came under fire, enemy shells straddling her hull – the German gunners were more than a match and the greater part of one salvo hit its mark.

However, at 1755 hours *Invincible* brought her own guns to bear with vengeance, followed minutes later by *Inflexible* and *Indomitable* (of the British Third Battlecruiser Squadron). The enemy squadron was only saved by the intervention of a force of battlecruisers which launched volleys of torpedoes at the British, forcing them to take avoiding action. In turning away from the torpedoes they lost vital ground on the enemy, who made their escape.

At around 1815 hours Rear Admiral Hood, CB, MVO, DSO, took his squadron into battle again, manoeuvring it ahead of Admiral Beatty's flagship the *Lion,* which headed her three sister ships. This formidable force brought its guns to bear on the German *Lutzow, Derfflinger, Koning, Grosser Kurfurst* and *Markgraf,* scoring numerous direct hits. Suddenly, a change in the prevailing wind parted a mist that had partly shrouded HMS *Invincible*, now exposed on the enemy's horizon. All available guns were trained on her, but only one salvo registered hits.

Vice Admiral D.R. Beatty.

A single shell pierced *Invincible*'s 'Q' turret causing an explosion that knocked out the turret. A cordite flash instantaneously shot down the shell hoist, detonating the magazine with catastrophic effects. Ripped in two by the explosion, an awesome sight was revealed once the flames and smoke had subsided. The battlecruiser had been torn apart almost in an instant, only the tips of the bow and the stern visible above the waves over 100ft apart.

Another vessel lost during the battle was HMS *Defence*. One of those who died on HMS *Defence*, flagship of Rear Admiral Sir K. Arbuthnot, Bart, CB, MVO, was Stafford's Leslie James Bagnall.

The *Defence* and *Warrior* were engaging the doomed *Wiesbaden*, holding fire until within 5,000yd range. As they closed in, the *Defence* and *Warrior* were straddled by fire from a German battlecruiser and four dreadnoughts. The Germans concentrated their fire with terrible effect. HMS *Defence* was hit by two heavy salvoes in quick succession, a round detonating her aft 9.2in magazine. A chain reaction sent a fireball which shot down the ammunition hoists to her 7.5in magazine which blew up. The *Defence* erupted in a ball of fire before disappearing below the waves; there were no survivors.

A further local casualty was 1st Class Stoker George Lester, who served on board HMS *Shark*. Lester's death was reported in the *Staffordshire Chronicle* of 3 July under the heading 'Stafford Boy Lost with the Shark':

> George Lester was the second son of Mr. Henry Lester . . . As a boy, George Lester attended Rowley Street School, his class teacher, Mr. Boon, explaining to a reporter from the *Staffordshire Chronicle*, that in June 1908 George had displayed bravery in saving the life of one James Preston, of Wright Street, who had fallen into the river [Sow].
>
> When he was only 14-years-old, Lester left school to work for Messers Mason and Marson, Boot and Shoe Manufacturers. He later found employment with Dormans, and then at Siemens. Unsettled and in search of adventure George, still only sixteen, joined the Royal Navy.
>
> Too young to go to sea on a battleship, Lester had initially trained on HMS *Victory* at Portsmouth, before being drafted to HMS *Flirt*. His next ship was HMS *Dominion*. He served on-board her in the Mediterranean as a part of the 3rd Fleet during the Balkan War, later transferring to HMS *Exmouth*, with whom he returned to England. Lester was posted to HMS *Flying Fish*, subsequently to HMS *Magnet*, and from that vessel he went, with others, by special train to join HMS *Shark* in the North Sea. George Lester was 21-years-old.

On 17 June the *Staffordshire Chronicle* report continued: 'HMS *Shark*, which took a prominent part in the opening of the naval battle in the North Sea, was sunk on 31 May.' The editorial added a note that: 'All accounts agree that the [crew of HMS] *Shark* maintained in a full degree the high traditions of the British Navy, and the men who

Survivors plucked from the icy seas.

were fortunate enough to survive speak of the great gallantry of the members of the ship's company.'

HMS *Shark*, commanded by Commander Loftus Jones, of the Fourth Flotilla, went into action at 1800 hours. *Shark* and three other destroyers engaged and pursued a stronger force of German destroyers and torpedo boats, but in so doing came within range of three battlecruisers. *Shark* was caught in a deadly fire which resulted in hits to her bridge and engine room. Her commander made his way to the aft wheel only to find that this too was out of action and that the vessel was crippled and still drawing fire. Lieutenant Commander J.O. Barron placed HMS *Acasta* between HMS *Shark* and the enemy and signalled to Commander Loftus, asking if he required assistance. Commander Loftus knew that *Shark* was lost and ordered Barron to save his own crew while he could. *Acasta* pulled away into the relative safety of lying mist.

Survivors of the *Shark* recalled how immediately after the *Acasta* left the scene the German battlecruisers closed in for the *coup de grâce*, pounding the steel hull with salvo after salvo. On board the *Shark*, Commander Loftus Jones ordered that the holes in the hull be plugged with collision mats in order to try to stem the rush of water. Meanwhile, the deckhands prepared the lifeboats for a possible evacuation. All efforts to save the ship were in vain, as the sea gradually crept up the decks. Still the surrounding German vessels continued their fire from all sides, despite the minimal return fire. Because of this the Captain refused to give in and personally took over one of the few remaining guns when its crew was reduced to two men. However, he was soon cut down, losing a leg and lay mortally wounded, but still issuing orders. With only fifty men unwounded, the Captain gave the order to abandon ship. But as the lifeboats were launched they were destroyed by fire from German vessels which by then were only 600yd away. The few survivors began jumping into the icy water. Suddenly a torpedo exploded and HMS *Shark* was engulfed in smoke and flames, before sinking along with Lester and her remaining crew.

It was after midnight when the dozen or so survivors were picked up by the crew of a Danish steamer. They had had to look on earlier as the rest of the Fleet sailed by in pursuit of the enemy. Eyewitnesses reported that Commander Loftus Jones rejoiced at the fact that the enemy was on the run, despite his own plight. Only six men, all other ranks, survived their time in the water, each being awarded the DSM. Commander Loftus Jones was awarded a posthumous Victoria Cross.

Jutland/Falkland (from the County War Memorial).

Stafford lost another of her sons off Jutland, with the death of Private William Alfred Found, a gunner with the Royal Marine Light Infantry. Found died on board HMS *Malaya* during a gunnery duel. He was the eldest son of Mr and Mrs W. Found, of 16 Albert Terrace, Stafford. During the naval engagement HMS *Malaya* was exposed at the rear of a British formation as it turned into position. Enemy rounds fell all round her at the rate of six a minute. By turning harder to port, however, she escaped, although for the next 20 minutes she was constantly straddled by salvoes and was twice badly hit below the water line and began to list. Before the order could be given to create a defensive smoke-screen, William Found's gun was hit by a heavy shell burst, which killed all of the gun crew and began a fire. Captain Godfrey H. Knollys, Royal Marine Artillery, commanding the Royal Marine Detachment wrote of the young Staffordian:

We know we have lost a very good comrade. He was always cheerful and keen on his work; in fact, I had a very high opinion of him. I am sure he was proud of the Corps, and wanted to make a success of his career. He was killed in action on May 31st, about 5pm, supplying ammunition to his gun in a fleet action, his death being instantaneous. He was buried that evening about 8.30pm at sea (as near as possible in the middle of the North Sea), the whole ship's company being present in the upper deck to pay their last respects to a brave man.

Yet another local sailor lost to the seas was Petty Officer Samuel Grant. He served on board HMS *Hampshire*, an armoured cruiser of the Devonshire class that played only a supporting role in the Battle of Jutland. HMS *Hampshire* set sail again from Scapa Flow a few days later, on 5 June 1916. Along with a crew of 800, the vessel was carrying a 'distinguished person' bound for an important meeting in Russia. Tight security had surrounded the whole mission and it was not until the VIP and his staff boarded the cruiser that he was recognized as Lord Kitchener of Khartoum. The *Hampshire* was to sail to Archangel from where he would travel with his party to meet with the Tsar and discuss plans for the forthcoming offensives, which would include the Battle of the Somme.

On boarding the *Hampshire*, Lord Kitchener was greeted by Captain Saville, who informed him of a change of plans. Admiral Sir John Jellicoe had despatched orders altering the proposed route of the convoy away from the open seas around the Orkneys to the more sheltered eastern passage. Although this plot avoided the worst of a gathering storm, it would also mean sailing through areas known to be mined.

HMS Hampshire.

HMS *Hampshire* sailed past Hoy Sound and soon rounded Stromness where it almost immediately hit rough seas. The Captain ordered all but one of her hatches to be sealed. Less than 1½ hours into her voyage the cruiser's hull was ripped open below the water line by a floating mine. Taking on water at an alarming rate, the *Hampshire* began to list heavily to starboard. The order was given to 'Abandon Ship'. As Samuel Grant and the other petty officers supervised the launching of the lifeboats, the terrible truth suddenly hit home – the derricks were electrically operated and the power had failed.

One crew managed to release their lifeboat by hacking away at its cabling. Once in the water, however, the small boat and its fifty occupants were picked up by a huge wave and dashed against the *Hampshire's* hull. Those who caught a glimpse of their own fate must have frozen for a moment – their lifebelts and cork waistcoats must have seemed pointless against the great walls of water that enveloped the men below. The options were grim: they could jump for it or they could wait for the waves to claim them. Some made for the Carley safety floats, huge oval lifebelts that could support up to fifty men clinging onto their sides or standing waist-high in water on a metal grid.

The accounts of the twelve survivors of the *Hampshire* record the last moments of the vessel and her crew. Of the terrible sights and sounds, the most pitiful surrounded those huddled in the lifeboats willing and praying that they would float clear as the ship slipped under – all were crushed or drowned when the *Hampshire* turned-turtle and disappeared almost without trace.

Only three of the Carley safety floats could be launched before the *Hampshire* sank. However, hypothermia soon took its toll on men already suffering from shock and burns, and one by one they simply slipped into unconsciousness and drowned. Sadly, Petty Officer Samuel Grant was not among the half-dozen survivors who were eventually washed up on the rocks of the Orkney coast. Later research revealed that during the build-up to the Battle of Jutland a few short days earlier, the German U-boat *U175* had laid a string of mines along what was later to be the path taken by *Hampshire* and her escorts, HMS *Victor* and HMS *Unity*. Ironically, Lord Kitchener did not live to see the fate of his Volunteer Army, which was largely destroyed on the Somme only a matter of weeks after his death.

Another local seaman, Petty Officer Frank Brown, of HMS *Thrasher*, saw service in home waters. Brown was a fitter with W.G. Bagnall Ltd before enlisting into the Royal Navy. He served on board the destroyer HMS *Thrasher*, which was largely engaged in patrolling Scapa Flow and protecting the British fishing fleet.

On 8 February 1917 HMS *Thrasher* engaged the German submarine *UC-39* off Bridlington Bay. The submarine had surfaced to shell the *Ida* when HMS *Thrasher's* crew intervened. Accurate fire from HMS *Thrasher* damaged the German submarine, which attempted to dive but was forced to resurface and surrender. While in the act of surfacing, a shell exploded near her conning tower, killing her commander, Oberleutnant Ehrentraut. The submarine was still making speed and so further rounds were fired, killing three crew members, three more falling overboard and drowning.

HMS Thrasher, whose crew included Frank Brown.

Eventually *UC-39* obeyed instructions to stop her engines and the remaining crew were taken as POWs. The submarine was taken under tow, but took on water and sank before reaching a port.

It was later discovered that the submarine had sunk the British merchantman *Hannan Larsen*, while 20 miles off Spurn Point. *UC-39* had surfaced and used her deck guns to shell the merchantman before taking the crew as prisoners and sending her to the bottom of the sea. Mr T. Read, late master of the *Hannan Larsen*, wrote to Lieutenant Ernest Hawkins, Captain of HMS *Thrasher*:

Dear Sir,
I am taking this opportunity of writing to you to thank you and your shipmates for the very kind way you treated Mr. Scott my Chief Engineer, and myself the day you rescued us from the German submarine.

The Germans gave us the choice of death, whether we preferred to be hung or shot. You gave us no choice at all, but only tried to kill us with kindness and if ever it lay in my power to return the compliment I will not be backward in doing so. I am sorry to say one of my Crew died in Grimsby hospital and two of the others are still detained there.

I have got everything square now, and am leaving Tyneside dock today as Captain of the SS *Primo of Newcastle* bound for Rouen in France and I only wish I could meet you and your shipmates there. I can assure you we would paint the town red.

If you are ashore in the Tyne when you come home and have time to call at the above address, I have left orders that you are to be treated to the best of everything and the password is to be '*Thrasher*'.

So best wishes to you and all your shipmates.
I remain
Yours truly,
T. Read. Late Master of SS *Hanna Larsen*.

CHAPTER 16

The Zeppelin 'Terror Weapon'

The first Zeppelin raids over British soil were made on 19 January 1915, and targeted the coastal towns of Great Yarmouth and Kings Lynn. The attacks, which killed two and injured another sixteen, were dubbed a 'terror raid' by an irresponsible press, which played directly into the Germans' hands. The coverage not only provided the enemy with a major propaganda coup, but also ensured that the raids, which had no military significance, would continue.

Former Stafford postman Corporal J.F. Edwards, of the Gloucester Regiment, wrote an account of a subsequent raid. Details of his letter were published in the *Staffordshire Chronicle* of 15 May 1915:

The Air Raid in Kent

His detachment was called out to witness a thrilling sight on Monday morning (10th May) – the attack on Southend. To the north the sky was clear and it was here that he had a view of what he made out to be three Zeppelins. They were at a great height, but no one could mistake their sausage like shape. He adds that now and again he could see large sheets of flames rise from the earth – probably some building on fire. 'I shall never forget,' he goes on to say, 'the bursting of the shells from the guns of the Thames forts. They lit up the sky, and often went near their mark. These same guns were responsible for the departure of the Zeppelins. There were no searchlights used, neither did I see any of our own aircraft in pursuit. We turned in again at 3.50am with sad hearts, not having been able to get a pop at the brutes.

Flying at over 20,000ft, Zeppelins operated above the ceiling of most of the Royal Naval Air Service's (RNAS's) aircraft. Anti-aircraft fire was not accurate enough to bring them down, even if they could be illuminated by searchlights. Meanwhile, even if fighter aircraft could get within firing range, .303 ammunition might pierce the

Zeppelins in their hangars.

Zeppelins pictured over London, illuminated by searchlights. The anti-aircraft guns fired shrapnel bursts but struggled to find the altitude and range of the enemy.

Zeppelin's gas cells but would not ignite the hydrogen gas (unless it hit a metal object to create a spark). The German airships, therefore, were able to raid with impunity, only being hampered by the blackout, which made navigation difficult. Only 10 per cent of bombs were dropped on their target area.

Emboldened by their early successes and the ineffectiveness of British air defences against the high-flying airships, the enemy turned their attention to London on 31 May 1915. The raid killed seven and wounded thirty-five, but caused little damage to infrastructure. The attack, however, created panic among the population, as a result of which vital aircraft were diverted from the front line for Home Defence.

Despite twelve RNAS squadrons being tied down as a part of Home Defence, the first aerial victory against an airship didn't come until the night of 6/7 June 1915. During an offensive raid, RNAS pilot Lieutenant Rex Warneford engaged and destroyed *LZ37* near Brussels. Warneford was flying a Morane-Saulnier on a bombing raid against the Zeppelin sheds at Evere when he intercepted *L237*. Placing his aircraft over the Zeppelin, he dropped six bombs onto the airship, which exploded in a fireball. Lieutenant Warneford's own aircraft was caught in the flames and he narrowly escaped death. Such was the jubilation at the destruction of the airship, that Lieutenant Warneford was awarded the Victoria Cross for gallantry. Victories against the Zeppelins remained rare, and they continued to be used to raid British soil almost unopposed.

The local press gave column inches to the Zeppelin raids which became the talk of the Home Front. On the night of 31 January/1 February 1916, the war came closer to Stafford when Zeppelins *L21* and *L19* accidentally raided the Midlands, their course taking them over the outskirts of the county town. The raid comprised of nine Zeppelins which crossed the North Sea targeting Manchester and Liverpool, in what was the biggest airship attack of the war to date. The lack of a long-range weather forecast meant that the airships' crews were unaware of winds that might take them off course and relied on ground observations for navigation. This was difficult at night and *L21*, commanded by Kapitanleutnant Max Dietrich, got lost soon after crossing the English coast due to a combination of inland mist and fog. Flying roughly on a westerly course, Dietrich passed over Derby, which he mistook for Manchester, but decided to save his bombs for Liverpool and turned south. A short while later, as he flew over the Staffordshire moorlands, unable to see any features below him, Dietrich believed he was over the Irish Sea. According to Dietrich's navigation, *L21* was closing on his prime target, the port of Liverpool.

Kapitanleutnant Dietrich continued flying south, thinking he was flying down the coast. Here the lumbering airship's path took it over the outskirts of Stafford, the droning of its engines causing alarm, bringing people onto the streets. But all along its flight path word had already been sent out and the blackout was nearly complete; the scene below the airship remained featureless. Meanwhile, as the airship approached Brocton Camp it passed over a group of soldiers who, fearing they might be a target, threw themselves into a ditch.

Not every district had heeded the warnings, mistakenly believing they were beyond the range of the airships or did not consider themselves a target. Soon Dietrich saw the lights of a town below him and to the south of it the lights of a second, the two separated by an area of darkness. These features he interpreted as Liverpool with Birkenhead to the south, separated by the River Mersey. He steered so as to attack what he believed to be Liverpool, making his approach from the south. His actual flight path, however, took the airship over Tipton, which was bombed at 8pm, killing fourteen, before raiding Wednesbury at 8.15pm, killing the same number. From Wednesbury *L21* turned and flew on over Lower Bradley, before passing over Walsall where it dropped further bombs.

Later that night *L19*, which was also lost, flew over the Black Country towards the fires created by *L21's* bombs, dropping its payload on West Midland targets but without causing further fatalities. During their combined attacks bombs were reported to have landed on Tipton, Burton-on-Trent, Walsall, Birmingham and Birchalls.

A ditched Zeppelin.

With the raid over, both Zeppelins headed back towards their base. *L19*, commanded by Kapitanleutnant Loewe, encountered difficulties and was forced to ditch into the North Sea, where in the early hours of the morning it was approached by the British fishing trawler the *King Stephen*. William Martin, the trawler captain, was worried that his men would be overpowered by the crew of sixteen and refused to rescue them. Martin was fishing illegally in a zone prohibited by the British authorities and feared discovery, so when he returned to port he gave the Royal Navy false co-ordinates for the ditched Zeppelin. A search was made for survivors but naturally no trace of the crew was found and they eventually drowned. The incident became a feature of anti-British propaganda.

One consequence of the raid locally was the establishment of a landing strip near Beacon Hill, on what, a generation later, became the site of RAF Stafford. From here fighter aircraft could mount patrols in defence of the northern approaches to the industrial Black Country. The press later reported that the raid led to an increase in local volunteers for the RFC. In late 1915, due to the lack of success against Zeppelins, responsibility for Home Defence, formerly assigned to the RNAS, was handed over to the RFC. This came at a time when innovations such as incendiary bullets began to give the fighter pilots the edge.

The first Zeppelin shot down in air-to air combat was *SL11*, the destruction of which was claimed by No. 39 Squadron's Lieutenant William Leefe-Robinson. The combat took place in the early hours of 3 September 1916. Flying a BE 2a, Leefe-Robinson fired several drums of ammunition, including the new incendiary bullets, into the Zeppelin before it caught fire and crashed, killing all on board. Leefe-Robinson was feted as a hero and awarded the Victoria Cross, also receiving a bounty of £3,500.

Second-Lieutenant Richard B. Levett, of Milford Hall, had earlier witnessed the destruction of an airship by anti-aircraft fire. He described the scene in a letter home:

> At 1.00am this Sunday [July 1916] morning I was watching the flashes of the guns firing at two Zeppelins North of Gravesend from here and saw the Zeppelin catch fire beautifully as funnily enough I was just watching that very piece of sky. There was first of all a glowing spark in the sky and then it got larger and larger and at last it became a great blazing mass but floating down quite slowly. Before it got to the ground it practically went out, only the glowing part showing but we could see the sky light up when the Zeppelin bumped on the ground, Soon after there was a curious light further down the Thames which might have been an airship burning on the ground. The Brigade officer telephoned here that two Zeppelins had been brought down so I hope it is true. It was an extraordinary sight watching the flames start out of nowhere in the sky and then gradually spread. All the men cheered and then there were scenes of great excitement and joy – but what a death! I couldn't help thinking of the wretched men inside as the envelope became more and more in flames. I don't know how far off she was, but some considerable distance.

At the time few people shared Richard Levett's compassion for Zeppelin crews, as their raids were directed against civilians.

Wreckage from the airships was highly prized and had to be guarded by the military against souvenir hunters. Salvaged sections of airships were displayed in Stafford and elsewhere as curiosities to help raise funds for the war effort. Smaller fragments of the soft aluminium were turned into jewellery and sold in the town on behalf of the British Red Cross.

CHAPTER 17

Stafford's Men in their Flying Machines

Staffordians fought in all of the armed services including the newly formed RFC. On 17 October 1914, it was reported in the *Staffordshire Chronicle* that 'Mr. Blackmore, of Messers Bagnall, who recently left to join the RFC, has passed the qualifying test, and has been given a machine.' Blackmore was not alone in his spirit of adventure and other early volunteers who joined the RFC included Reginald O. Wain, Francis V. Webb and B.J. Woodhouse, all of whose names were mentioned in the press in November 1914.

Two more early volunteers were the Wood brothers, who enlisted on 8 September. Initially Bill and George Wood served in the Grenadier Guards, but later answered a call for men to join the RFC. Bill was promoted to corporal and later to flight sergeant, serving in France. He was badly burned when an aircraft crashed into a hangar where he was servicing another machine. Bill spent a part of his convalescence at nearby Sandon Hall Red Cross Hospital.

No doubt all of these volunteers had been inspired by the visits to the county town by the aviator Gustav Hamel, a British national who had a few years earlier made demonstration flights in his Bleriot monoplane from the Common Plot and the Lammascote. Aerial warfare was initially limited to reconnaissance flights and close encounters with the enemy only resulted in the exchange of pistol or rifle fire. Later the aircraft carried machine guns, but these could only be fired over the propeller or from swivelled gun mounts – gunners had to be careful not to hit their own aircraft in the melee.

Stafford played an important role in the advancement of air-to-air combat following the invention of a system that allowed machine guns to be fired between the blades of a rotating propeller. Known as the Constantinesco and Colley Interrupter-gear, the equipment was manufactured under licence at W.H. Dorman & Co. Ltd.

Of the Staffordians who flew combat operations, perhaps the most notable was an observer who came up against the German top aces. In May 1917 news reached

Stafford that local man 21-year-old Air Mechanic 1st Class Ernest George Perry, RFC had been shot down in combat. Perry was the twelfth victim of Lothar von Richthofen, brother of the Red Baron. Ernest Perry survived the air battle but was to remain a POW until 1918. He was only repatriated early the following year.

The first flying machines were largely made of wood and fabric and were often manufactured and serviced by men who were in peacetime more accustomed to producing furniture. Mechanics were recruited to maintain the aircraft's engines. Ernest Perry, of 82 Peel Terrace, Stafford, had worked in the engineering trade, hence his selection for the role of air mechanic. With his initial training completed, Perry was posted to No. 11 Squadron RFC, stationed in France. Perry was evidently 'noticed' by his NCO and recommended for flying duties. Ernest had expressed an interest in flying, the first stage of which was taking a trip as a passenger. This proved to be a fairly pleasant experience and he soon became one of the Squadron's observers.

An FE2b reconnaissance aircraft.

As observer/air gunner on the obsolete FE2b, Perry's position was in the nose of the bi-plane, ahead of both the wings and the pilot. While he had a good forward vision, his sight to the rear was very limited. Fighter tactics had already developed, and the favoured method of attack was from above and behind, and preferably from out of the sun. This and the aircraft's relatively slow air speed compared to the Germans' best fighters made the FE2b a sitting duck.

Perry's role was to navigate and to help his pilot identify enemy targets before mapping their location and taking reconnaissance photographs. This information was used both to plan advances and target enemy positions for bombardment. He had a defensive role too and was armed with two Lewis machine guns with spare drums of bullets. As an air gunner, Perry was trained to deal with blockages in the guns and to change magazines – difficult enough on the ground, but doubly so when flying at speed and in a combat situation.

Anti-aircraft fire became quite accurate as the war progressed and slow-moving reconnaissance aircraft became easy targets.

The American Frederick Libby, MC described his role as an FE2b gunner and its inherent dangers: 'When you stood up to shoot, all of you from the knees up was exposed to the elements. There was no belt to hold you.' The air gunner relied on his grip on the gun and the sides of his compartment, which as Libby put it were all that 'stood between you and eternity'. He continued: 'Toward the front was a hollow steel rod with a swivel mount to which the gun was anchored. This gun covered a huge field of fire forward. Between the observer and the pilot a second gun was mounted, for firing over the FE2b's upper wing to protect the aircraft from rear attack.'

To adjust and fire the rear-facing gun meant that Perry would have to stand with his feet only just inside the lip of the gunner's position, his whole body exposed as the aircraft flew through the air at 80mph. Libby explained: 'You had nothing to worry about except being blown out of the aircraft by the blast of air or tossed out bodily if the pilot made a wrong move.'

While the parachute had been invented, the authorities feared that if issued with them, air crew might bail-out of damaged aircraft rather than try to land them. This policy led to the unnecessary loss of thousands of lives. The nightmare of most pilots was burning to death in their open cockpits as engine oil or petrol caught fire, the flames blowing back at them in the aircraft's slipstream.

Die fünf erfolgreichsten Flieger der Jagdstaffel Richthofen.

Vizefeldwebel Festner †Leutnant Schäfer †
Leutnant Frhr. von Richthofen
Rittmeister Frhr. von Richthofen †† Leutnant Wolff †

Members of Jasta II – the Richthofen brothers.

Air Mechanic Perry's aircraft was lost while on an evening patrol on 27 April 1917. The news of his plight came to his mother in a letter written by his Commanding Officer, a major in the RFC. It transpired that Perry and his pilot, Second Lieutenant John Arthur Cairns, took off in their FE2b fighter (Serial No. 4850) at 1720 hours. They were over an hour into a line patrol when their formation was attacked by the much-feared Jasta II, led by Manfred von Richthofen. The Red Baron had already shot down two of No. 11 Squadron's aircraft in the previous few weeks. His claims included the FE2bs of Lieutenant C.E. Robertson and Second Lieutenant H.D. Duncan (flying A827), his forty-second 'kill' on 13 April and of Lieutenants C.A. Parker and J.C.B. Hesketh (flying A820), his forty-sixth 'kill' on 22 April.

At 2015 hours Cairns' aircraft was seen to be in a combat with an enemy aircraft. Working as a team, Perry had tried to direct his pilot to avoid incoming fire, while at the same time using his machine gun to fend off the enemy. The air battle continued for several minutes as the pilots vied for position. But the Albatros V had the advantage. Despite his best efforts the FE2b was damaged sufficiently enough for Second Lieutenant Cairns to have to make a forced landing behind enemy lines. Wrestling with the controls, he put the aircraft down safely near Fresnes, to the south-west of Vitry. The landing was witnessed from the air. Consequently it was reported that there was 'reasonable hope that both men had survived the combat and resultant forced-landing'.

In truth, the British airmen had stood little chance against the aircraft of Jasta II. Out-gunned and with a 40mph speed disadvantage, they were easy targets for a pack

Lothar von Richthofen.

of seasoned, highly motivated and disciplined German airmen flying the Albatros V, then the fastest and most manoeuvrable aircraft in production.

Of the two aircraft damaged or destroyed by Richthofen's men one, Cairns', fell to the guns of the Red Baron's younger brother, Lothar von Richthofen. Confirmation of the men's capture eventually reached their families via the Red Cross. The pilot and his observer were separated soon after they fell into enemy hands, the Germans sending them to different POW Camps, Cairns being an officer.

The second FE2b of No. 11 Squadron destroyed (Serial No. 7698) was flown by Second Lieutenant P.R. Robinson with Air Mechanic 2nd Class M.H. Tilley acting as observer/air gunner. The FE2b was shot down at 2020 hours by Kurt Wolff (his twenty-second 'kill'). The FE2b crash-landed behind British lines south of Gavrelle, with both men wounded. Wolff, already an ace with Jasta 11, was to achieve twenty victories during April alone, being awarded the *Pour le Merite* on 1 May (on his twenty-ninth out of a total of thirty-three victories).

Stafford's Ernest Perry was shot down in April 1917, known to the RFC as 'Bloody April'. During this month the British flew countless sorties in support of the Arras Offensive, while the French Army was also in the throes of a major offensive on the Aisne. The RFC paid a terrible price for the information they provided for the planners on the General Staff, suffering a 40 per cent casualty rate. This was at a time when the operational life of air crew was rated at only 17½ hours.

The Battle of Arras began on 7 April. Flying reconnaissance sorties in support of the advance, the RFC deployed some twenty-five squadrons, including Perry's No. 11 Squadron. These units were pitched against just five well-equipped German Jasta. This figure rose to eight by the end of the month. Much of the success of the Arras Offensive was down to the skill and bravery of the airmen of the RFC. During the build-up to the battle men like Stafford's Ernest Perry took thousands of aerial photographs and drew an equal number of sketch maps pinpointing every German gun position and strongpoint. This intelligence was crucial to the success of the offensive, allowing the British artillery to destroy the enemy positions prior to the infantry's advance. In addition, the pilots flew ground strafes during the battle itself. One pilot recalled:

Leutnant Kurt Wolff.

We were detailed to fly at a low altitude over the advancing infantry, firing into the enemy's trenches. Working with the infantry in a big attack is a most exciting business. It means flying close to the ground and passing through our own shells and those of the enemy.

The air seemed shaken and literally full of shells on their missions of death and destruction. Over and over again one felt a sudden jerk under a wing tip, and the machine would heave quickly. This meant that a shell had passed within a few feet of you.

Despite their numerical advantage, however, the RFC was largely equipped with slower reconnaissance aircraft or scouts, and light bombers. The new pilots arrived in France after only 10 hours' flying time on trainers and none on the aircraft they were to fly in combat. Although the RFC had a few Sopwith Pups, these were reserved for the experienced British aces. The newly trained pilots could do little more than take off, fly straight and level, and perform a few basic manoeuvres. They learned air-to-air firing in the field – as such they were cannon-fodder for the Albatros pilots.

During April the RFC lost 245 aircraft, with 211 air crew killed or reported as 'missing'. A further 108, including Cairns and Perry, became POWs. One-third of the RFC's losses during this period fell to the guns of von Richthofen's Jasta II. By contrast, the Germans lost sixty-six aircraft, with many of their pilots returning to combat before the end of the month.

Lothar von Richthofen was already a seasoned fighter pilot when he claimed Cairns'

FE2b. His flying career was as remarkable as his more famous older brother's. Like Manfred, he had initially been a pre-war officer cadet in the cavalry, winning the Iron Cross 2nd Class. Lothar took his brother's advice and applied for re-training, and by the winter of 1915 he had qualified as an observer and a year later gained his pilot's badge.

On 10 March 1917, Lothar became operational and was assigned, at his own request, to Manfred's Jasta II, based at La Brayelle. In stark contrast to the rapid turnover of the British pilots, it was a full two weeks into his posting before Lothar made his first operational sortie. By this date his brother, Manfred, was already the holder of the *Poure le Merite*, or 'Blue Max', and was well on his way to his fiftieth 'kill'. Manfred ordered the young oberleutnant to act as his wingman and to stay close by his side at all times.

Fighter pilots are generally superstitious and Lothar was no exception. Manfred gave him a pair of his 'lucky' gloves – Manfred had shot down his first ten 'kills' while wearing them. For good measure, Lothar was allowed to fly his elder brother's cast-off fighter, in which he had destroyed his nineteenth to twenty-ninth enemy aircraft. It should be noted that even with their speed and armament advantage, the Luftwaffe pilots were not totally invincible, as Lothar was shot down on three occasions (13 May 1917, 13 May 1918 and 13 August 1918).

When writing about his brother, the Red Baron noted: 'After the third flight with him [Lothar] I suddenly saw him break away from me and jump an Englishman and kill him. My heart leapt with joy as I watched him.' Lothar von Richthofen lacked none of the combat skills of his brother. Within four weeks of his first air battle, he had been credited with twenty British aircraft and was commanding the Jasta in his brother's absence.

Lothar von Richthoven's twentieth victory was against one of the RFC's top aces, Albert Ball, VC, DSO **, MC, then flying with No. 56 Squadron. Between May and August 1916, Ball had flown Nieuports with Perry's No. 11 Squadron and it is possible that Perry served under the future VC winner. The two adversaries, Ball and Lothar, faced each other in combat on the evening of 7 May 1917, only a few days after Perry had been shot down. Both pilots crashed as a result of the engagement; Lothar survived but Ball was killed. His SE5 fighter was seen to emerge from cloud inverted before falling to the ground. Later research, however, suggests that Ball died as a result of becoming disorientated in thick cloud, leading to him stalling his aircraft.

When the wreckage of Albert Ball's SE5 was found there were no signs of combat damage. Apparently one of Lothar's fellow pilots fired his pistol into the engine to validate Lothar being credited with the 'kill'. Lothar had suffered a leg wound and was taken off flying duties and probably knew nothing of the conspiracy. He ended the war with forty victories. Albert Ball, who had already won the DSO with two Bars, and the MC, was posthumously awarded the Victoria Cross.

CHAPTER 18

The Battle of the Somme

⸭

Over a million men became casualties in the long and bitter struggle on the Somme. The offensive, which began on 1 July 1916, dragged on until mid-November and cost Great Britain and her Empire 125,000 dead, with a further 294,654 gassed or wounded. But the battle was not totally one-sided, and following the initial assault the Germans suffered heavy losses. An estimated 437,000 to 680,000 Germans became casualties, leading a German Staff officer to describe the Somme as 'the muddy grave of the German field army'.

In Britain the impact of the losses was severe, particularly in the north of England where many of the Pals battalions had been recruited. Some battalions went into action for the first time on 1 July and were decimated. Not all of the regiments that fought on the first day of the Somme were a part of Kitchener's New Army. Among the local battalions engaged were the 1/5th and 1/6th Battalions of the North and South Staffordshire Regiments, which fought at Gommecourt.

The Allies had originally intended that the Battle of the Somme would be the push that ended the war. This plan was altered as a result of a pre-emptive attack by the Germans in the Verdun Sector. French reserves were severely drained, losing 250,000 men by the end of May. The revised plan was designed to relieve pressure on the French, although the assault in the northern sector on Gommecourt was in itself only a diversion for the main attack further south. The assault fell to the men of the 1/5th and 1/6th Battalions of the North and South Staffordshire Regiments, along with the 1/5th Battalion, Lincolnshire Regiment. Together they formed the 137th Brigade under the command of Brigadier General H.B. Williams.

The task of the 137th Division was to advance and form a pocket in a German position which lay to the north of Gommecourt, establishing, with the aid of the 1/3rd and 2/1st North Midland Company's Royal Engineers, ten new strongholds. The second phase of the Division's objectives, a southward sweep involving the capture of the village of Gommecourt, was to be launched from these new positions at 1030 hours.

An artillery bombardment along most of the Somme Front raged for seven days, longer than originally intended owing to the date of the assault being pushed back due to heavy showers. The combination of a million shells and the rain created a morass of thick mud in no man's land along the whole 40-mile front.

The troops had arrived at the Somme section of the front full of confidence, but there was a rude awakening for those who had not yet seen combat; a portent of things to come. It had become common practice before major offensives for mass graves to be dug in advance. As the Staffords marched towards the reserve trenches, they would have passed in silence as they looked upon what could prove to be their own 'final' resting place.

Due to the flooding of the assembly trenches, the assault troops found themselves cramped in old French trenches which zigzagged about the battlefield. To avoid confusion in this labyrinth, lines of red tape were laid late the previous night, taking the men forward to their starting point. On reaching the front-line trenches they crouched down for hours awaiting the order to attack. The 1/6th Battalions of the North and South Staffordshire Regiments formed the first line of the attack, which was planned in six waves. Zero Hour was set for 0730 hours. At the appointed time, as the barrage began to lift, the shrill of whistles was heard along the front. This was the signal for the men of the first wave to scramble out of their trenches and advance towards the enemy's lines.

The senior planning staff were so confident that the German defences would have been obliterated by the barrage, that the British troops were ordered to walk across no man's land at a steady pace. Every man had been assigned individual duties. Some men carried reels of barbed wire, others materials to rebuild what remained of the enemy trench systems.

Once the advance began, the shell-churned mud severely hampered the men's progress which, with 90lb on their back, was never going to be faster than the prescribed walking pace. With the Staffords only halfway across no man's land, at the point of no return, a strong wind picked up and the smoke shells screening their advance began to disperse, leaving the men dangerously exposed. Meanwhile, the Germans had already begun to emerge from their dug-outs, which, far from being destroyed, were set 40ft deep in the earth. British High Command had chosen to ignore intelligence reports that, during the two years of preparation, the Germans had constructed these shell-proof bunkers.

The German front-line trenches had largely been replaced by a patchwork of shell craters but these, however, served the same purpose. It was, therefore, only a matter of a few seconds before the German machine-gunners were in position and mowing down the advancing British troops. In addition, German artillery was able to pinpoint strategic positions and lay down a deadly shrapnel fire which cut the troops to ribbons.

And so it was into a hail of machine-gun fire and shrapnel that the men of the 1/6th Battalions of the North and South Staffordshire Regiments made their advance. Men dived for the temporary shelter of shell-holes, moving forward in short rushes. Some reached the German wire, which lay in two bands, 40ft thick, and remained largely intact and impenetrable. Here they were cut down by the enemy machine-gunners and

The first wave goes off in the Battle of the Somme.

The second wave goes off.

by rifle fire from their front and flanks. A few men penetrated the enemy wire and reached the German trenches, but by then the rear waves of the assault were being blown to pieces in the British front line or in no man's land. The remainder of the first wave were either killed in front of the German lines or forced to retreat through lack of support.

By 0900 hours the situation was so desperate that even the 'Top Brass' were aware that the 137th Brigade was in trouble. Unable to cancel the operation, which was a part of a wider plan, Brigadier General Williams decided to renew the attack in four waves, using the 1/5th Battalions of the North and South Staffordshire Regiments, held in reserve, along with the 1/5th Battalion, Leicestershire Regiment. By this stage the 1/5th Battalion, North Staffordshire Regiment, which was being pounded by enemy artillery in the communication trenches, could only muster 200 men, while the Leicesters were similarly depleted and were led by a junior officer.

These reinforcements were weighed down with wire, line-pins, wire cutters etc., each man ready to perform what had been his allotted task – so confident were the generals of the attack's success. It became a devil of a job for the officers and NCOs to get their men to offload their additional kit and instead prepare for a bayonet charge across 400yd of bullet-raked open ground. Delays in finding smoke shells meant that the attack was put on hold. It wasn't until 1520 hours that the first rounds landed in no man's land, creating a haze that quickly dissipated. When the first twenty men left the relative safety of their trench, all but two were shot within 20yd of the British lines. As a result, the remainder of the assault was not ordered off.

In late October the following account of the advance, written anonymously by L.A.L. and relating to actions on 1 July, was published in the *Staffordshire Advertiser*:

Saturday Morning 7am. We are to charge at 7.30am. Six of us are sitting in a little group round a small brazier in the dug-out; every eye dwells thoughtfully on the remaining embers. In 30 minutes we go over. The call to 'battle positions' may come at any moment. The row made by the artillery is terrific. Our own shells pour ceaselessly onto the German positions. We have silenced many of their Batteries, but they keep sending over some more heavy stuff. Suddenly, the curtain (sacking) is pulled aside and Mr. F.B. – who stands in the opening, curtly gives the order to stand to positions. We grasp rifles and bayonets and grimly march out.

7.15am My God the din is fearful. The guns are roaring now to terrible purpose. Our own huge shells roar over our heads like trains over an iron bridge, and burst on the Bosche [sic] lines with explosions that seem to rend the very earth in two. Terrific explosions around us testify that the Bosche's artillery also is busy. His whiz-bang batteries are sweeping our trenches.

7.25am Five minutes to go. We shake hands all round, with expressions of 'Good Luck'.

7.28am The officers stand watches in hand, and we wait tensely at the foot of each ladder. The Colonel comes along, cheerfully climbs on the parapet, and gazing over at [the] Germans, says, 'Safe as Piccadilly, boys'. The cry comes along, 'The [censored] are over'. Then 'Over you go'. We scramble over the parapets and the wreckage of our own barbed wire. Machine gun and rifle bullets are whistling round us, shrapnel begins to fly too. It is all a terrible dream

– only one word can adequately describe it – HELL. [Our] captain [standing] in front [of the advancing troops] falls shot through the neck, and Cecil R. on my left pitches forward silently on his face. Captain [censored] is on his feet again, covered with blood and raving mad. He drags himself after us, banging away with his revolver. We are near the front line trench now, and the Germans are leaning over the parapets blazing away and hurling bombs. Men are going down everywhere. As the two men on my immediate right and the man on my left drops, I begin to wonder when my turn is coming. However, luck favours me and I land in their front trenches.

Most of the Germans have rushed to their second line, and those that now remain throw down their rifles and up with hands with their infernal 'Mercy, Kamerad'. We press on to the second line, and again the brutes are busy with their rifles. One big fellow as I neared the trench blazed away at me, and how he missed me I am hanged if I know. I felt the heat of the bullet pass me, but before he had time to shoot again I had him through the head. To my right, three Germans threw up their arms as prisoners, to be immediately shot from behind from their own men. The German dead are all over the place, forming barricades in parts, over which it is necessary to climb. As I scrambled over one heap, the top German, a huge brute, scrambled up, but a whack over the head with my rifle butt did the necessary. Hurrah! the second line is ours, but as one looks around, it can easily be seen at how big a cost. Men are lying everywhere, some horribly still, others wrestling about and slowly going. We press on to the third line. The Germans are firing furiously, and our lads going down rapidly. A curse on the machine guns! The third line and the [censored] Redoubt fall into our hands, and the enemy are in full flight. It is funny what a peculiar sensation a charge instills into you. You don't care a tap what happens, and have only ambition to kill, kill, kill. We are victorious and know it, and though we should have stopped at the redoubt, some of us in the flush of victory race after the retreating enemy, until a corporal suddenly discovers we have gone too far. We drop into a huge shell crater and open rapid fire. In front of us lie a mass of greenish-grey and khaki forms. One or two of our men endeavour to rise to drag themselves to the trenches. They are immediately shot by snipers. Rotten brutes, shooting wounded men.

Elsewhere, the battle plan had fallen apart while there had been few gains. In fact the division that the remnants of the 1/5th Battalion, North Staffordshire Regiment would have been sacrificed for, in their diversionary attack, had already been pushed right back. The whole operation was officially called off at the exact moment that the Territorials should have gone 'over the top' to what must have been an almost certain death. Instead they sat out the German barrage which had already lasted an hour-and-a-half. Finally, at 1630 hours the 1/5th Battalion, North Staffordshire Regiment was ordered to file out of the trenches and 'stand down'.

The Somme inscription (from the County War Memorial).

The battle had cost the 1/6th Battalion, North Staffordshire Regiment 14 officers and 205 NCOs and other ranks killed, while many more were wounded, and this out of an initial strength of around 520 all ranks. Meanwhile, the 1/6th Battalion, South Staffordshire Regiment lost 13 officers and 292 NCOs and other ranks killed out of an initial strength of around 740.

Around 19,240 British soldiers died or were posted as 'missing in action' on the first day of the Somme, twice that number (38,230) being wounded, out of a total of 120,000 engaged. Among the dead lay 25 Staffordians, most having no known grave, only a line among the 73,367 names on the mountainous wall otherwise known as the Thiepval Memorial. A nominal list of Stafford's casualties on the first day of the Somme includes the following:

Private Frederick Allen*, 1/6th Battalion, North Staffordshire Regiment (TF)
Private Sydney Allard, 11th Battalion, Notts and Derby Regiment
Private Arthur Allport*, 1/5th Battalion, North Staffordshire Regiment (TF)
Private C.H. Anthony*, 1/6th Battalion, North Staffordshire Regiment (TF)
Second Lieutenant Richard Gordon Bagnall, 14th Battery, Heavy Battery, RA
Private Ernest Baker*, 1/5th Battalion, North Staffordshire Regiment (TF)
Private George Batten*, 1/5th Battalion, North Staffordshire Regiment (TF)
Private Frances N. Birch, 1/6th Battalion, North Staffordshire Regiment (TF)
Major Charles Edward Boote*, TD, 1/5th Battalion, North Staffordshire Regiment (TF)
Private Arthur Daniels*, 1/5th Battalion, North Staffordshire Regiment (TF)
Second Lieutenant Percival Harry Emberton, 1st Battalion, South Staffordshire Regiment
Private James Evans, 7th Battalion, Queen's Regiment

Sapper Albert Edwin Hackett, 92nd Field Company, RE
Private Harry Holden*, 1/6th Battalion, North Staffordshire Regiment (TF)
Private Harry Houlding, 1/6th Battalion, North Staffordshire Regiment (TF)
Private B.F. Hurst, Lancashire Fusiliers
Private William Joseph Johnson*, 1/6th Battalion, North Staffordshire Regiment (TF)
Private Harry Stanley Lant, 1/6th Battalion, North Staffordshire Regiment (TF)
Private William Lloyd*, 1/6th Battalion, North Staffordshire Regiment (TF)
Private Thomas Matthewman*, 1/6th Battalion, North Staffordshire Regiment (TF)
Lance Corporal Alfred Mills*, 1/6th Battalion, North Staffordshire Regiment (TF)
Private Bertram Joseph Norton, MM, 1/8th Battalion, Royal Warwick Regiment (TF)
Lance Corporal Henry E. Steventon, 1/6th Battalion, North Staffordshire Regiment (TF)
Lance Corporal Ernest John Thorpe*, 1/6th Battalion, North Staffordshire Regiment (TF)
Second Lieutenant Henry Egerton Whitgreave, King's Shropshire Light Infantry
Private Horace Wilson, 1/6th Battalion, North Staffordshire Regiment (TF)

* No known grave.

Just because a soldier is listed as having no known grave does not necessarily mean that they were not given a Christian burial at the front. In the height of battle, men were often buried in shell-holes or in temporary burial grounds immediately to the rear of the action, even under battle-field conditions the padres reading the committal words of the prayer book burial service over the deceased. Grave markers might very easily be lost as the tide of the front line ebbed and flowed, a soldier's resting place being destroyed by artillery fire before it could be recorded by the Grave Registration Commission (renamed the Imperial War Graves Commission in 1917, and from 1960 the Commonwealth War Graves Commission). Similarly, the Germans buried bodies recovered from no man's land or POWs who died at their dressing stations. Often these graves were not properly recorded and were consequently lost during the British advance.

Of the Stafford casualties listed above, the following is known.

Private Allard's uncle received a letter from his Commanding Officer, Second Lieutenant Arthur Bennett, which read: 'I am terribly grieved to tell you that your nephew was killed-in-action on 1 July. Everyone of his platoon spoke highly of him, and I (his officer) found him a good soldier, and can guess something of the sorrow this will bring to you all.'

Ernest Baker was twice turned down for military service on medical grounds before finally being accepted into the army in early 1915. Following a period of basic training, Ernest was sent to France in March 1916. His officers were all killed or badly wounded during the battle and it fell on the regiment's army chaplain to write: 'He was killed "instantaneously" while carrying out his duty as one of a "carrying party". He was buried near to the British Lines.' Like so many men who were buried close to where they were killed, his grave marked only with a rifle and helmet, Baker's final resting place was destroyed due to shelling.

Evidence of impromptu graveyards close to the front line has only recently become the subject of modern investigations using original reconnaissance photographs. Consequently a number of burial sites have already been located and excavated under the auspices of the Commonwealth War Graves Commission; only in a handful of cases thus far has it prove possible to identify the remains using a combination of personal effects and DNA.

Another casualty was Second Lieutenant Richard Bagnall, who was one of three brothers serving at the front. Richard was killed while acting as a Field Artillery Forward Observation Officer. It was his role to locate enemy targets and send their co-ordinates back to the gunners. Bagnall's family ran the local engineering firm, which was heavily involved in manufacturing munitions and locomotives, playing a vital role in the war effort. All of the Bagnall brothers could have claimed they were in reserved occupations, but instead chose to join the colours.

Private Thorpe was among the first Staffordians to volunteer in August 1914. Like Privates Birch, Matthewman and Wilson, who had only been in France for three weeks, he was initially reported as 'missing'. No one knew his exact fate, as those who bore witness to his death were themselves killed. It could take a very long time before the families of such men received a communication to say they had been officially declared as 'missing presumed dead'. The following letter arrived at Private Matthewman's parents' address nearly a year after he was first reported as 'missing'. It may be seen as representative of the letters received by the next of kin of Birch, Thorpe, Wilson and countless others:

I have made full enquires about your son, and can find nothing for certain. I am afraid, however, that there is but little doubt that he fell in the great attack on 1 July. If he did, he died in a glorious battle and died a glorious death. I wish I had more comforting news. God bless and support you in your trouble.

(signed) The Reverend S.A. Studders Kennedy

Also killed in action was Lieutenant Colonel C.E. Boote, who had served as a captain with the Stafford Volunteer Contingent during the Boer War before becoming a member of the new Territorial Army in 1908. He was the most senior officer serving with 1/5th Battalion, North Staffordshire Regiment, taking command of his battalion only a week before the attack on Gommecourt. Boote was initially reported as 'missing'. It was later confirmed that he died at the head of his men.

Of the remaining Staffordians who were killed, two fought alongside other regiments, their names inadvertently being omitted from the Corporation War Memorial. One, Private Thomas Holland, served in the 11th Battalion, Royal Fusiliers. The other was Second Lieutenant Henry Egerton Whitgreave, who fought with the 1st Battalion, King's Shropshire Light Infantry, a part of the 29th Division. Whitgreave was killed in action leading his troops in the advance at Beaumont Hamel.

The Advance at Mametz

As the Battle of the Somme continued, some small successes were made further to the south. Using more imaginative tactics and assisted by the French artillery which was on their immediate right, the 18th and 30th Divisions took their objectives, including Montauban, while the 7th Division captured Mametz. Elsewhere, at Thiepval the 36th (Ulster) Division seized the Schwaben Redoubt but was forced to withdraw because of lack of progress on its flanks. These limited gains cost 57,470 British casualties, but there could be no question of suspending the offensive with the French still under immense pressure at Verdun.

One of the survivors of the Battle of the Somme later wrote of his experiences at Mametz, where the advance of the 1st Battalion, South Staffordshire Regiment had met with greater success. His letter was published in the *Staffordshire Advertiser* of 22 July:

The Charge of the Staffords at Mametz
Working up the two sides parallels of the Quadrangle, we could get close up to the strong positions but they resisted every attempt upon them, whether made by direct attack, with bombs or with trench mortar. Between 4 July and 9 July we made three separate frontal attacks. The first two failed. In the third, made shortly before midnight on the 9th, our men crept out in dead silence till within a few yards of the trench.

Then with one yell of 'Staffords' they rushed the parapets, and literally fell headlong on the enemy inside. Here there was real bayonet work of the sternest kind, and it is believed that not a German got away. With daylight the enemy began to sweep it with machine-gun and rifle fire from both ends. It was impossible to stay, because no one who stayed could have lived. Most reluctantly those of our men who were left made their way back in small parties.

With the fall of Contalmaison and Mametz Wood on the following day another battalion of the same brigade again rushed the support, and as this time it was no longer raked by fire from the two ends, held it for good.

In the course of the ten days' fighting the brigade lost many men. It could not be otherwise. But they have a magnificent result to show for it, for to them fell all the ground right up from Fricourt to the top of the Quadrangle, and with it over 1,500 prisoners, ten machine-guns, and three field guns, and a lot of other booty.

It is not suggested that other troops did not do work as fine: indeed, it seems impossible to say that any troops have shown greater gallantry than any others, even if some have won more ground, others had tasks set them which from unforeseen causes proved impossible.

Captain John Glyn Jones, MC, assistant master at the Corporation Street School, distinguished himself during the latter phases of the attack on Mametz Wood. A renewed assault was ordered for 0415 hours on 10 July. But the attack was poorly coordinated and chaotically executed. Captain Jones, 14th Battalion, Royal Welsh Fusiliers described the scene: 'Presently the silent waves of men started moving forward, and I, with my third wave joined in. Machine guns and rifles began to rattle, and there was a general state of pandemonium, little of which I can remember except that I myself was moving down the slope at a rapid rate, with bullet-holes in my pocket.' As his battalion reached the wood, Captain Jones was confronted by about forty German soldiers who emerged with their hands up in surrender.

Meanwhile, a report appeared in the *Staffordshire Chronicle* of 2 September that was based on an interview with a local officer of the South Staffordshire Regiment who described some of the fighting on the Somme:

The officer at the head of the leading company was conspicuous for the way he encouraged his men at a crucial period. He paid the price. As he fell his men came to a halt. 'Carry on men,' he called with his last breath, and then fell back. The men rallied quickly, and dashed forward.

The rain of projectiles became more pitiless if that were possible, and it soon looked as though it were impossible for flesh and blood to make headway against that dead-weight of metal. The advancing companies came to a halt. One was forced back for a few yards.

The crucial moment had now come, and if the South Staffords had not responded to the call made on them, the day would have been lost so far as that part of the field were concerned. The colonel placed himself at the head of the battalion, and led them in a bee-line for what was understood to be the weakest part of the enemy's position. 'Forward, Staffords; that position must be won at all costs,' he cried. The men never answered a word, but set their teeth and dashed forward.

There seemed to be a machine gun to every foot of ground, and the fire was kept up incessantly. It became too hot for the men to advance any further. They retired a little, and sought shelter in the ploughed-up ground. Bombing parties were sent forward to dislodge the enemy from a commanding position they held. This attack was successful. The enemy was thrown back, and then our advance was resumed.

The South Staffords quickly pressed through the captured trenches and joined hands with the other attacking parties, thus completing the capture of the position.

Lance Corporal H. Howard, of Stafford, had been at the front for a year prior to the Battle of the Somme. He received a bullet wound to the face and neck during 8 July but was rescued from the battlefield and taken back to 10th Stationary Hospital, France. Howard was reported to be responding well to treatment. Writing home, he explained:

> Our latest 'do' with the Germans was a few nights back, when we made a bombing raid on them. We brought back a dozen prisoners, and left a few in their trenches to finish shouting 'Mercy, comrade.' Of course they gave us a bit of a hot time after for it with a few of Bertha Krupps [heavy shells].'

Howard added a sentiment that could be found in letters from as early as the spring of 1915 when he wrote: 'The Boys out here think the war will not last much longer now. The biggest majority you speak to think it will finish in a very short time.'

Another casualty of the battle was Private J.B. Ellis, 8th Battalion, North Staffordshire Regiment. Ellis had gone out to the front on 3 July and was killed in action twenty days later. Notification of his death appeared in the *Staffordshire Chronicle*, and this stated he was only 16 years old and that formerly he had worked for the Stafford Corporation.

Despite the terrible losses on the first day the battle, which lasted another four months, made some headway and cannot be dismissed as a complete failure, not at least in the eyes of the top brass of the time. The following extract is from an order issued by General Erich von Falkenhayn, commander of the German forces on the Somme, to his officers: 'The first principle in position of warfare must be to yield not one foot of ground; and if it is to be lost to retake it by immediate counter-attack, even to the use of the last man.' It was the carrying out of these orders that cost the German Army dearly and led to Falkenhayn's replacement by General Erich Ludendorff and Field Marshal Paul von Hindenburg.

First Day of the Somme (1916)

Despite the regular publication of casualty lists and letters from the front, the public still had no real concept of the brutality of trench warfare, the effects of poison gases or the terrible wounds caused by shrapnel shells. There had, however, been a steady flow of wounded soldiers arriving at Stafford railway station, destined for Stafford General Infirmary or one of the many temporary hospitals or convalescent homes dotted around the area. The majority of these cases were relatively lightly wounded and would recover well in time and be sufficiently fit to return to active service.

The silent short entitled *First Day of the Somme*, shot by official war cinematographers Geoffrey Malins and John McDowell, was released on 21 August and played at cinemas across the country, including at Stafford. The film was to prove a pivotal moment in the public's perception of war, causing shock and dismay, bringing the cost of war into sharp focus.

Another view of the first wave going off in the Battle of the Somme.

Some of the combat footage in *First Day of the Somme* was filmed on a training ground and would be regarded as extremely tame by today's standards. The film did, however, include genuine images of the dead and wounded; one audience member was reported as having recognized her husband being carried on a stretcher, only weeks after being informed that he had died from his wounds. When first shown, some of the imagery caused such distress that members of the audience had to be helped out from cinemas. In particular, the sight of a British soldier stumbling as he tried to follow his comrades 'over the top' into the haze of battle caused great upset. In response cinemas placed age restrictions on admissions. Despite this, over 1 million people saw *First Day of the Somme* in its first week, the film eventually reaching a staggering 20 million.

The film was released at a time when most streets had suffered casualties. Many of the men who came home on leave or suffered from wounds were often withdrawn and uncommunicative and eager to return to their comrades. For those who had lost friends or family, or who were in constant fear of losing someone, the silent movie, for the first time, gave them a dreadful image of a 'Tommy' in combat and supposedly being wounded or worse – the stumbling soldier symbolized their son, their brother, their father, their friend.

CHAPTER 19

The Tank Corps and the Breakthrough at the Battle of Cambrai

Experimental tanks were in production as early as December 1915, but were not used in action until 15 September the following year, when they were deployed on the Somme. Naturally, there was great secrecy surrounding the new weapon, which many of the 'Top Brass' believed might make the breakthrough that led to the end of the war. Everything about the new weapon was kept top secret. While under production they were referred to as water tanks, hence the name 'tank', which stuck.

Initially the tank crews were largely drawn from the Machine Gun Corps, and became known as the 'Heavy Machine Gun Corps', before being redesignated the Tank Corps. These men were to be among the brightest and fittest, as set out in *Instructions for the Training of the Tank Corps in France*:

> The object of all training is to create a 'Corps d'Elite'; that is a body of men who are not only capable of helping to win this war, but are determined to do so. It cannot be emphasized too often that all training, at all times and in all places, must aim at the cultivation of the offensive spirit in all ranks.

On 15 September thirty-six Mark I tanks of 'C' and 'D' Companies took part in the engagement on the Somme, which became known as the Battle of Flers-Courcelette.

Powered by a 105hp Daimler engine, the tanks were built in two types, which were essentially the same except for their armament. The 'Male' type carried two Hotchkiss 6-pounder (57mm) guns and four machine guns; the 'Female', five machine guns.

Turning was a complex manoeuvre which required the officer in control of the brake levers to pull down hard on the right track, while the driver accelerated, making the tank slewed slowly on the stationary right track, the left still in motion. This process

A Mark IV tank advances at Bapaume.

A Mark IV tank clearing a ditch.

9. - Char lourd franchissant un fossé.

was reversed in order to turn to the left. In combat it was essential for the tank to zigzag in order to avoid enemy artillery, which would be zoned in on its position by spotters. This was made all the more dangerous as a tank's maximum speed was 4mph, making them an easy target.

The machines were crewed by a junior officer, three drivers and four gunners, of which one was an NCO. Conditions inside the tank were appalling, due to a combination of intense heat, noise and engine exhaust fumes. The armour-plating was meant to stop bullets, but their impact resulted in splashes of molten metal flying about inside the hull (the side armour was even less efficient and might be pierced by high-calibre bullets and shells).

Staffordshire-born Gunner Alfred Reiffer, of Tank D17, 'D' Company, Heavy Branch, MGC, wrote: 'We were fired on by German machine guns . . . the impact of their bullets was making the inside of the armour white hot. And white-hot flakes were coming off, and if you happened to be near enough you could have been blinded by them.' It was difficult to communicate both within the tank and with the outside world, making co-ordinated attacks more difficult to pull off. Vision was poor and so the tank commander often had to get out in order to reconnoitre his surroundings, making him vulnerable to enemy fire.

The first deployment of tanks caused considerable alarm among the Germans until they realized their shortcomings and began to organize tactics against them. Sergeant Harold Bisgood, a Staffordshire man who served with the 1/2nd Battalion, London Regiment (Royal Fusiliers), witnessed the destruction of a Mark I tank in 1916:

The Germans seemed at first awestruck at the tank, but they soon pulled round and offered a most stubborn resistance.

A Hun shell hit one of the caterpillar bands [tracks]. You may well imagine how we felt, perched in already smashed-up trenches. However, our friend held his own, firing from his Maxims every shot he had, and using up all his shells in the Hotchkiss gun. The mechanics then set the petrol tank alight and retired into our trenches.

At the Battle of Flers-Courcelette, the tanks were sent into action ahead of the infantry. It was recognized that an artillery barrage would churn the ground up and hinder the tank's advance, and so the artillery gunners left corridors along which the tanks could travel.

Even in trials the early tanks were notoriously unreliable. Consequently, only thirty-six of the forty-nine deployed even made it as far as the British front line. Of those that advanced, fourteen had to be abandoned, while two were put out of action by enemy fire; another seven were slightly damaged. Some reached the enemy positions but could not make the hoped for breakthrough.

The next major use of tanks came during the Battle of Arras in April 1917. Sixty tanks went into action, but many were lost through mechanical issues, while others

A damaged Mark IV tank. Note the open hatch behind the machine gun and the broken right-hand track.

A captured anti-tank rifle.

were severely hampered by the muddy conditions. Meanwhile, the designers had already acted to strengthen the tank's armour. The resulting developments led to the Mark IV tank, which first saw service at the Battle of Messines in June 1917. Previous combat experience had demonstrated that tanks might easily be stopped by wide or deep trenches. Many of the newer types carried fascines, which were huge bundles of wood that could be dropped to bridge wide trenches, shell craters and ditches. Despite these improvements, the tanks that fought at the Third Battle of Ypres (July–November 1917) fared little better and their only real victory came at St Julien.

On 20 November 1917, Byng's Third Army launched a limited but tactically radical attack at Cambrai (often erroneously referred to as the first tank battle of the war), where a combination of better drainage and the lack of a heavy barrage prior to the assault meant the ground was more solid. Following a relatively light artillery bombardment, 378 Mark IV tanks smashed through positions on the Hindenburg Line, a heavily defended complex of concrete bunkers and emplacements. Unfortunately, despite the confusion in the enemy's ranks, the infantry was unable to make sufficient headway and a major opportunity was lost.

Cambrai/Hindenburg Line inscriptions (from the County War Memorial).

Among the men who fought and were killed during the Battle of Cambrai was Gunner Louis Haynes, youngest son of Mr and Mrs W. Haynes, of 1 Herbert Road. Prior to being conscripted in April 1916, Haynes, who was 26 years old, was employed as a fitter at Siemens Brothers Electrical Engineering Works. He went out to France in November of 1916 and was a member of the 9th Battalion, Tank Corps, initially known as 'I' Battalion, which was formed in late 1916 and comprised the 25th, 26th and 27th Tank Companies.

'I' Battalion fought throughout the Battle of the Hindenburg Line, taking part in

A head-on view of a Mark IV tank climbing out of a ditch.

the opening stages of the Battle of Cambrai. Here they saw action in the fighting near La Vacquerie, in support of 61st Infantry Brigade, part of 20th Light Division. Their initial action was inconclusive. Of the thirty-five tanks that crossed the start line on 20 November 1917, four were destroyed by enemy artillery fire, while eleven more suffered breakdowns. Of these four were subsequently recovered. Unfortunately, the infantry were ordered to advance 400yd behind the tanks, which consequently lacked close support and suffered heavily. In places, however, there were some gains.

A further tank assault was launched at 1435 hours on 23 November 1917. Twelve tanks of 'I' Battalion, including Haynes', took part in the assault on the village of Fontaine Notre Dame. The attack, commanded by Major Penn-Gaskell, resulted in the destruction of a number of machine guns and damage to the enemy's defences, but made no real headway. From the battalion's operational reports a picture of the engagement may be pieced together.

'A' Section advanced to the southern edge of the village, engaging the enemy, but failed to push any further. 'B' Section's tank No. 118 (commanded by Second Lieutenant C.H. Sykes) was penetrated by armour-piercing ammunition and bombed. Four of its Lewis guns were put out of action. 'C' Section, however, suffered the loss of tank No. 132 (commanded by Second Lieutenant A.W. Russell) which engaged enemy machine-gunners and then went down the main street of the village under heavy fire. A mortar round penetrated the radiator but the tank kept moving along Station Road, turned right and went back through the village. Here it overheated and broke down and had to be abandoned.

Another tank, No. 124 (commanded by Second Lieutenant E.J. Mecredy) went through the village under heavy machine-gun fire. It was forced to withdraw from the fight, having developed mechanical trouble. Meanwhile, 'D' Section's tank No. 141 (commanded by Second Lieutenant G.E. Williams) entered the village before suffering a direct hit which damaged one of its tracks. During the action Stafford-born Louis Haynes was killed; the remainder of the crew was captured.

The following day another dozen tanks supported the assault on the village of Bourlon. Five were destroyed, while another five suffered mechanical damage or fires. Throughout the battle Haynes' battalion had been deployed as a part of the spearhead of the attack. Despite the losses in terms of tanks, only two officers and four ORs were killed during the battle. Thirteen Military Medals were awarded to members of the Battalion for their actions (ten of these being for the action on 20 November).

Lance Corporal W.H. Potts, of the Duke of Wellington Regiment, fought in a support role during the attack on Cambrai. Potts was hospitalized as a result of a wound received during the attack. In a letter home to his father, which was published in the *Staffordshire Chronicle* of 1 December, Potts wrote:

> And what a sight to see the Tanks, and my boys. The [enemy] lines [were] one blaze of fire. The Tanks crawling to them, sweeping them with machine guns. Then the barrage lifted and the Tanks went on to the next objective. As soon as the Tanks had gone over the trenches, in the boys got [with] the bayonet. Poor devils! Didn't they hold up their hands and give souvenirs away.
>
> It was exactly the same with the next objective, and it was quite amusing to see them being brought in. Then our turn came. We had to get two cottages and two lines of trenches, and here comes the worst part of the whole section. We were going forward to our kicking off position when an enemy sniper and machine gun opened out. We rushed them and straight away they put their hands up.
>
> Then we got to our objectives, and just as I was jumping into the trench something hit my right ankle. When I got to a dug-out I had a look at it. It had all swollen up, so I was a casualty because I could not walk. I think a Johnny [German] must have tried to bayonet me. So I started back, and what a time I had dodging shells, falling into shell holes, and having a rest now and then.

Potts finally made his own way back across no-man's-land and into the British trenches, following a communications trench as far back as a Dressing Station. Here he was tended by two POWs: 'Who could come up to me but a German doctor and his assistant, who had been captured earlier in the morning, and had been working all day amongst the wounded. He was a fine chap. In fact both were a treat. They bandaged me up well.' Lance-Corporal Potts' wounds were serious enough for him to be taken out of the line. He was sent back to a Field Hospital where he was treated by Australian nurses, who he referred to as 'Angels of Mercy'. His letter continued to the effect that he hoped to be home for Christmas, adding, 'but if I am here in the Australian hospital, I shall not grumble'.

Another of the units engaged at the Battle of Cambrai was the 7th Tank Battalion, which formed a part of the 1st Tank Brigade. From 20 November the Battalion, which included Private T.G. Beardmore of Stafford, fought in the action near Lens, north of Arras. The Battalion's next major engagement wasn't until 21 August the following Year (1918), when it was deployed north of the Somme. Their crews were a part of one of the lead battalions in the assault against the Hindenburg Line. Bitter fighting resulted in heavy losses, both in tanks and men. On 27 September the 7th Battalion crossed the Canal du Nord in advance of the Canadian Corps' attack which captured the village of Bourlon and the nearby wood.

The 7th Battalion remained in action, fighting to the west of Cambrai, losing eight officers, four sergeants and twenty other ranks killed in action. The Battalion made good progress during the heavy fighting, which led to the award of six DSOs, twenty MCs, four DCMs and twenty-seven MMs. Included in the tally was the Military Medal awarded to Private T.G. Beardmore, of Stafford, which was not announced in the *London Gazette* until 14 May 1919.

CHAPTER 20

1918: The Breakthrough

✦

The USA had entered the war in 1917. But despite supplying armaments to the Allies, they were ill-prepared to go to war. The American armed forces had to be trained and equipped ready to go into action and it wasn't until 1918 that their servicemen were in France in any numbers. With the industrial might of the USA now numbered among the Allies, the German High Command realized that their only possibility of victory lay in one last all-out assault.

On 21 March 1918, German storm-troopers (well-armed soldiers unburdened by heavy 'kit') launched their Spring Offensive, recapturing much of the territory lost over the previous two-and-a-half years. A further attack was made in the Amiens Sector on the 28th, but was halted by the British. Meanwhile, the Germans made smaller scale assaults near Ypres on 9 April and along the Somme on the 24th. In a further development the French were pushed back 40 miles in three days during an assault that began at Chemin des Dames. The German offensive nearly pulled off a miracle, reaching within 37 miles of Paris, but the momentum could not be sustained. The French then counter-attacked on 18 July, pushing the enemy back to the River Aisne.

Meanwhile, the reality of their situation dawned on many of the German troops when they discovered the vast reserves of munitions in captured Allied military dumps. They were further disheartened at the variety and quantity of cigarettes, tobacco, chocolate bars, home-made cakes and other treats in the Tommies' parcels from home. The Germans had been led to believe that the British were on their knees and on the verge of surrender.

The advances had been made at a terrible cost. By June the Germans had suffered a further 1,000,000 casualties, while the British had suffered 380,000 dead, wounded and POWs. After nearly four years of bitter fighting, the BEF had lost the better part of the Regular Army, the Special Reservist, the Reserves and the Volunteer Army. So many waves of reinforcements had been decimated that by the second half of 1918 the men at the front were composed largely of conscripts, most of whom were just 18 years old. This youthful army began their counter-attack at Amiens on 8 August, quickly

The Staffords pose on the bank of the St Quentin Canal.

capturing a swath of land 8 miles deep. The new positions were quickly consolidated and the Germans were unable to make a counter-attack.

Propaganda leaflets dropped behind German lines accurately summed up the situation facing the enemy:

> Arithmetic!
> 1) Between 15 July and 24 August more than 100,000 German soldiers were captured by the Allied troops in France. In addition to this, the German army has suffered extreme losses in wounded and killed.
> 2) Monthly reinforcements of 300,000 fresh American troops are arriving in France with the armies of the Entente.

The Allies' general assault forced a major breakthrough in early October as the fighting focused on the crossing of the St Quentin Canal. Here the men of the North and South Staffordshire Regiments played a crucial role. The 1/6th Battalion, North Staffordshire Regiment captured the vital Riqueval Bridge over the canal on 29 September. Remarkably the troops took both ends of the 150yd-long bridge before enemy engineers could blow the demolition charges. This lay the path open for an advance on the third line of defences of the Hindenburg Line (known as the Beaurevoir Line), which were breached on 2 October.

This proved to be the defining moment in the attack in the British Sector and left the way open for an advance on Germany. The Central Powers were on the verge of defeat on all fronts, and on 3 November Austria-Hungary surrendered, while eight days later Kaiser Wilhelm II was forced to agree to an Armistice. After over four years of near stalemate, during which the tide of war had ebbed and flowed, on 11 November some British regiments found themselves literally yards away from the positions they had held when they fired their first shots in August 1914.

One of the many heroes of the 1918 campaign was Private George Crewe. While serving with the 13th (Service) Battalion, Royal Scots, probably in the Fampoux/Roeux area, Crewe won the Military Medal and the French *Croix de Guerre* in June or July. The *Staffordshire Chronicle* of 21 September 1918 recorded the presentation of the French *Croix de Guerre* to George while on Home Leave. He was invited to attend a session of

George Crewe, MM.

the Stafford Borough Police Court where the Mayor of Stafford, Councillor R.J. Young, presented him with the French award for gallantry (the Military Medal not then being available) announcing that 'Private Crewe, at great risk, brought in a wounded soldier and also saved two machine guns.'

The *London Gazette* of 13 November 1918 carried the official announcement of George's Military Medal, while that of 22 November granted him permission to wear the French decoration. The awards were for the same act of gallantry when George Crewe 'risked his own life to bring in a wounded comrade. He then prevented the enemy from capturing his own Lewis light machine gun and that of the wounded gunner, both of which had put down suppressive fire during a general retreat before becoming dangerously exposed.' George's actions were particularly selfless as machine-gunners were only rarely taken as prisoners during the heat of the battle due to the extreme losses they inflicted on the enemy.

On the Home Front the suddenness of the final victory caught many by surprise. Stafford was still on a war footing and in the midst of a fundraising campaign, the *Staffordshire Chronicle* of 16 November announcing: 'Captured German Guns at Stafford. Five captured German guns arrived at Stafford on Monday morning [11th November], and were placed in the Market Square for public inspection.' In the event, the war drive took place but under a new banner, raising money for comforts for the troops rather than munitions.

With over 1,100 fatalities and many more gassed or wounded, news of the 11 November Armistice was greeted with muted celebrations. The Staffordshire County

Council, however, was quick to pick up on the role of the county's regiments in the final push, passing a resolution congratulating the 46th Division on the gallant attacks at St Quentin on 29 September and 3 October. Meanwhile, the end of the hostilities was marked with due solemnity with a thanksgiving service held at the Borough Hall on 17 November.

Having won the war, the nation now had to fight a second, almost as deadly terror – the Spanish flu. During mid-October the virus struck Stafford, spreading with fearsome speed, and in fatal cases killing its victims within hours of the first signs of infection. Glasgow physician Professor Roy Grist described the disease as 'the most vicious type of pneumonia that has ever been seen' and recorded the symptoms as they presented themselves: 'Two hours after admission, they have mahogany spots over the cheek bones and a few hours later you can begin to see the cyanosis (blueness due to lack of oxygen) extending from their ears and spreading all over their face. It is only a matter of a few hours then until death comes.'

While influenza is normally most dangerous for the young, infirm and elderly, the 1918 variety seemed to affect the fit and healthy worst of all. The highest death rate was among those aged 20 to 45, the demographic with the strongest natural immune systems. Scientists now believe that these victims died because their immune systems went into overdrive, producing an overreaction to the virus which often proved fatal. There was no cure for the influenza, which had to run its course, and best government advice at the time was to take additional preventative measures: 'Avoid sneezing and coughing in public, carry plenty of fresh handkerchiefs, wash hands regularly and gargle with disinfectant mouthwash.' A mixture of mustard and Bovril was thought to boost the immune system, as was alcohol. If any of the above did actually work, they would only have served to increase the likelihood of a fatal outcome. One advert, published in the *Staffordshire Chronicle* of 23 November read:

Influenza. Bovril Ltd. wish to express their regret at the shortage of Bovril during the recent Influenza epidemic. Those who are deprived of the Bovril may more easily fall victims to the epidemics. It is suggested that those customers who have a stock of Bovril should avoid purchasing at present, and thus leave the available Bovril for those who have more pressing need of it at this critical time.

The *Staffordshire Chronicle* of 2 November reported the death of 21-year-old Edith Colley, of 101 Marston Road, one of the town's early influenza fatalities. Edith had returned home from work on Friday complaining of a cold. Feeling somewhat better by Sunday, she suddenly deteriorated on Monday evening, dying at 9.45pm, only 15 minutes after her symptoms worsened.

It was only as the death toll mounted that many schools, theatres and dance halls were closed and people were urged to stay at home. In early November the Picture Palace, Stafford, restricted admissions, the proprietor announcing that: 'during the continuation of the Influenza epidemic children will not be allowed to the cinema for the next fortnight.' Stafford's schools had been closed, temporarily reopening on 6 November. Cases of influenza continued and the Medical Officer, Dr Reid, ordered a further closure until 6 January, by which time the epidemic was over.

Stafford Hospital was inundated with the sick and dying, while elsewhere some wards were closed due to the nursing staff falling ill. Reminiscent of the plagues of the medieval era, many towns demanded signed health certificates before strangers were admitted. Nationally there was a shortage of coffins, morticians and grave-diggers, while funerals had to be limited to 15 minutes.

As is often so, where people gathered in large numbers or were confined in small spaces the disease spread more virulently. The greatest fatalities locally were at the training camps on Cannock Chase, near Hendesford and at Brocton, and in the Brocton German POW Camp. Many of those interred in the war cemeteries on Cannock Chase were victims of what became known as the Spanish flu.

CHAPTER 21

The Wounded

⁙

During the four years of trench warfare around half of the British serviceman who served at the front became casualties; many were gassed or wounded on several occasions, returning to combat following treatment and a period of recuperation.

The Evacuation Chain

A wounded soldier's chances of survival depended on many factors: the nature of their wound; how quickly they received medical attention; the medical facilities available; whether there were foreign bodies in the wound which could lead to infection; and their aftercare. There were no antibiotics and few antiseptics available to counter infection, while blood transfusions didn't come into general use until after November 1917. Consequently, many servicemen died from shock if bleeding could not be stemmed early, or following major wounds or amputations. If dirt or germs entered a wound with shrapnel, gas gangrene often took hold. This was particularly prevalent in wounds received in Flanders due to the peaty soil. Gas gangrene was very difficult to treat and could re-enter a wound even after amputation.

Unless wounded while in the relative safety of a trench, the casualty needed first to crawl, crater by crater, back to their lines or had to be assisted from no man's land. Rescuing the wounded could normally only be attempted under cover of darkness, as enemy snipers were always a deadly threat. This meant that soldiers might remain exposed to further shrapnel and small arms fire for hours, if not days, before they could be brought in. Under such circumstances even a flesh wound could result in a dangerous loss of blood, infection or blood poisoning. This was what happened in the case of former Edwin Bostock & Co. employee Leonard Booth, who volunteered in August 1914 and served at the front from 22 December 1914. He was first wounded while cooking in the advanced trench. A bullet penetrated the sandbag redoubt. It struck him in the cheek, and carried away the fleshy portion of his ear. He had to remain in the trench until dark before he could be removed. Booth recovered from his wounds and was soon back in the firing line. But this was only the first time that Booth was wounded; he was not so lucky on the second occasion.

Bringing in the wounded.

On 2 December 1916, the *Staffordshire Chronicle* reported the 'death of Private Leonard Booth, of the Coldstream Guards, at Plant House Hospital, Gillingham, Dorset, from the effects of wounds received in action during the advance on the Western Front in September'. The article revealed: 'He was wounded in the right arm, and for some time he was reported to be doing well, but blood poisoning resulted from a wound in the hand, and he subsequently contracted pneumonia. His strength being undermined, he was unable to withstand the strain on his constitution, death taking place.' Booth had been among the 'walking wounded' and had received fairly rapid attention, but infection had proved fatal.

The more seriously wounded had little chance of survival unless they were quickly rescued or could somehow crawl back to the trenches. One such casualty was reported in the *Staffordshire Chronicle* of 12 June 1916, and was typical of many cases:

Lance-Corporal A. Dobson, of the 1st Grenadier Guards, was wounded in action last Tuesday last week [8th], and now lies in Birmingham Hospital with three shrapnel wounds in the calf of the leg and one on the shoulder. Dobson was on duty in the trench at the time and he managed to crawl about a quarter of a mile, when he was picked up by a comrade, who carried him a mile and a half to the dressing station.

Dobson was one of the lucky ones. His determination to survive meant that he was seen by medics before it was too late and, as the press reported, was 'making satisfactory progress'.

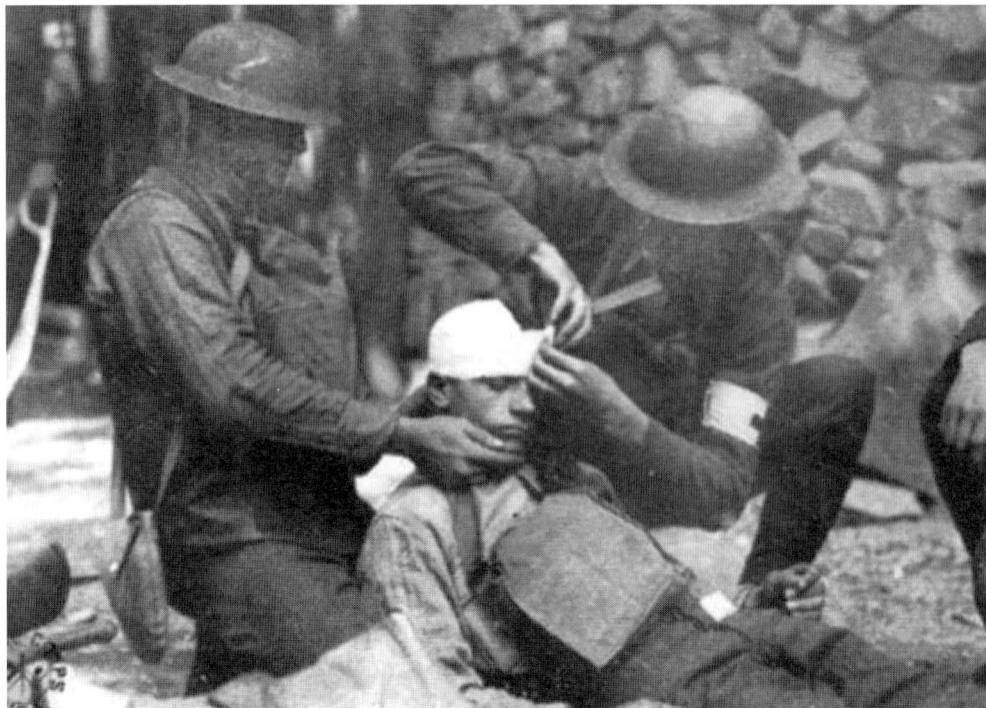

Treating a head wound at a Regimental Aid Post.

The wounded had to pass through a chain of medical stations where they were assessed, treated and moved on. The stretcher-bearers could only give very basic first aid in the field, stemming blood loss or applying splints, before moving the wounded to their Regimental Aid Post.

Regimental Aid Post
The Regimental Aid Post was located in a dug-out a little behind the front line, in a communication or a reserve trench. Here additional treatment was administered by the Medical Officer, his orderlies or stretcher-bearers (often bandsmen or conscientious objectors). The post was equipped with an assortment of bandages, shell dressings and 1st Field Dressings, along with anti-tetanus serum, Boric ointment (an antiseptic) and brandy. Once the wounded had been dealt with they returned to duty, if their injuries were considered only superficial, or were passed further down the line to the Advanced Dressing Station.

Advanced Dressing Station
The more seriously wounded were generally transported 300–400yd to the rear of the front line to the Advanced Dressing Station. The transfer was normally made at night so as not to attract shelling or sniper-fire. To avoid congestion along the trenches, men were held at collection posts, with teams of stretcher-bearers carrying the wounded back in stages. When a front was more 'active', each of the posts could have tens of stretcher-cases lying out in the open waiting to make the next leg of the journey.

When the men were seen at the Advanced Dressing Station, their wounds were more thoroughly assessed, with an orderly writing out an ID card giving the soldier's name, regiment, particulars of wounds etc. Wounds were redressed, while some emergency operations were carried out, and by 1916 the stations housed a Field Surgical Team. During 'active' periods wounded men lay outside on stretchers for hours while waiting their turn to be examined. Many died under such circumstances, without having been seen by a doctor.

Treatment was normally rudimentary but nevertheless could be life-saving. The story of one local officer seen at an Advanced Dressing Station, however, was untypical; the details of his rescue were reported in the *Staffordshire Chronicle*. While convalescing at Sandon Hall, Lord Sandon and his mother, Lady Harrowby, played host to Private Robert King, brother-in-law of Mr Walker, headmaster of Sandon School. Robert King, who was on Home Leave recovering from wounds, had been instrumental in saving Lord Sandon's life. Along with another stretcher-bearer, King had run a considerable distance, carrying Lord Sandon under heavy fire to the nearest Advanced Dressing Station. Here the dangerously wounded Lord Sandon received immediate attention from Stafford's Major Hodder.

Another Staffordian fortunate enough to undergo emergency surgery was Lieutenant Humphrey Thomas Bostock, MC, 1/6th Battalion, North Staffordshire Regiment. Bostock was hit in the right arm and thigh when a shell exploded in his trench. He was immediately stretchered to the Advanced Dressing Station where Major Hodder was forced to make an amputation at the elbow. This was a complicated and

Carrying back the wounded.

dangerous operation not normally undertaken at the front, but which undoubtedly saved his life.

The Main Dressing Station

Once assessed, the more serious casualties were moved further back down the line to the Main Dressing Station. This was usually located at least a mile behind the front line, sometimes in a commandeered building, but more likely a tented 'village'. Initially the stations lacked any surgical facilities but this soon changed. On less 'active' areas of the front the station had a holding capacity of a week. Soldiers who were expected to be fit within this period of time were treated before being sent back to their units. Otherwise, the casualties were sent further back down the line to the Casualty Clearing Station.

The Casualty Clearing Station

This was generally the first large well-equipped medical facility that the wounded man would visit. Here the staff treated all serious cases that were unfit for further travel; other casualties were evacuated. The Casualty Clearing Station was often a tented camp of 1,000 beds, covering about half a square mile. They were usually located adjacent to a railway line and had surgical theatres. If it was anticipated that a wounded soldier would be out of action for over a month, he would be transferred from the Casualty Clearing Station to a Stationary Hospital (400 beds), a General Hospital (1,000-plus beds) or a Base Area Hospital (1,000-plus beds).

The General Hospital

The General Hospitals were near the Army's principal bases at Boulogne, Le Havre, Rouen, Le Touquet and Étaples. Here the medical staff included volunteers from the British Red Cross and St John's Ambulance, often supported by ladies from upper class families. Two such volunteers were Lady Sandon and her eldest daughter. Another volunteer serving in France was Miss E. Bailey. The *Staffordshire Chronicle* of 24 March 1917 carried the following article:

News reached Mr. T. Booth, of 239, Oxford Gardens, Stafford, on Wednesday morning, that his youngest son, Pte. Leonard Booth, of the Coldstream Guards, has been wounded in his right arm during the recent advance, and is now in hospital at Cosham, Hants.

Pte. Booth, who is nearly 21 years of age, and was in the clicking department at Messrs. Bostock's factory, enlisted at the end of August, 1914, and was sent to France on the 22nd of December of that year. In April, 1915, he was slightly wounded, but recovered and returned to the firing line.

Pte. L. Booth.

Information was received on Wednesday morning by Mr. J. Coates, 17, Victoria Terrace, Stafford, that his eldest son, Pte. Frank Coates, of the Coldstream Guards, has been slightly wounded in a recent engagement, and is now at a base hospital.

Pte. Coates, who is 22 years of age, enlisted at the end of August, 1914, was sent to the front on the 22nd of January, 1915, and has been on active service since that date. He has two other brothers also serving with the Colours—Pte. Sydney Coates, of the Coldstream Guards, who has also been on active service since the 22nd of January, 1915, and Sapper Cyril Coates, who was in the telegraph department at Stafford Post-office, and is now in the Signal Section Royal Engineers).

Pte. Frank Coates.

Prior to the enlistment of Pte. Frank Coates, he was employed in the cutting department at Messrs. E. Bostock and Co.'s boot factory. His brother Sydney was on the office staff. Cyril was assistant organist at the Primitive Methodist Church, and Frank was a member of the choir. Sydney is a well-known footballer. He was a member of Christ Church team at Stafford, and has played in several important battalion matches. He was the recipient of a wristlet watch from the late Capt. Agar Robartes, M.P., and assisted that officer when he was wounded. From letters received which give a graphic account of the fighting it appears that Pte. Frank Coates was wounded in the hand and badly shaken, while his brother Sydney came through the action unscathed. The former states that the late Lieut. Raymond Asquith, who was killed in the same engagement, was close by them.

Sep 1916.

A press announcement of two of Stafford's wounded.

Miss Elsie Bailey, second daughter of the Deputy-Mayor of Stafford (Mr. T.S. Bailey) left Stafford on Monday to take up her duties as an ambulance driver with a convoy of the British Red Cross in France. On offering her services in the autumn of last year, after obtaining her First Aid certificate, she was called up to London for a three week's course but passed her examination in motor car driving and management in about three days. She received orders to report for service on Tuesday last, and left for France on Thursday. She is the first lady who has been accepted for this class of foreign service.

The article continued: '[She] was recognized as one of the most skilled drivers in the district. Her technical knowledge of the mechanism will make her services all the more valuable whilst engaged on foreign service.'

The nature of the evacuation chain meant that the wounded might be moved from one location to another and it could often be difficult for their next of kin to keep in touch, or keep pace with their progress. In a letter published in the *Staffordshire Chronicle* of 26 January 1916, a Lieutenant E.J. Allen wrote from France to thank Miss E. Tunnicliffe for a letter and parcel sent to her brother, Private W. Tunnicliffe, of Peel Terrace, Stafford (formerly an employee at Edwin Bostock & Co.). His commanding officer, Lieutenant Allen, paid a high tribute to Private Tunnicliffe when he wrote:

I feel I ought to enclose a note with the letter of appreciation of the men of the parcel you sent your brother, as they say he is slightly wounded, and is therefore in hospital.

At times like these one is being constantly moved from one hospital to another, and if a parcel comes for a man who has been moved it is, I believe, invariably opened at the hospital and distributed there so it is just as well to distribute it amongst his own pals, as is always done, and I am sure this will meet with your approval, especially if you only know how they appreciate any parcel.

It is only just to say a few words about your brother. He was, of course [at 40], one of the oldest men in the company, and there is no doubt the work is beyond him. Try to imagine him wearing heavy equipment, carrying a rifle, 170 rounds of ammunition, eight or nine bombs, four sandbags, some barbed-wire iron stakes, a shovel, and food for three days, tumbling along in the dark for four or five miles over wet, marshy country, pitted with shell holes about six feet deep. And yet he never complained; he could not do another stroke. I am very glad indeed to have met him and know him, for he is a splendid example to us younger fellows. He was one of the cheerful men of the company.

A 'Blighty-One'

Casualties whose wounds were debilitating but permitted them to travel would be moved directly to a port of embarkation. The troops referred to these wounds as a

'Blighty-One'. Many soldiers acknowledged that the possibility of seeing home and family was more attractive than remaining unwounded in the trenches.

Hospital Ships

The wounded were evacuated home in Hospital Ships, which were clearly painted with the symbol of the Red Cross. There were, however, numerous instances of Hospital Ships coming under fire, despite their use being covered by international convention. The attacks culminated in the sinking of HMS *Lanfranc*, which was lost while fully laden with wounded men. The attack constituted a war crime, while the treatment of some of the German POWs who survived the initial action but were drowned when the vessel went down was regrettable.

It was at about 1935 hours on 17 April 1917 when a torpedo, fired by an enemy submarine, hit the *Lanfranc*. In a matter of minutes the vessel was listing heavily and crew were ordered to abandon ship. There were 166 wounded German POWs and 220 wounded British soldiers on board. According to the account of Staffordian Private Smith of the RAMC, attached to HMS *Lanfranc*, the British were picked up first, while only twenty-two Germans were saved. Smith recalled: 'We had to fight them off with our fists to keep them clear of the boats.' Smith, who prior to the war had worked at the Vik Heel Factory, Stafford, had received a leg wound while jumping clear of the boat, and was sent to the 2nd Eastern Hospital in Brighton. It is not clear if he took an active part in repelling the German survivors or if, as a consequence, they drowned or found other boats.

The *Staffordshire Chronicle* carried tens of stories relating to local men who had passed along the chain back to hospitals in Great Britain for further treatment. For instance, on 9 September 1915, it was reported that: 'Rifleman Frederick Charles Perry, of Stafford, of the 1st Battalion Rifle Brigade, who was dangerously wounded in France on 14 June in the left arm and lung, is making a slow recovery in the Norfolk and Norwich Hospital. Previous to this he was in a Base Hospital for three weeks.' Despite the seriousness of his wounds, Perry made a near complete recovery and survived the war.

Red Cross Hospitals and Convalescent Units

In Great Britain a network of Red Cross hospitals and convalescent units was established, while general hospitals made beds available to war casualties. Locally, invalided troops were treated at Stafford General Infirmary, the Sister Dora Home and Sandon Hall Red Cross hospital, to name but a few. Here the men exchanged their uniforms for Hospital Blue (or 'Blighty' Blue), which was similar to military uniform, but manufactured in blue fabric.

Soldiers who returned to military service following wounds wore a brass badge known as a 'wounded stripe' on their left sleeve. It was not uncommon for an infantry soldier to be wounded two or three times during his time in the trenches. The *Staffordshire Chronicle* of 8 June 1918, carried the following, one of many reports of men suffering multiple wounds:

The wounded arrive at Stafford station, May 1915.

Private Arthur Heath at Sandon Hall.

Mr. F.E. Clews, 1, Back Browning Street, Stafford, has received news from the War Office that his son, Private F.L. Clews, 7th King's Shropshire Light Infantry, has been severely wounded by a gas shell and has been sent to Oxford. This is the 8th time he has been wounded, and twice that he has been gassed. He has been serving at the Front since 1915, and has only been home once. He was previously employed at Messers Bostock's factory.

The official casualty figures for the British armed forces may be broken down:

Mobilized	5,397,000
KIA or DOW	702,917
Wounded	1,663,000
Amputees	250,000
Shell shock	80,000
Casualties	49.9 per cent

Poison Gas

The Germans first used poison gas at 1500 hours on 22 April 1915, when they released 120 tonnes of chlorine gas against French and colonial troops on the Ypres Sector. A total of 402 officers and 11,778 other ranks were reported as casualties. The first gas masks were simply pieces of cloth soaked in urine. Purpose-made masks (simple pads of horsehair and cotton waste soaked in hypo-sulphate of soda) and goggles were issued later. A further development was the use of phosgene, which was a lighter gas and tended to dissipate and therefore had to be mixed with chlorine.

Originally gas could only be used under favourable winds as it was released from cylinders along the front-line trenches, or from forward saps, and needed to drift over the enemy trenches. Once detected, gas attacks were signalled by the ringing of a make-shift bell, usually made from a used shell case. Strong winds would help disperse the vapour, while a change in wind direction might carry it back over the aggressor's lines. A more accurate method of concentrating poison gas in enemy trenches was via the use of shells, something that was banned by the Hague Convention, the signatories of which agreed not to 'deploy projectiles the sole use of which is the diffusion of asphyxiating or harmful gas'.

In late May 1915 a member of the Stafford Battery wrote home and included a reference to the Germans' use of chlorine gas shells:

The use of the asphyxiating gas is a terrible thing and getting more frequent, for they are using it in shells now. I dug a shell up a few days ago which had gone right into the ground and made a poor 'burst'. It was full of shrapnel embedded in a sort of chloride, and it did stink, I can tell you.

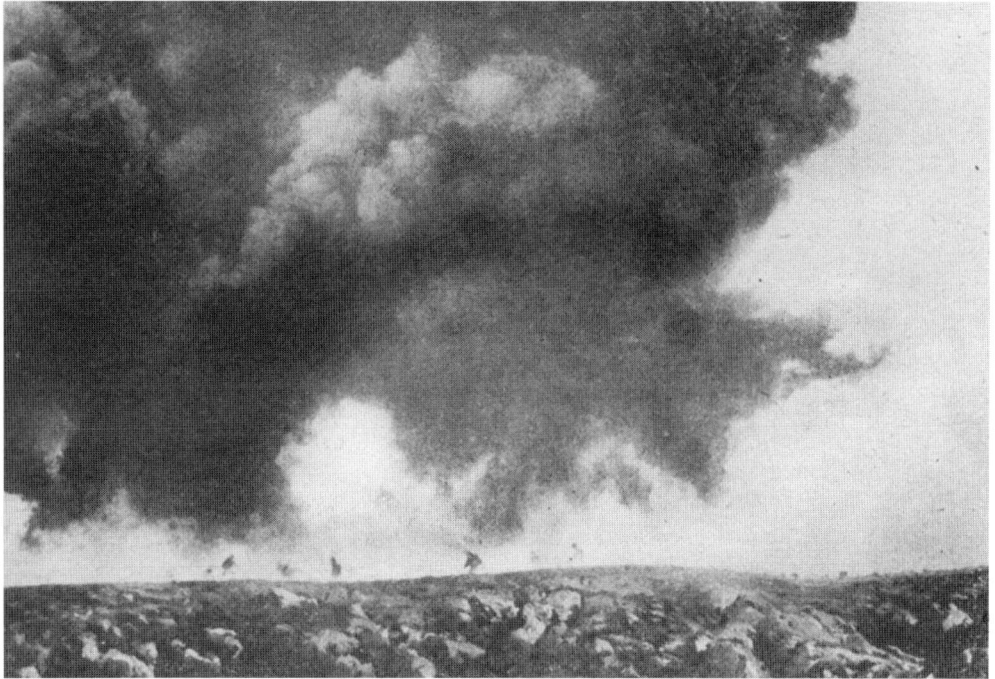

A gas attack on the front.

The use of gas shells became much more prevalent and by 1918 around one-quarter of the shells fired on the Western Front contained poison gas. As the use of poison gas proliferated anti-gas hoods were developed, and later the Box Respirator, which had separate goggles (the Long Box Respirator being introduced from 1916, which covered the whole head and had a tub leading to a filter). One officer, Captain F.C. Hitchcock, of the Leinster Regiment, described the early gas hood: 'It had talc eye pieces and a rubber tube for the mouth; the ends of the respirator had to be tucked under the jacket collar. They were all drenched with a solution of hypo [hypo-sulphate of soda], and were very sticky, messy gadgets.'

Sadly, many Staffordians suffered the effects of poison gas. The *Staffordshire Chronicle* of 6 May 1916 reported that: 'Lieutenant J. Fisher, of Alexander Road, Stafford, has succumbed to the effects of the inhalation of noxious gas which the Germans discharged over the British trenches last Sunday [1 May].' Second Lieutenant Joseph Fisher, who died on 2 May, had earlier served in the ranks. He had been wounded by machine-gun fire and was sent home to recover. Fisher received a commission with the North Staffordshire Regiment. He had only returned to the front from Home Leave the day before being gassed.

Many of the poison gases used were heavier than air and could linger in bomb craters and trenches for weeks, while they also clung to clothing. Poison gas blackened men's brass buttons and could stop watches. Soldiers were ordered to keep the bolt actions of their weapons moving during an attack in order to prevent them seizing up. Some of the gases used were invisible and if they were delivered by gas shells they could only be detected if they had a distinctive smell. Around 181,000 British soldiers were gassed during the war, and many of those who survived suffered respiratory problems for the remainder of their lives, which were often cut short.

Mustard Gas

One of the most potent killers was mustard gas, which was first used by the Germans in September 1917. Exposure damaged the victim's sense of smell, which often led to the premature removal of gas masks. Effective gas masks were quickly put into service and were carried 'at the ready', but they could only protect the face and lungs. The gas also clung to clothing, and there were instances of medical staff suffering the effects simply by removing a patient's clothing. Mustard gas, the effects of which can be delayed for up to 12 hours, causes blistering to the skin and can penetrate clothing. The gas is particularly unpleasant as it destroys body cells from both within and without, leading to a very painful death which can occur up to four to five weeks after exposure.

Trench Foot

While serving at the front, men might spend over a fortnight at a time in the trenches. Extreme stress and lack of sleep were just two of the effects of serving on the front line. When standing for days on end in trenches that were inundated with water, the soldier's skin broke down, exposing the muscles underneath; this was known as trench foot. The dangers of trench foot were quickly realized and daily inspections were carried out. Any man found developing the ailment could be put on a charge as it was seen as a route out of active service. Despite this, unofficial estimates place the number of cases at over 200,000 men.

Shell Shock

The stresses that men were under at the front were unimaginable and many who escaped physical injury were nevertheless traumatized for life. Shell shock, now known as post-traumatic stress disorder, was first identified by Dr C.S. Myers in an article published in the *Lancet* in February 1915. The authorities were initially unsympathetic to the effects of combat fatigue, and the condition was not considered a genuine ailment. Officers, who were considered to be 'made of sterner stuff', were often diagnosed with neurasthenia, while the other ranks might be tried for cowardice. Eventually specialist hospitals were established to treat some of the 80,000-plus men suffering from the condition.

A report appeared in the *Staffordshire Chronicle* in early November 1915 concerning a soldier who was found wandering the streets of Stafford, breaking shop windows and apparently unaware of who he was or what he was doing. The soldier was taken to the workhouse, where he received a warm meal and a change of clothes. It later transpired that the man's name was Peters and that he came from Birmingham. Private Peters had seen his brother killed at his side while in the trenches. It was only once away from the immediate danger of the front that the symptoms of 'shell shock' manifested themselves. Private Peters was sent to a military hospital, but once deemed 'fit' he would almost certainly have been sent back to the front.

On 13 October 1917, it was reported in the *Staffordshire Chronicle* that Captain Humphrey J. Bostock, MC, was confined to hospital suffering from a nervous breakdown, otherwise known then as 'shell shock'. Captain Bostock had lost his right arm at Messines in 1915, while serving with the 1st Battalion, North Staffordshire Regiment. With his combat status lost, Humphrey Bostock returned to duty, but with the Labour Corps, volunteering to go back to France in February 1917. His unit's role included digging and repairing trenches at the front, infilling shell-cratered roads and the burial of the dead. Their work was frequently carried out under heavy shell fire. It was while patrolling an important road on 31 July 1917 that Captain Bostock was wounded in the knee by shrapnel from an enemy shell. He was removed from the front and was treated for his wounds. However, on 13 October 1917 it was reported in the *Staffordshire Chronicle* that he was confined to hospital suffering from a nervous breakdown. He resigned his commission on 25 January 1918.

CHAPTER 22

The Treatment of Prisoners of War

Initially there was no formal method for the independent inspection of German POW camps. As a neutral, the role fell to Mr James W. Gerard, the American ambassador in Berlin. Although he had no formal authority to demand access, from early 1915 Gerard visited POW camps and compiled reports which were published as White Papers. Gerard and his team were responsible for publicizing a number of atrocities, although he frequently found the Germans un-cooperative and the prisoners too fearful of retaliations to speak freely. Consequently, many incidents could not be investigated more fully until after the war.

All repatriated POWs were required to file a report of the circumstances surrounding their surrender and their subsequent movement and treatment. Through these independent reports it became apparent that many men were kept in inhumane conditions and badly treated. Other men bore witness to war crimes. Their statements later helped bring a number of the perpetrators to justice, although many more escaped through an unwillingness of the authorities to pursue war criminals after the cessation of hostilities. Private F.G. Haywood, Royal West Kent Regiment, of White Lion Street, wrote:

I was taken prisoner on the 28 October 1914 [having been cut off for two days without food or re-supplies of ammunition], and was taken to a barn not fit for human beings. We stayed there for eight hours, and from there we were transferred to Lille station, and embarked [on a three-day journey] in cattle trucks and were hit and kicked in a most disgraceful manner. There were forty-seven men in one truck.

The diet we received at Göttingen Camp [situated on the side of a hill on the outskirts of Göttingen], Hanover, Germany was as follows:

Breakfast, 6am: so-called coffee, which was water, with just a slight colour, without sugar or milk, one small black loaf, which had to last us three days;

soup at 12 noon, consisted of horse beans, horse chestnuts, cabbage water, and a good many things too numerous to mention; tea at 5pm, consisted of barley water (flour water), which would have been used by billposters in England.

On the 1 December 1914, Pte. McEwen, of the Scots Guards [Private 8934 C. McEwan, 2nd Battalion, Scots Guards], was shot dead on the promenade [forced march], because, owing to a wound in the leg, he was unable to walk quickly enough to the Germans' liking.

On 22 December 1914, I stood [up to the ankles in snow, and without boots, or coats and caps] for four hours undergoing punishment with the rest of the prisoners there.

As the potato carts came to the camp they were always raided by the English, as they were absolutely starving. We would often go to the pig tub, and get the potato peelings out and take them to our barrack room [and] cook them in our washing basin.

The men were very resourceful and in the absence of tobacco used to dry peat or tea bags which they smoked: 'and can assure you greatly enjoyed them'. Conditions in the camp remained harsh, with a poor diet, few medicines, little in the way of bedding and only the clothes the prisoners were captured in.

The plight of local POWs very quickly became public knowledge. Almost from the outbreak of the war, a number of Stafford's factories raised funds to send POWs creature comforts, including mittens and balaclavas, along with tobacco and food parcels.

Private Haywood's living conditions were so poor that he contracted tuberculosis and, as a result of failing health, was eventually repatriated via neutral Switzerland. Here he was nursed under improved conditions and was able to put back on some of the weight lost during his time in German hands. Haywood wrote about his steady decline and subsequent

STAFFORD SOLDIER A PRISONER MAY 11. OF WAR. 1918

Mr. and Mrs. E. W. Gask, of Lovatt-street, Stafford, have received news that their son, Signaller E. W. Gask, of the North Staffordshire Regiment, is a prisoner of war in Germany. He took part in the early stages of the German offensive on the Western front.

Signaller Gask, who is 22 years of age, was educated at Corporation-street School, and after working for a short time at a local newspaper office, entered the service of the County Council, where he was employed on the clerical staff. He enlisted in November, 1915, and was promoted lance-corporal about May of the following year. He passed as instructor in signalling at Otley, and did duty in that capacity at Lincoln for several months. On May 5 of last year, he proceeded to France, and after serving at various places on the front, came home on leave last January. Returning on Feb. 13, his regiment was engaged in the severe fighting which marked the opening stages of the German attack, and he was taken prisoner. The anxiety which was felt by his parents as to his whereabouts was relieved on May 4, when a post-card, dated March 27, was received from him from Germany stating that he was quite well.

The announcement of the capture of Private E.W. Gask.

release: 'I was taken to hospital on the 23 August 1915, and remained there until June, 1916. From that time the camp life was a little better, owing to the prisoners receiving the parcels from England from their friends. I was discharged from hospital in June, but did not arrive in Switzerland until 12 August 1916.' Once considered well enough to be moved, Haywood returned to Britain and, eventually, to his home town, where he was greeted by a small reception at the railway station. Among the crowds of well-wishers were his wife and four young children. Following the very briefest periods with his family, he was sent to rest in a sanatorium, then the only recourse for TB sufferers.

Prior to enlistment, Haywood had been employed at the Siemens Brothers Electrical Engineering Works, where he was a member of the works' football team. Haywood's former workmates organized a collection, and on the day after his return a reception was arranged at the works. On behalf of the men, Mr W. Parker, the general manager, presented Private Haywood with the sum of £20 in recognition of his service during the Battle of Mons, and in sympathy with him for the suffering he had endured while a captive in German hands. In a speech, Private Haywood thanked his former colleagues for their kindness and for the parcels that he had received while still a prisoner, which he believed saved him from dying of starvation.

The *Staffordshire Chronicle* of 25 May 1916 revealed that every fortnight, the Stafford Prisoner of War Fund sent out parcels to Stafford men who were POWs in Germany. They received letters of thanks from the prisoners which helped to confirm that the parcels had reached the men for whom they were intended.

As the war progressed more former POWs were repatriated due to illness or their wounds. The *Stafford Newsletter* of 15 February 1918 reported a special presentation:

> On 8 February 1918 ninety-five local former PoWs attended a function held at the Co-operative Hall, where each man was presented with a cheque for £2. 6s. 6d. from the fund raised by Mr. Jack Peaple, of Stafford.
>
> The guests sat down to a light meal provided by the Stafford Co-operative Society while tea was laid on by the Women's Guild of the Co-operative Society.
>
> A Colour Certificate, marking their service, was presented to all of those gathered who had been POWs.

Among the men to receive a cheque and certificate from the fund was Private Albert Boult, of Stafford, formerly a prisoner at Gustrow POW Camp. Boult served with the 2/5th Battalion, North Staffordshire Regiment from 5 September 1916, but was later taken prisoner. Conditions in the camp were harsh, as related by another former POW, Private E. Caine, 1st Battalion, Dorset Regiment:

> The food ration was barely sufficient to keep one alive; Breakfast: Soup (rice water). Dinner: Cabbage water or foul-smelling soup made from boar's head. Supper: Soup, and sometimes raw herring. Every four days a loaf weighing about a kilo was served to each man. This bread was very hard and heavy, sometimes almost uneatable; we frequently found whole potatoes embedded in it.

The camp doctor refused to treat the English POWs, claiming as his justification 'if they had not come into the war they would not be there'. Caine continued:

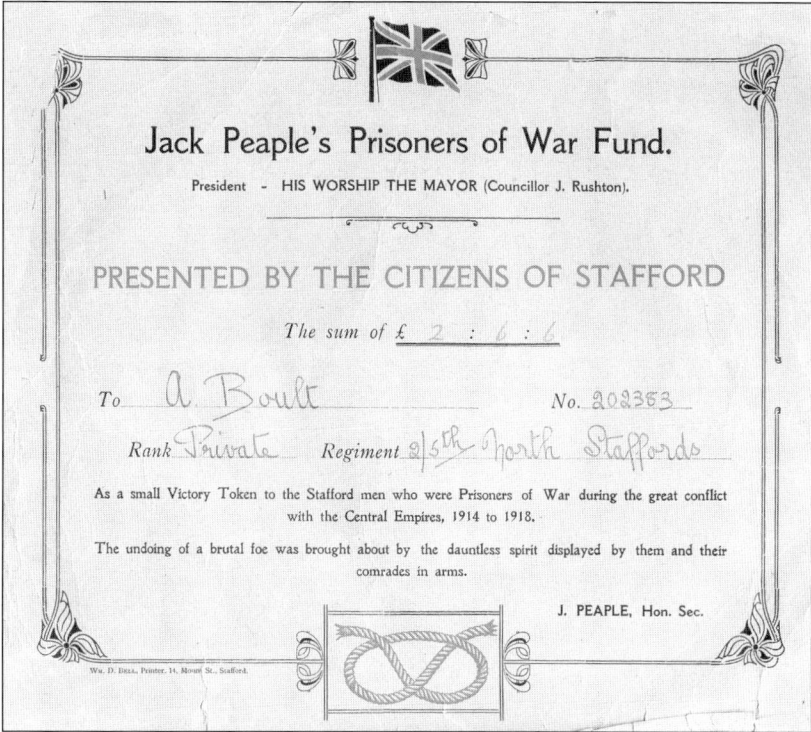

A POW certificate presented to Private Albert Boult.

The Gustrow POW Camp.

A post-war photograph of Private Albert Boult.

We paraded every morning at 7am for roll call and telling off [i.e. selection of] working parties, and were dismissed at between 10 and 11am. At 1pm we were paraded again and not dismissed till 3 or 4pm. Parades were always in the open regardless of weather; consequently many men suffered from frostbite, and one, Drummer Eaglefield, Grenadier Guards, lost both his feet as a result of this. All had to be in the tents at 8pm and to quit [refuse to do so] after that time was to risk one's life, as sentries made free use of their bayonets and police dogs were let loose. Men were made to work about six hours a day.

Here Unteroffizier Deutschmann had a reputation for strutting about carrying a heavy wooden truncheon, 'with which he used to hit our men promiscuously for no reason'.

In his de-briefing one former POW, Private W. Butcher, 1st Battalion, Queen's Regiment, reported that he was discovered to have stolen a loaf of bread. As a punishment he was tied to a post in the snow for 3 hours and had his boots taken from him. Butcher developed frostbite and lost several of his toes, removed by the German doctor, without the aid of anaesthetic.

Brocton POW Camp

As the war progressed there was a greater need for POW camps in Great Britain, one of which was constructed at Anson Bank, near Brocton. It was run under Camp Commandant Lieutenant Colonel Sir Arthur Grant, Bart.

Work on the camp was well underway by January 1917, with the barbed wire perimeter fence already complete and the prisoners' huts nearly in place. The first prisoners were sent to the camp in April, with 300 arriving via Milford station on the 10th, another 500 a week later and 600 more early the following month. Meanwhile, on 14 October, a train arrived full of severely wounded German prisoners who were transported to the camp on stretchers by Red Cross motor ambulances.

A scale model of the Messines battlefield at the neighbouring training camp is said to have been built by the prisoners. This was done under the instruction of the New Zealanders who had occupied the site since mid-1917. Such models were not uncommon, although most were in France, and were on a much larger scale. The High Command, meanwhile, used smaller 3-D contour models which had trench systems, gun emplacements and other strongholds mapped out on them, and these often formed the basis of their battle plans.

One of the best surviving features of the Great War model at Brocton Camp is an L-shaped fortified building known as 'Fanny's Farm'. The farm was on the northern boundary of what was the New Zealand Division's sector on 7 June 1917. During the battle they were held up by machine-gun fire from the farm. The bunker was only taken after a Mk IV tank was called upon to give assistance. The tank's gunner was able to breach the wall, allowing the capture of the machine-gun crew.

The Messines model had become overgrown by 1921, when volunteers made it accessible again. A small shack was erected close by and a warden appointed to give tours, but the site had fallen into disuse within a decade. By the 1980s the footprint of the miniature village was only visible to the trained eye, while recent excavations have revealed that much of the layout still survived below a thin layer of vegetation and topsoil.

Many of the prisoners were allowed out on licence, working on local farms during the day and returning to the camp ahead of their evening curfew. Not all of the prisoners were so co-operative and in 1918 a successful escape was made by five men. Most of the escapees were quickly rounded up, but a few were still at large a fortnight later. A further escape was made in July of the following year, when two POWs absconded only a matter of a few days before the peace treaty was signed.

While the POWs in German hands often suffered intolerably, those captured by the British were treated considerably better, as revealed in a complaint made by two local serving soldiers while on Home Leave. Their letter was published in the *Staffordshire Chronicle* of 9 November 1918 and relates to the fact that German prisoners held at Brocton POW Camp were allowed out to work on local farms on licence:

> While on leave in Stafford a short time ago we were surprised to see German prisoners leisurely making their way about the town, and country lanes at night, unattended by any escort.
>
> We even saw one in sole charge of a milk float, moving about the town calling for goods.
>
> Do you think this fair to allow them to roam about and laugh and jeer at our own boys being marched under escort to and from the Detention Barracks. It seems to us that Stafford is a town of pure delight where happy Huns do roam.

The camp, which was in use until 1919, housed upwards of 3,000 other ranks and 200 officers. A report into its general maintenance and the treatment and health of its inmates was 'excellent' at the end of 1918. This, however, did not prevent the deaths of 178 prisoners who perished at the end of the year as a result of the Spanish flu epidemic. They are buried in the nearby German Cemetery on Cannock Chase.

CHAPTER 23

The Post-War Years

The Armistice took effect on the eleventh hour of the eleventh day of the eleventh month in 1918, when across all fronts the guns finally fell silent. Many officers didn't know exactly what to do, and for the time being at least both sides remained in their own positions wary of accidental fatalities. Gradually, however, German troops came over to surrender, while others simply left their positions and began the long march home.

In Stafford, and elsewhere in the country, church bells rang, while the placards of the *Staffordshire Advertiser*, *Staffordshire Chronicle* and the *Stafford Newsletter* all heralded news of the Armistice. On Saturday, 15 November the local press announced that there would be a thanksgiving service conducted at the Borough Hall the following day.

Although the 'war to end all wars' was over, there were still millions of men and women in uniform. Many would not be de-mobbed for a further eighteen months. In addition, the gassed and wounded filled hospitals at home and abroad, and there were many Staffordians languishing in POW camps across Germany; all needed to be nursed back to health and assisted into employment. The campaign to care for our country's servicemen and women had only just begun and on 12 December 1918 the following announcement appeared in the *Staffordshire Chronicle*:

Thanksgiving Week

Thanksgiving Week is the new name for the process of 'feeding the guns'. The war savings campaign must be continued in order to pay for the demobilization and fair treatment for the men and women who have done the nation's work on land, sea, and air, and in the field, factory, and workshop. The Stafford Borough Committee have changed their title to Stafford War Savings Committee, writing to the War Office requesting something more novel to be sent than the German guns, to help raise funds during the campaign.

At a meeting held at the County Buildings, Stafford, the Disablement Sub-committee of the Staffordshire Naval and Military Pensions Committee adopted a scheme for the retraining of gassed and wounded discharged soldiers. This scheme involved the schooling of men in farm and garden work, and was run in conjunction with the Staffordshire War Agricultural Educational Committee. An experimental farm had already been established at Harper Adams Agricultural College, near Stafford, through which hundreds of soldiers passed.

While local people were turning their attention to winning the peace, the events of the previous four years remained at the forefront of the nation's conscience. A thanksgiving service was held at St Mary's, Stafford, on 29 June 1919, nearly a week ahead of the formal signing of the peace treaty at Versailles (5 July). In addition, 13 July was officially designated as National Thanksgiving Day and was marked by events throughout the Empire.

A number of old comrades' associations were already in existence prior to the war. Naturally their membership swelled during the immediate post-war years as there was a need for clubs and associations to help men adapt to civilian life. These groups offered comradeship and helped men to bridge the gulf between army life and civvy street. Many found comfort simply from being in the company of men who had shared the common experiences of the front – it was impossible to convey the horrors they had endured to anyone who was not there.

A meeting of 600 local members of the Discharged Soldiers Federation was held in Stafford on 8 August 1919. A number of motions were put forward including that a dinner should be given for those who were invalided out of the services. Another, less practical suggestion from the floor was that this should be extended to all 6,500 men formerly under arms. A further proposal, also rejected, was to produce an illuminated scroll inscribed to the town's servicemen and women as a mark of appreciation from the Corporation. During the proceedings it was suggested that a veterans' club might be established in the town. There was no consensus of opinion and the meeting ended without any agreement on the way forward.

It would appear that the existing local organizations did not fulfil the needs of all ex-servicemen. The *Staffordshire Chronicle* of 19 August 1919 carried a feature on the proposed formation of a Stafford branch of the National Federation of Demobilized Soldiers and Sailors. The same edition announced that a drumhead ceremony was to be held on the Grammar School field. This was to honour the local men and women who had served in uniform during the war. Headed by civic dignitaries, the parade formed up in front of the Shire Hall, which for many years had been the town's recruitment centre. On the command, the band struck-up and the veterans and their loved ones marched and walked through the town centre, making their way to the service. In the military tradition, this was performed, as it had been out on the battlefields of France and Flanders, by constructing a temporary altar out of drums. The service was brief but poignant, particularly for those who had attended similar services alongside comrades who had subsequently been killed in action.

The need for veterans' associations continued and as late February 1920 a meeting of around 150 former servicemen was held at the Drill Hall on Newport Road. The

A post-war veterans' parade in Stafford.

prime point of discussion was the formation of a Stafford branch of the Old Comrades Association (one of the associations that later amalgamated to become the British Legion, only later given the 'Royal' designation).

Over 1,165 Staffordians had died during military service, with still more seriously wounded or disabled as a result of poison gas attacks. Hundreds of children were left fatherless and many families were in desperate need of financial aid. During the war, some local factories had paid a percentage of their former workers' wages to their dependants, while a separation allowance could be claimed by those who were in financial difficulty. Nationally, the Ivy Leaf League was formed in order to help raise money for the relief of the tens of thousands of children who lost their father as a result of the Great War. The Stafford branch arranged a number of fundraising events, which were promoted through the press. As a part of the general campaign to recognize the plight of fatherless children an Ivy Leaf Day commemorative service was held on 30 August 1919.

CHAPTER 24

Gallantry Medals and Awards

❖

Over 200 Staffordians were recognized for gallantry and distinguished service during the war. Those men and women not mentioned elsewhere in the main body of the book are recorded here, along with their rank and unit. Where possible, the circumstances surrounding the award are given, along with the date of the official announcement in the *London Gazette* and/or report(s) in the local press.

Press reports came from various sources, official and unofficial, and sometimes awards were not forthcoming. For instance, it was reported that two early volunteers, both of whom became members of the Coldstream Guards, had been recommended for the Distinguished Conduct Medal. In the event, one was awarded the DCM while the other only received a Mention in Despatches (the Military Medal was not instituted until 1916, and might well have been issued in the latter instance for what was evidently considered a lesser act of bravery).

Letters home often carried details of awards, news of which might appear in the press months ahead of any official announcement. In one widely publicized letter, Private Edward Harry Millward revealed that he had been recommended for the Victoria Cross. The rare distinction was even mentioned in the council chambers, but no award was forthcoming. Similarly, the commanding officer of another man, Driver George Godwin, wrote to his parents stating that he too had been recommended for the highest award for gallantry, but Godwin received no award.

Abbreviations
LG – London Gazette
SA – Staffordshire Advertiser
SC – Staffordshire Chronicle
SN – Stafford Newsletter

Private Edward William Millward, 14th Battery, RFA
SN, 16 January 1915, announcement of the recommendation for the Victoria Cross

A Stafford man has earned the VC and the townspeople are naturally very proud of the fact. Private Edward William Millward, of the 14th Battery RFA, has written to his parents at 19, Brook Street, saying that he had won the coveted distinction.

Millward gave no particulars of the circumstances under which it was obtained but says that it took place on New Year's Eve, and that no doubt they would see it in the paper. Millward has been in the Army a number of years, and went to the Front from India, where he had been stationed for six years. His parents are naturally very proud of their son's achievements and they have three other sons with the Colours. The matter was mentioned at Tuesday's meeting of the Council, and doubtless when the fact is officially announced public notices will be written of the distinction.

Despite being wounded on no fewer than four occasions and suffering from the effects of poison gas, Edward Millward survived the war. His 'award of the VC' remains a mystery but must have been indicated by his commanding officer. The VC could only be awarded following a regimental level recommendation. This had to be supported by three independent eyewitness accounts. The process was escalated and had to pass through several levels of scrutiny, with the final submission and approval being by the Secretary of State for War before it was put before His Majesty the King. There were, therefore, many levels at which an award could be downgraded.

Sergeant John James Murrough, Suffolk Regiment
LG, 18 June 1915, Mentioned in Despatches

Sergeant J.A. Dutton, 2nd Battalion, Royal Enniskillen Fusiliers
LG, 22 June 1915, Mentioned in Despatches

Captain Stanley Alwyn Smith, No. 3 Field Ambulance, Canadian Army Medical Corps
LG, 25 August 1915, Distinguished Service Order (Festubert, 20 May)

For conspicuous gallantry at devotion to duty at Festubert, on the night of 20 May 1915. Captain Smith, with a party of eight men, went out voluntarily to remove the wounded from an orchard whilst under heavy fire, and eventually succeeded in bringing all into safety. Four of the eight men of the rescue party were wounded, and two have since died.

Quartermaster Sergeant Williams, RE
SC, 18 December 1915, announcement of the award of the Distinguished Conduct Medal

The original press report provided only the recipient's rank, surname and unit. The most likely candidate is: **Sergeant C.E. Williams, 42nd East Lancaster Divisional Signal Company, RE (TF)**
LG, 15 September 1915

> For conspicuous gallantry and coolness on the Gallipoli Peninsula during 1915. He has frequently laid wires under heavy rifle and shrapnel fire, and has consistently shown great bravery and resource.

Sergeant (later Battery Sergeant Major) G. Bostock, 1/2nd North Midland Brigade Ammunition Column, Royal Field Artillery, (TF) (formerly of the Stafford Battery)
LG, 10 March 1916, Distinguished Conduct Medal

Distinguished Conduct Medal. (obverse and reverse)

> For conspicuous gallantry and resource. When in charge of fourteen wagons the road was heavily shelled, some men being wounded and several horses killed and badly injured. Sergeant Bostock handled the situation with great skill, attended to the wounded men, and extracted the injured horses under heavy fire, and by his fine example of coolness and personal courage, not only prevented any panic, but on each occasion completed his task and brought the convoy back in good order.

Lance Corporal C.F. Emberton, 1st Battalion, North Staffordshire Regiment
LG, 31 May 1916, Distinguished Conduct Medal

> For conspicuous gallantry when in charge of a patrol. Seeing that there was danger from the enemy, although he was in an exposed position in the front, he shouted back [a] warning to the front line of his company. He then sent back his patrol, but remained out himself till satisfied as to the situation. He then returned and reported.

Staff Nurse 1st Class Miss D. McLelland
LG, 2 June 1916, Royal Red Cross Decoration, 2nd Class
SC, 10 June 1916, announcement of the award of the Royal Red Cross Decoration, 2nd Class

Sergeant J.A. Dutton, 2nd Battalion, Royal Enniskillen Fusiliers
LG, 3 June 1916, Military Medal
SC, 2 December 1916, news of the award of the Military Medal

Stafford soldier honoured twice

Sergeant J.A. Dutton, Royal Enniskillen Fusiliers, has been awarded the Military Medal for bravery in the field. He is at present in a hospital in France. He was a Reservist, and prior to outbreak of war was employed at Siemens Bros. He re-joined his old regiment, and proceeded to France early in August, 1914, and has served continuously with his battalion. He was Mentioned-in-Despatches for gallantry in June 1915, and won his MM on the Somme.

Dutton died of his wounds on 10 October 1919.

Lance Corporal Frederick G. Madeley, 4th Battalion, Grenadier Guards

LG, 3 June 1916, Military Medal (Ypres, trench raid on the night of 19/20 April)
SN, 15 September 1917, details of the award of the Military Medal

The [police] officer who has twice been wounded while serving with the Grenadier Guards was awarded the decoration for bravery in taking up ammunition to the trenches and reconnoitring [when he captured one prisoner]. He has returned to the [police] force on being discharged from the Army [in September] as a result of wounds.

Corporal T.A. Plant, Rifle Depot (late of 12th (Service) Battalion, Kings Royal Rifle Brigade)

LG, 3 June 1916, Military Medal (Ypres)
SC, 1 July 1916, details of the award of the Military Medal

Awarded for gallantry in the field at Ypres. After being wounded he went out to fetch in a wounded officer. He has been at the Front for over a year.

Temporary Lieutenant Herbert John Hill, RE

LG, 16 June 1916, Mentioned in Despatches (later Member of the Order of the British Empire as a major on the RE's GHQ Staff)

Temporary Captain John Glyn Jones, 'C' Company, 14th Battalion, Royal Welsh Fusiliers

LG, 23 June 1916, Military Cross (later Member of the Order of the British Empire, King's Birthday Honours List, 1938)

Captain Jones was assistant master at Corporation Street School, Stafford. Writing to his head, Mr. J. Wheeldon, he revealed some details of the action that earned him the award. His letter formed the basis of an article which appeared in the *Staffordshire Chronicle*:

STAFFORD OFFICER GAINS THE MILITARY CROSS.

CAPT. GLYNNE JONES'S EXPERIENCE.

The second Stafford officer to win the Military Cross is Capt. J. Glynne Jones, of the Welsh Fusiliers. Capt. Jones gained the distinction for bringing back wounded soldiers to the trenches at night. Prior to mobilising with the Lincolnshire Territorials in August, 1914, Capt. Jones was assistant master at Corporation-street Boys' School, Stafford, under Mr. J. Wheeldon, head-master. He came to Stafford on Feb. 2, 1914, from Louth, Lincolnshire, where he had been assistant master since leaving the Training College at Bangor. He is a native of Llanrwst, North Wales.

Capt. Jones has had a successful military career, and his promotion, which has been rapid, was well

...rned. He received a commission in the Royal Welsh Fusiliers in February, 1915, was gazetted ...utenant in April, and was awarded his captaincy ...June.

Writing to Mr. J. Wheeldon, he graphically ...rrates his experiences, in which he says the ...rgeant and a little fellow and himself volunteered go out to get in wounded after a small attack the British on the German trenches about 200 rds away. They managed to bring 10 wounded ...n in and guide stragglers back. On the last ...rney back to the British lines—they always ...d to crawl—a poor chap was found lying near ...e German trench and was groaning and drawing ...e on them. As he was badly wounded they ...nt back for a big stretcher and risked their ...es by carrying him on that all the way. The ...k was extremely dangerous on account of star ...lls continually going up from the German ...es and revealing their position. When they ...; to the British lines they had to go slowly to ...k a way through the barbed wire. As the ...btain was walking backwards he tripped over ...iece of wire and fell back, the stretcher and the ...n falling on him. Happily, no serious injury ...ulted from the fall. They reached the ...aches at daybreak in an exhausted condition, ...r a very trying experience, as there were "all ...s of little deaths and big deaths flying round." ...t. Jones is only 25 years of age.

A press article about Captain Jones.

The sergeant and a little fellow and himself volunteered to go out to get in wounded after a small attack by the British on the German trenches about 200 yards away. They managed to bring ten wounded men in and guided stragglers back. On the last journey back to the British lines – they always had to crawl – a poor chap was found lying near the German trench and was groaning and drawing attention on them. As he was badly wounded they went back for a stretcher and risked their necks by carrying him on that all the way. The walk was extremely dangerous on account of star shells continually going up from the German lines and revealing their position. When they got to the British lines they had to go slowly to make a way through the barbed wire. They reached their trenches at daybreak in an exhausted condition, after a very trying experience – there were 'all types of little deaths and big deaths flying around'.

Temporary Captain F.H. Troop, Gloucester Regiment (attached to the 14th (Service) Battalion)
LG, 27 July 1916, Distinguished Service Order

For conspicuous gallantry and ability during a successful raid on the enemy. When his CO had become a casualty he took charge, behaved with great gallantry, and was largely responsible for the success of the operation.

Sapper Harold J. Holland, RE
LG, 10 August 1916, Military Medal

Sergeant Edward Robins (later Second Lieutenant), Royal Fusiliers
LG, 26 September 1916, Distinguished Conduct Medal (Pozières, 3 August 1916)

> For conspicuous gallantry during a night attack on an enemy trench. When his officer was shot he bayoneted the man who shot him. He then did fine work in the trench, and accounted for many of the enemy, though wounded, he refused to retire till he was ordered.

Corporal William James Richards, RE
LG, 26 September 1916, Distinguished Conduct Medal

> For conspicuous gallantly. When his section officer was wounded, he dragged him into a shell hole under heavy machine gun fire, bandaged his wound and got him back to the trenches. On five other occasions during the afternoon he went out into the open and dragged wounded men into safety.

Company Quartermaster Sergeant (acting Colour Sergeant) F. Middleton, 'C' Company, 1st Battalion, North Staffordshire Regiment
LG, 11 October 1916, Military Medal

Sergeant Walter J. Dean, 19th (Service) Battalion, Northumberland Fusiliers
LG, 20 October 1916, Distinguished Conduct Medal

> For conspicuous gallantry. When the party repairing roads was several times dispersed by shrapnel, he voluntarily went back and searched for missing men. During the fortnight that the division was in action he did fine work steadying his men under very heavy fire.

Private W. Coram, 6th Battalion, North Staffordshire Regiment
LG, 11 November 1916, Military Medal
SN, 4 August 1917, presentation of a silver wristwatch and details of the award of the Military Medal

> On Friday afternoon, Private William Coram visited his old school, St Austin's, where he was cordially welcomed. The Very Reverend Cannon Keating presented him with a handsome silver wristlet watch on which was engraved 'From the teachers and children of St Austin's School to a brave "Old Boy"'.

The deed for which he obtained the MM is officially described as follows:

> 'Private Coram came out to France with the Battalion in March 1915, and on several occasions has shown great courage and devotion to duty, notably on one occasion when the enemy exploded a mine near Hill 60 and there was very

heavy shelling. He was sentry over the ammunition reserve. The whole of the remainder of the guard were killed and his sentry box blown in, but he stuck to his post until ordered to leave.'

SN, 20 April 1918, presentation of the Military Medal
A number of presentations of gallantry awards were made by the Lord Lieutenant of Staffordshire, Lord Dartmouth. Included in the line-up of Staffordshire men was Private W. Coram of the North Staffordshire Regiment.

Private B.J. Norton, 1/8th Battalion, Royal Warwickshire Regiment (TF)
LG, 11 November 1916, Military Medal

Bombardier C.H. Glover, RFA
LG, 11 November 1916, Military Medal
SC, 26 October 1918, presentation of the Military Medal

> The Mayor [J. Rushton] pinned the MM onto the tunic of Sergeant Glover, RFA, awarded to him for conspicuous bravery in the field.

Private R. Bee, 1st Battalion, North Staffordshire Regiment
LG, 14 November 1916, Distinguished Conduct Medal

> For conspicuous bravery and devotion to duty. While attending wounded in the open Private Bee's leg was broken. He managed to put the limb into improvised splints and crawl back, being again wounded in the head and shoulders. He dressed his own injuries, and continued to attend to his duties.

SN, 8 September 1917, presentation of the Distinguished Conduct Medal and French *Croix de Guerre* in the Council Chamber, Guild Hall, on 4 September. The mayor, Mr R.J. Young, presented an inscribed silver watch.

Second Lieutenant Richard Melville Hall, South Staffordshire Regiment
LG, 14 November 1916, Military Cross

> For conspicuous gallantry in action. He displayed great gallantry and devotion to duty in carrying orders under very heavy fire, and in conducting parties with stores.

Private B. Lymer, 3rd Battalion, Coldstream Guards
LG, 16 November 1916, Military Medal (Cuinchy, September 1916)
SC, 28 October 1916, presentation of a gold watch

STAFFORD SOLDIER WINS THE MILITARY MEDAL.

STAFFORD SOLDIER WINS THE MILITARY MEDAL.

Oct 14. 1916

Another Stafford soldier—a native of the town —has won distinction on the battlefield. Pte. Benjamin Lymer, of the Coldstream Guards, having been awarded the Military Medal for conspicuous gallantry and devotion to duty. He is the youngest son of the late Mr. Frank Lymer, of North Castle-street, Stafford.

Official intimation was received last week that Pte. Lymer had been wounded in action between Sept. 14 and 16, and on Oct. 5 Mr. J. Lymer, of Erncroft, Wright-street, received a letter from his brother stating that he was going on satisfactorily, adding: "I got through two engagements with a slight wound, but I stuck with the battalion all through." In his letter Pte. Lymer mentioned that his cousin, George Lymer, of Doxey, was wounded (as already reported) in the first attack; that Corp. Harry Logan, of Stafford, was reported missing, and that Bert Wilson, a well-known member of Stafford Range football team, was with the battalion.

Pte. B. Lymer.

Modestly, at the end his letter Pte. Lymer mentions that he has g the Military Medal, and adds: "I hope I sh soon be able to see you now." The welcome ne is confirmed in a letter which Mr. and Mrs. Rea of 3, Tillington-street, Stafford, have receiv from their son, Pte. W. A. Read, of the Col stream Guards, who states that Pte. Lym although wounded, "stuck to his Lewis gun aft most of his mates had been put out of action."

Pte. Lymer, who is unmarried and about 3 years of age, served his apprenticeship at t engineering works of Messrs. W. G. Bagnall, Lt Stafford, and went out to Chili for the Angl Chilian Nitrate Railway Company. After som years' residence there he returned to this countr and entered Messrs. W. H. Dorman and Co. employ. He enlisted from their works and wen out to the front in February of last year. He ha a brother in Chili, Mr. William Lymer, who re turned to England, after war broke out and volunteered, but was rejected for military service

A press article about Private Lymer.

After the taking of Cuinchy, the Coldstreams had advanced to further trenches, and had dug themselves in. This trench was held against all the assaults of the Germans. Private Lymer did wonders with his Lewis gun, and when all his companions were killed or wounded, he fought on and brought his gun safely out of action.

Three days later, attacking another village, Private Lymer again greatly distinguished himself with his Lewis gun, doing great execution.

Private Lymer had also been an employee of W.H. Dorman & Co., of Stafford. The company presented each of its gallantry award winners with a suitably inscribed gold pocket watch 'as soon as the opportunity afforded'.

SC, 28 October 1916

At Messers W.H. Dorman & Co.'s works on Monday evenings a gold watch and chain was presented to Private Benjamin Lymer, of the Coldstream Guards, in recognition of his having won the Military Medal for conspicuous bravery in the field. The presentation, which was made by the Directors of the firm and the workpeople, took place in the works, a temporary platform having been erected for the purpose.

Mr. John Dorman, one of the directors, made the presentation on behalf of the subscribers. He said that they had met to congratulate and to express their thanks to a very gallant comrade, who had won great distinction on the battlefields of France, and of whom they were very proud – Private Lymer, of the Coldstream Guards, late of Dormans.

Applause.

At Guinchy [sic], in September, when the Coldstreams, in a long and sanguinary engagement, covered themselves with glory. Private Lymer was awarded the Military Medal. It was difficult for those who stayed at home to realise what was meant by modern warfare – the thunder of the guns, the shrieking of shells, the bombing, the bayonet fighting – death, carnage, danger everywhere; and so they did not know really how to appraise the heroism of their friend, but they might be very sure that no ordinary measure of bravery had been commemorated by the medal.

Applause.

Private Lymer, like most brave men, was a modest man, and had not talked much about his deeds.

Reflecting on Lymer's enlistment, the article continued:

On September 14th, very shortly after the outbreak of war, his patriotic energy led him to offer his services to his country, with this splendid result. They at Dormans were proud of him, England was proud of him. They welcomed him home, they wished him long life and prosperity, and safe return, and, to show their appreciation of the honour he had done them, they asked him to accept the watch from the directors and workpeople of Dormans as a token of their esteem and gratitude.

Cheers.

Private Lymer, who was loudly cheered by the men, said that such a gift was more than he had expected. He was gratified with the honour they had done him, and he should go back to the Front, and do the same again if he could. Applause.

For He's a Jolly Good Fellow.

Driver George Godwin, ASC

SC, 16 June 1917, recommended for the Victoria Cross (not awarded)

VC For Stafford Soldier

Information has been received that Driver George Godwin, aged 24-years-old, late of Weston Road, Littleworth, Stafford, who is in the Army Service Corps, has been recommended for the Victoria Cross.

Lieutenant Jones, in a letter states:

'Driver Godwin is now my batman, and has been this last few months. I must express my feelings towards him as a very good man indeed, and also I may inform you that he has been recommended for the Victoria Cross for bravery whilst under heavy fire, rallying his comrades over the parapet, and also for bringing in three wounded officers under rifle fire to safety. I have the honour to inform you that I am one of the officers. I can assure you that he is a soldier and a man worth thinking of. Hoping that he will be able to come home to you shortly and be happy.'

Corporal J. Holmes, RE

LG, 18 July 1917, Military Medal (near Ypres)

SN, 26 January 1918, details of the award of the Military Medal

Corporal Holmes received the Military Medal for bravery in the fighting for one of the ridges round Ypres. He was in charge of a working party company of Royal Engineers in fixing water pipelines close to a battery of artillery. The enemy, no doubt by the help of his aeroplanes, spotted the battery, and trained his heavy guns upon it, with the result that the gunners had to take cover; but unfortunately before they could do so some were killed, and two wounded lay out in the open. Corporal Holmes . . . [who] had taken shelter in a shell-hole. . . bravely went across to their aid, and dragged them into his shell-hole, where he attended to their wounds, and later they were successfully sent down to the Dressing Station. Corporal Holmes was wounded before he rescued the men; in fact; whilst he was getting his own working party under cover. Corporal Holmes was not recommended by his own officer, but by the artillery major belonging to the battery.

Temporary Lieutenant Colonel Andrew Edward Hodder, MD, 1/3rd North Midland Field Ambulance, RAMC (TF)
LG, 1 January 1917, Distinguished Service Order

1st Class Staff Sergeant Major W.H. Dean, ASC
LG, 1 January 1917, Mentioned in Despatches

1st Class Staff Sergeant Major W.H. Dean, ASC
LG, 1 January 1917, Meritorious Service Medal

Second Lieutenant Francis Herbert Clarke, RFA (Special Reserve), attached to the 124th Battery, 28th Brigade (formerly an NCO with the Stafford Battery)
LG, 4 January 1917, Mentioned in Despatches

Lieutenant Colonel Andrew Edward Hodder, MD, DSO, 1/3rd North Midland Field Ambulance, RAMC (TF)
LG, 4 January 1917, Mentioned in Despatches (wounded)
Company Sergeant Major F. Middleton, MM, 'C' Company, 1st Battalion, North Staffordshire Regiment
LG, 4 January 1917, Mentioned in Despatches

Colonel J.S. Nicholson, CB, CMG, DSO
LG, 4 January 1917, Mentioned in Despatches

Sergeant S. Morris, RE
LG, 13 February 1917, Distinguished Conduct Medal

For conspicuous gallantry and devotion to duty. He has rendered most valuable services, and at all times under fire set a splendid example.

SC, 20 March 1918, details of the award of the Distinguished Conduct Medal

> For conspicuous gallantry and devotion to duty while working on Tank tracks and causeways, during lengthy operations.

Sergeant S.A. Powell, RE
LG, 19 February 1917, Military Medal

Company Sergeant Major F. Middleton, MM, 'C' Company, 1st Battalion, North Staffordshire Regiment
LG, 26 March 1917, Distinguished Conduct Medal (near Lens, 10 February) (later awarded the French *Légion d'honneur)*

> For conspicuous gallantry and devotion to duty. He brought in two of the enemy who were wounded under heavy fire, and captured an enemy officer. He has at all times set a splendid example.

The events leading to this award occurred on 10 February 1917, during the aftermath of a German trench raid near Lens, and were later reported in the press:

> A party of the enemy were spotted picking their way through the wire entanglements and across No-Man's-Land. As they drew close to one of our machine-gun positions, a Verey light was shot into the air illuminating the sorry group for the gunner to pick them off at will. The few survivors hid in craters or ran back to their own line as best they could. As the gun-fire died down, the air was filled with the cries of the wounded and dying, scattered as they were across No-Man's-Land.

Middleton brought in two wounded soldiers, before going out again with an officer and returning with an unwounded enemy private and a German officer. They also dragged in the corpses of four Germans. This was primarily to search the bodies for any documents that might give information on the enemy troops stationed opposite their line.

All raiding parties were meant to hand over their personal effects before going 'over the top', but this did not always happen. The enemy were found to be carrying a map of the British trenches, while personal papers revealed that they were crack troops of the 72nd Infantry Regiment, specially trained for raiding duties.

A trench raid planned for the 1st Battalion the following day went ahead despite the intelligence already gained from his prisoners. In a tragic reversal of the previous night's event, the British raid stumbled into the field of fire of enemy machine guns which cut down six men, thirteen more suffering bullet or shrapnel wounds.

Corporal D. Lowndes, Leicestershire Regiment
LG, 26 April 1917, Military Medal

Private R. Bee, 1st North Staffordshire Regiment
LG, 1 May 1917, French *Croix de Guerre* (Delville Wood, 31 August 1916)
SC, 1917, details of the Mentioned in Despatches

> For action at Delve Wood [sic] on 31 August 1916 when Bee went out to tend
> to the wounded of the 8th Queen's Own Regiment.

Private J.G. Robinson, 1st Battalion, Black Watch
LG, 11 May 1917, Military Medal

Flight Sergeant B.W. Felton, RFC
LG, 15 May 1917, Mentioned in Despatches

Private George Edward Parker, 1/6th Battalion, North Staffordshire Regiment (TF)
SC, 12 May 1917, commended for bravery

> Private George Edward Parker [of Hyde Lea], 1/6th North Staffordshire
> Regiment (TF) has received the following: 'Your Commanding Officer and
> Brigade Commander have informed me that you have distinguished yourself
> by conspicuous bravery in the field.'

Temporary Lieutenant Herbert John Hill, RE
LG, 18 May 1917, Mentioned in Despatches

Corporal W.A. Cliff, RFA
LG, 9 July 1917, Military Medal (Arras, 23 May)
SC, 17 November 1917, presentation of a gold watch and chain
On Saturday morning Mr. T.F.L. Howard, loco foreman at the L & NW, Railway
Engine Sheds presented, on behalf of his fellow workers, a gold watch and chain
to Corporal W.A. Cliff of the Royal Field Artillery, in recognition of his award
of the Military Medal for bravery.

SC, 1 December 1917, presentation of the Military Medal

> At a whist drive organised by the Discharged Sailors' and Soldiers' Association
> at the Central Co-operative Hall, Stafford, on Wednesday evening, the Mayoress
> of Stafford (accompanied by the Mayor) publicly presented the Military Medal,
> which had been awarded for conspicuous gallantry on the battlefield, of
> Corporal W.A. Cliff, of the RFA.

In making the presentation, the Mayoress said that the medal was won on 23 May by conspicuous bravery during the Battle of Arras. The recipient of it was wounded in the head and shoulder in late July, and they were glad to know that Corporal Cliff had recovered. He had seen much fighting at the Front, and had been in the battles of the Somme, Arras, Messines, and Ypres.

Private W.D. Flamack, RAMC
LG, 18 July 1917, Military Medal

Sergeant E.W. Vaughan, MGC
LG, 18 July 1917, Military Medal

Corporal F. Hawkins, West Yorkshire Regiment
LG, 18 July 1917, Military Medal
SN, 20 April 1918, presentation of the Military Medal
A number of presentations of gallantry awards were made by the Lord Lieutenant of Staffordshire, Lord Dartmouth. Included in the line-up of Staffordshire men was Corporal Hawkins of the West Yorkshire Regiment.

Corporal W.E. Smith, Worcestershire Regiment
LG, 18 July 1917, Military Medal

Temporary Captain Colin James Smithells, Gloucester Regiment
LG, 25 July 1917, Military Cross

> For conspicuous gallantry and devotion to duty. He led his Company in the assault with great courage and ability in the face of heavy fire. On being ordered to withdraw to our own lines it was entirely due to his fine leading that the Company suffered so few casualties.

Sergeant W.H. Salt, 1/8th City of London Post Office Rifles
SN, 7 July 1917, details of the award of the Military Medal
LG, 16 August 1917, Military Medal (Messines, 7 June)

> For conspicuous bravery at the Battle of Messines on 7 June.

Private Percy W. Clewlow, 'late of the Hussars'
LG, 29 August 1917, Distinguished Conduct Medal

> For gallant and distinguished service. In command of a cable wagon detachment he has laid his lines under heavy fire and shown great devotion to duty.

Sapper A.T. Hicks, RE
LG, 28 September 1917, Military Medal

Corporal A.J. Moulding, 2nd Battalion, Grenadier Guards
LG, 28 September 1917, Military Medal

Sapper J. Francis Bagnall, RE
SC, 13 October 1917, presentation of the award of the Military Medal ('For conspicuous bravery in the field.')

> The Officer Commanding the regiment [*sic*] has decorated Sapper Bagnall in the field. His special work is that of maintaining the telegraphic and telephonic communications, and the way in which he has discharged the duties allotted to him is indicated by the awarding of the Military Medal.

LG, 19 November 1917, Military Medal

Private F. Fowler, Liverpool Regiment
LG, 22 October 1917, Distinguished Conduct Medal
LG, 24 January 1919, citation to the Distinguished Conduct Medal

> For conspicuous gallantry and devotion to duty. He displayed great gallantry and initiative in bombing the enemy, and when his supply of bombs was finished he used those which he had captured. Through his efforts at least a dozen prisoners were taken and his gallant conduct was an inspiration to all.

Temporary Second Lieutenant William Henry Rebbeck, RE
LG, 27 October 1917, Military Cross

Frederick John Heath, RN
LG, 2 November 1917, Mentioned in Despatches

> In recognition of his service on a submarine in enemy waters.

Sapper A.E. Buxton, 20th Divisional Signal Company, RE
LG, 11 November 1917, Military Medal
SC, 1 December 1917, announcement of the award of the Military Medal and a Certificate for Bravery (near Largemarck, 19–24 September)

> Sapper A.E. Buxton 20th Divisional Signal Company has received a certificate from Major-General Douglas Smith, mentioning his gallant conduct near

Largemarck, from 19–24 September 1917, in mending telephone lines under most heavy shell fire and machine gun fire. And he congratulated Buxton on this fine behaviour.

This is the second certificate of honour that Sapper Buxton has received. He has also been decorated with the Military Medal at the Front.

Lance Corporal David Johnson, 6th (Service) Battalion, King's Shropshire Light Infantry
LG, 12 December 1917, Military Medal (Villiers Pluich, 19–23 September)

William Francis 'Frank' Lyons, 103rd Company, Royal Engineers
LG, 12 December 1917, Military Medal

Corporal V.H. Mitchell, RFA
LG, 12 December 1917, Military Medal

Sapper A.E. Buxton, 20th Divisional Signal Company, RE
LG, 12 December 1917, Mentioned in Despatches (see announcement of the award of a Certificate for Bravery above)

Lieutenant Herbert John Hill, RE
LG, 14 December 1917, Mentioned in Despatches

Lance Sergeant (acting Sergeant) Oliver John Paskin, 2nd Battalion, Coldstream Guards (attached Trench Mortar Battery, Guards Brigade)
LG, 17 December 1917, Belgian *Croix de Guerre*

Lance Corporal R.J. Cooper, 4th (Pioneer) Battalion, Coldstream Guards
LG, 17 December 1917, Meritorious Service Medal

Temporary Quartermaster and Honorary Lieutenant F. Crewe, North Staffordshire Regiment
LG, 21 December 1917, Mentioned in Despatches

Captain W.G. Thomson, AVC
LG, 24 December 1917, Mentioned in Despatches

Lieutenant (Acting Captain) Herbert John Hill, RE
LG, 1 January 1918, Distinguished Service Order

Ammunition Staff Sergeant T.M. Wood, AOC
LG, 1 January 1918, Meritorious Service Medal

Dr George Reid, MB, Medical Officer of Health, Staffordshire County Council
LG, 4 January 1918, Member of the Order of the British Empire (Home Front)
SN, 12 January 1918, announcement of the appointment to be a Member of the Order of the British Empire

Sapper Arthur Housby, RE
SC, 5 January 1918, announcement of the award of the Distinguished Conduct Medal
LG, 28 March 1918, citation to the Distinguished Conduct Medal

> For conspicuous gallantry and devotion to duty. During the advance on the enemy, two hostile machine guns were enfilading the flank. He, with two other sappers [one of whom was Sapper Douglas Rutty, see below], attacked the machine-gun crews, killing both crews save one N.C.O., who was taken prisoner. The guns were captured, and the attack on the flank was thereby enabled to continue.

Private H.H. Bartle, 8th Battalion, Lincolnshire Regiment
LG, 14 January 1917, Military Medal

Sergeant W.T. Reynolds, 1st Battalion Coldstream Guards
LG, 14 January 1918, Military Medal
SN, 3 November 1917, details of the award of the Military Medal

> Sergeant William T. Reynolds, 1st Battalion, Coldstream Guards won his honour through taking charge of a section [under heavy shellfire] when his officer was wounded, taking the objective and retaining it against a counter-attack.

Acting Corporal G.A. Bramhall, ASC
LG, 16 January 1918, Mentioned in Despatches

Corporal (acting Sergeant) Arthur Dann, RE
LG, 16 January 1918, Mentioned in Despatches

Corporal George Lymer, 3rd Battalion, Coldstream Guards
LG, 28 January 1918, Military Medal (Third Battle of Ypres)

Presentation by L&NWR to Corporal George Lymer MM by *Staffordshire Chronicle*, 26 October 1918

Corporal George Lymer, Coldstream Guards, of The Hill, Doxey was presented by his colleagues in the rolling stock department of the L & NW Railway, with a silver service tea service and salver in recognition of his having won the Military Medal for bravery in action during a stiff engagement in France.

Corporal Lymer had been in France for three years, and was severely wounded in September 1916. After recovering he re-joined his regiment in France and has been through many stiff engagements with the Coldstream Guards. He was recommended by his CO for bravery in action at a critical moment, when his company was in a tight corner.

Pioneer W. Fryer, RE
LG, 4 February 1918, Military Medal
SN, 9 February 1918, announcement of the award of the Military Medal

Second Lieutenant Maurice McFerran, Royal Irish Rifles
SC, 4 February 1918, announcement of the award of the Military Cross

Sergeant John James Murrough, Suffolk Regiment
LG, 12 October 1916, Military Medal
SC, 16 February 1918, announcement of the award of the Military Medal (earlier awarded the Long Service Good Conduct Medal)

The Military Medal (obverse and reverse).

Sergeant W.E. Smith, RFA
LG, 23 February 1918, Military Medal

Private A. Hicks, Pioneer Battalion, RE
LG, 23 February 1918, Military Medal

Private William J. Whittaker, RAMC
LG, 23 February 1918, Military Medal

Lance Corporal J.N. Aston, Hussars
LG, 4 April 1918, Distinguished Conduct Medal

> For conspicuous gallantry and devotion to duty. During a heavy enemy attack he took command of his machine-gun troop at a critical moment and handled the guns with marked ability and coolness, thereby greatly assisting in repelling the enemy's attack. He showed no regard for his own safety and set a fine example to his men.

SN, 9 March 1918, announcement of the award of the Distinguished Conduct Medal

Private (acting Corporal) Herbert W. Wilson, 1st Battalion, Coldstream Guards
SN, 16 March 1918, announcement of the award of the Military Medal

> Private H.W. Wilson had been awarded the Military Medal for gallantry-in-the-field during the big push at Cambrai. Wilson had enlisted into the Coldstream Guards on the outbreak of the war and had served in the trenches for three years.

LG, 30 January 1920, Military Medal (Cambrai)

The Croix de Guerre *(Belgium).*

Lance Corporal Herbert John Mountford, 8th Battalion, North Staffordshire Regiment (TF)
SC, 2 March 1918, announcement of the award of the Belgian *Croix de Guerre*
LG, 12 July 1918, Belgian *Croix de Guerre*

Sapper Douglas Rutty, RE
LG, 28 March 1918, Distinguished Conduct Medal
During the advance on the enemy two machine-guns were enfilading the flank. He, with two other sappers, attacked the machine-gun crews, killing both crews save one NCO, who was taken prisoner. The guns were captured, and the attack on the flank was thereby able to continue.

Private William Rupert Banton, Royal Welsh Fulsiliers
LG, 2 April 1918, Military Medal

Corporal W. Lomas, Norfolk Regiment
LG, 10 April 1918, Military Medal

Battery Sergeant Major Frederick Arthur Broomfield, RFA
LG, 5 April 1918, Belgian *Croix de Guerre*

Sergeant William Thomas Plant, 'A' Battery, 160th Brigade, RFA
SC, 9 March 1918, announcement of a Mention in Despatches
LG, 6 November 1918, Mentioned in Despatches

Major F.W. Peach, 1/6th Battalion, North Staffordshire Regiment (TF)
LG, 22 May 1918, Territorial Decoration

Gunner Thomas Frost, RGA
LG, 31 May 1918, Distinguished Conduct Medal (Italy)

For distinguished services in connection with Military Operations with the British Forces in Italy.

LG, 21 October 1918, citation of the Distinguished Conduct Medal

Major Peach, TD.

For conspicuous gallantry and devotion to duty on many occasions as a despatch rider, frequently under very heavy shell fire. He never failed to get his despatches through, and his courage, energy and resource were worthy of the highest praise.

Sergeant Cyril Baker, 8th Battalion, Oxfordshire & Buckinghamshire Light Infantry

LG, 11 June 1918, Mentioned in Despatches (Macedonia)
SC, 20 July 1918, announcement of the Mention in Despatches 'for devotion to duty in the field'.

Corporal W. Lomas, Norfolk Regiment, MM

LG, 12 June 1918, Bar to the Military Medal

Sergeant Percy Lowe, RFA

LG, 17 June 1918, Military Medal

Captain Alfred Edward Gore, North Staffordshire Regiment (Special Reserve)

SC, July 1918, announcement of the award of the French *Croix de Guerre* (Bligny mountain, 6 June 1918)

The Croix de Guerre *(France).*

The following extracts are from the French Army Orders and cover the events leading to the award:

On 6 June 1918, charged with the defence of an important position of the mountain of Bligny, they maintained their position for many hours against the attacks of an enemy superior in numbers, and who had almost surrounded them. Obliged by the last attack to give ground, they counter-attacked immediately. This attempt being checked, a new counter-attack led with magnificent dash by the battalion in reserve, threw the enemy from Bligny mountain, took three prisoners, and re-established entirely the line, which was then maintained in spite of violent bombardment.

This officer showed remarkable bravery during the operations on the 6 June 1918 at the mountain of Bligny. During a difficult situation he rallied the men of his battalion, and organised the counter-attack which retook all the ground temporarily lost. He afterwards took command of his battalion successfully when his Colonel was wounded.

LG, 6 November, French *Croix de Guerre* (Bligny mountain, 6 June 1918)

Lance Corporal Benjamin Morris, 2/6th Battalion, North Staffordshire Regiment

SN, 18 June 1918, announcement of the award of the Distinguished Conduct Medal
LG, 21 October 1918, Distinguished Conduct Medal

For conspicuous gallantry and devotion to duty as battalion scout. While the battalion was in the front line, he went out on patrol night after night, and by his daring and resource obtained much valuable information.

Sapper J. Pritchard, RE

LG, 21 June 1918, French *Croix de Guerre* (later awarded the Military Medal)

Private T. Crates, Coldstream Guards

LG, 27 June 1918, Military Medal

Lance Corporal Herbert John Mountford, 8th Battalion, North Staffordshire Regiment

LG, 12 July 1918, Military Medal
SC, 20 July 1918, announcement of the award of the Military Medal

Corporal H.G. Coe, South Staffordshire Regiment

LG, 16 July 1918, Military Medal
SC, 20 July 1918, announcement of the award of the Military Medal

Sergeant J. Ellis, Yorkshire Light Infantry

LG, 12 July 1918, Military Medal
SC, 20 July 1918, announcement of the award of the Military Medal

Temporary Lieutenant W.J. Dean, DCM, 19th Battalion, Northumberland Fusiliers

LG, 26 July 1918, Military Cross (later Mentioned in Despatches)

For Conspicuous gallantry and devotion to duty. During a retirement, his company commander becoming a casualty, he took over command and worked unceasingly for five days. He led a successful counter-attack over the railway, driving back vastly superior numbers of the enemy. By this timely stroke he allowed time to the supporting troops to come up.

Temporary Second Lieutenant Leonard Joy Spilsbury, RE

LG, 26 July 1918, Military Cross

For conspicuous gallantry and devotion to duty. When in charge of a demolition party orders to destroy the water tank and bridges had failed to reach him. Seeing the near approach of the enemy, he laid and connected up the charges and fired them on his own initiative. He effected these demolitions under a heavy fire and set an excellent example of initiative and courage to his men.

Private C.R. Johnson, King's Royal Rifle Regiment

LG, 6 August 1918, Military Medal
SC, 10 August 1918, details of the award of the Military Medal
'For gallantry in the field'.

The Military Cross.

Private T.H. Whittaker, Lincolnshire Regiment
LG, 6 August 1918, Military Medal

Lieutenant V.G. Robins, RE (attached to Labour Corps of Signals Company)
LG, 6 August 1918, Mentioned in Despatches (East Africa)

Lance Corporal David Johnson, MM, 6th (Service) Battalion, King's Shropshire Light Infantry
LG, 6 August 1918, Bar to the Military Medal (Battle of St Quentin, 22 March–1 April)

Frederick John Heath, RN
SC, 31 August 1918, announcement of the award of the Distinguished Service Medal

In recognition of his service on a submarine in enemy waters.

Sergeant Percy Lowe, MM, RFA
LG, 3 September 1918, Distinguished Conduct Medal

For conspicuous gallantry and devotion to duty while acting battery Sergeant-Major at the gun position. The battery was subjected to a terrific bombardment of high explosive and gas shells, which necessitated the use of masks for five hours. During all this time this non-commissioned officer did magnificent work in keeping the guns in action, assisting in the supply of ammunition, and encouraging the detachments. He also went through a barrage to obtain stretchers for the wounded. He displayed wonderful courage, and set a fine example to the men of his battery.

SC, 9 November 1918, referred to the presentation of an inscribed gold pocket watch and Albert to Sergeant Lowe by Mr Ivor James, Managing Director of W.H. Dorman & Co. Ltd, who 'Congratulated Sergeant Lowe on the honour he had won, and expressed the pleasure felt by all at the old firm in being able to make the presentation. In accepting the watch, Lowe urged those present to renew their efforts on the shop-floor "until the Hun was finally crushed".'

Private Green, North Staffordshire Regiment
LG, 13 September 1918, Military Medal

Sapper J. Pritchard, RE
LG, 7 October 1918, Military Medal
SC, 12 October 1918, presentation of the Military Medal

MMs have been awarded to Sapper J. Pritchard, RE, Castle Church, Sergeant G. Taylor, RFA, Stafford, and Fitter Staff Sergeant H.W. Weymouth, RFA, Stafford.

Fitter Sergeant H.W. Weymouth, RFA
LG, 7 October 1918, Military Medal (Fonquevillens, 15 May)

For conspicuous bravery and devotion to duty near Fonquevillens on 15 May.

SC, 12 October 1918, presentation of the Military Medal

MMs have been awarded to Sapper J. Pritchard, RE, Castle Church, Sergeant G. Taylor, RFA, Stafford, and Fitter Staff Sergeant H.W. Weymouth, RFA, Stafford.

Sergeant G. Taylor, 130th Battery, RFA
LG, 7 October 1918, Military Medal (Fonquevillens)
SC, 12 October 1918, presentation of the Military Medal

MMs have been awarded to Sapper J. Pritchard, RE, Castle Church, Sergeant G. Taylor, RFA, Stafford, and Fitter Staff Sergeant H.W. Weymouth, RFA, Stafford.
For conspicuous bravery and devotion to duty, near Fonquevillens on May 15th.

Private H.H. Bartle, MM, 8th Battalion, Lincolnshire Regiment
LG, 21 October 1918, Bar to the Military Medal

Gunner T. Frost, RGA
LG, 31 May 1918, Distinguished Conduct Medal (Italy)
LG, 21 October, citation to the Distinguished Conduct Medal

For conspicuous gallantry and devotion to duty on many occasions as a despatch rider, frequently under very heavy shell fire. He never failed to get his despatches through, and his courage, energy and resource were worthy of the highest praise.

Corporal T. Venables, RFA
LG, 30 October 1918, Distinguished Conduct Medal

For conspicuous gallantry and devotion to duty. He was in charge of two heavy trench mortars, which were in action immediately behind our front line. When our attack began the enemy put down a heavy barrage on the trenches occupied by these mortars, the detachments of which suffered heavy casualties. Corporal Venables showed an admirable example of coolness and fortitude and by his

A gallantry award presentation at the front.

conduct steadied and encouraged what was left of his detachments, and carried out the firing programme in its entirety. After the bombardment ended, the detachments, now reduced to two men each, stood by for twenty-four hours to respond to SOS calls with a resolution and courage which were largely inspired by this non-commissioned officer's fine behaviour.

Sergeant William Thomas Plant, 'A' Battery, 160th Brigade, RFA
SC, 6 November 1918, announcement of the award of the French *Croix de Guerre*
LG, 19 June 1919, French *Croix de Guerre*
Lieutenant John Claude Verney Morgan, RNR
LG, 26 November 1918, Distinguished Service Cross

For service in action with enemy submarines.

Second Lieutenant Francis Herbert Clarke, RFA (Special Reserve), attached to the 124th Battery, 28th Brigade (formerly an NCO with the Stafford Battery)
LG, 2 December 1918, Military Cross

For conspicuous gallantry and initiative. When acting as forward observation officer during an attack he showed great resources in rallying the infantry, who were held up by machine-gun fire. Being the only officer on the spot, he took command, reconnoitered [sic] the situation, and then led the attack forward. When the situation became obscure he made a daring reconnaissance, and sent back valuable information.

Temporary Captain F. Crewe, 3rd Battalion (attached to the 8th Battalion), North Staffordshire Regiment
LG, 28 December 1918, Mentioned in Despatches

Acting Captain A.E. Gore, 3rd Battalion, North Staffordshire Regiment (attached 8th Battalion, North Staffordshire Regiment)
LG, 28 December 1918, Mentioned in Despatches (Bligny mountain – see French *Croix de Guerre*)

Acting Lance Corporal P.C. Bullock, 3rd Mobile X-Ray Unit, RAMC
LG, 30 December 1918, Mentioned in Despatches

Temporary Captain Joseph Devlin, 6th Battalion, North Staffordshire Regiment
LG, 1 January 1919, Member of the Order of the British Empire (Calais Base)

Sergeant S.W. Taylor, 1st Battalion, North Staffordshire Regiment
LG, 1 January 1919, Distinguished Conduct Medal (Somme, 23 March–6 April)
LG, 2 September 1919, citation to the Distinguished Conduct Medal

> For conspicuous gallantry and devotion to duty during operations on the Somme in March 1918. From 23 March – 6 April he was in charge of a platoon, and carried out a number of difficult rearguard actions most skilfully. Although greatly out-numbered he, with his platoon, frequently held up the enemy and successfully covered the withdrawal of other units. By his gallantry and devotion to duty he set an inspiring example to his men.

Private (acting Sergeant) J.H.V. Busby, AVC
LG, 17 January 1919, Meritorious Service Medal

Private (acting Lance Corporal) A.D. Wright, AOC
LG, 18 January 1919, Meritorious Service Medal

Private H.H. Bartle, 8th Battalion, Lincolnshire Regiment, MM and Bar
LG, 24 January 1919, a Second Bar to the Military Medal (announced as a First Bar)
LG, 22 November 1919, correction to the earlier announcement

Sergeant F.A. Critchley, 37th Divisional Signals Company, RE
LG, 24 January 1919, Military Medal

Staff Sergeant Alfred Henry Ducie, RE (attached to the Staff of the Chief Engineer, VIIth Corps)
LG, 29 January 1919, French *Croix de Guerre*

Driver B. Wooldridge, 30th Divisional Ammunition Column, RFA
LG, 11 February 1919, Military Medal (Dranoutre)
SC, 16 November 1919, details of the award of the Military Medal

For gallantry and services rendered at Dranoutre.

Corporal S.C. Tomlinson, 1/16th Battalion, London Regiment
LG, 18 February 1919, Distinguished Conduct Medal

Private L. Swanwick, 3rd Battalion, Rifle Brigade
LG, 18 February 1919, Distinguished Conduct Medal

Driver T. Egerton, 'F' Battery, 14th Brigade, RHA
LG, 18 February 1919, Military Medal

Sapper S.H. Gisby, 62nd Divisional Signals Company of the Royal Engineers
LG, 13 March 1919, Military Medal

Battery Sergeant Major Frederick Arthur Broomfield, RFA
LG, 13 March 1919, Belgian *Croix de Guerre*

Private (acting Corporal) H. Bill, 3rd Field Ambulance, RAMC
LG, 14 May 1919, Military Medal

Sergeant H. Bayliss, 85th Battery, 11th Army Brigade, RFA
LG, 14 May 1919, Military Medal
Company Quartermaster Sergeant G. Addison, 59th Divisional Signal Company, RE
LG, 3 June 1919, Meritorious Service Medal

Lieutenant (acting Major) George Cecil Lowbridge, 468th (North Midland) Field Company, RE (TF)
LG, 3 June 1919, Military Cross

Temporary Lieutenant Cecil Rhodes Arnott, 33rd Battalion, MGC
LG, 3 June 1919, Military Cross

Private A.B. Bristow, ASC
LG, 3 June 1919, Meritorious Service Medal

Sergeant (later Company Sergeant Major) A.A. Dann, 'V' Corps Signal Company, RE
LG, 5 June 1919, Mentioned in Despatches

Fight Sergeant (Temporary Sergeant Major) B.W. Felton, RAF
Flight Magazine, 12 June 1919, announcement of the award of the Meritorious Service Medal

Private John Brown, 7th (Pioneer) Battalion, Durham Light Infantry
LG, 17 June 1919, Military Medal

Lieutenant Charles E. Morgan, RN
LG, 27 June 1919, Distinguished Service Order

For distinguished service as Navigation Officer, HMS *Caledon*, 1st Light Cruiser Squadron.

Lieutenant C.E. Morgan (later Rear Admiral C.E. Morgan, KCB, DSO) was the son of Mr C. Morgan, of Morgan's Beer and Wine Merchants. His mother organised the members of the Brocton Golf Club into running the Welcome Club at the newly built Carnegie Free Lending Library, for which she was later made a Member of the Order of the British Empire.

Sapper E. Stone, Indian Army Corps, RE
LG, 3 July 1919, Military Medal (Mesopotamia)

Temporary Captain F. Crewe, 8th Battalion, North Staffordshire Regiment
LG, 9 July 1919, Mentioned in Despatches

Sapper P. Packman, 70th Field Company, RE
LG, 23 July 1919, Military Medal

Private A.P. Willson, 9th Field Ambulance, RAMC
LG, 23 July 1919, Military Medal

Sergeant Samuel Jones, RFA
LG, 20 August 1919, Military Medal
Samuel Jones was from Woolwich and presumably came to Stafford with his family due to the transfer of workers from the Siemen's Brothers Electrical Engineering Works, Woolwich.

Private Francis Victor Wright Till, 8th Battalion, North Staffordshire Regiment
LG, 20 August 1919, Military Medal
In a letter to his mother dated 3 October 1917, Till wrote:

The Distinguished Service Order.
(obverse and reverse)

Dear Mother, You will be proud to hear that I have been recommended for devotion to duty and carrying out my work in a most amiable manner. When my officer read the recommendation to me, my thoughts flew to you at once and wondering how proud you would feel of your son when you knew of it. I have heard no more of it since. I don't know for certain of it, there may be others more deserving you see.

Till's officer, while reading his letter for censorship purposes, added a separate sheet on which he wrote a personal message:

Dear Madam,
Your son is the best Boy I think I Ever met, certainly out here.
I am doing my very best to get him a decoration. He deserves all that can be given him. He is brave, honest and the most willing. I am only sorry that officers who knew him well in the Battalion [who were] of higher rank than myself were alive now, then the matter would be simple.
I have done all I can, and will continue to do so.

Signed (A.H. Bainbridge) 8th North Stafford

Sergeant S.W. Taylor, 1st Battalion, North Staffordshire Regiment
LG, 3 September 1919, Distinguished Conduct Medal (Somme, 23 March–6 April 1918)

For conspicuous gallantry and devotion to duty during operations on the Somme in March 1918. From 23 March to 6 April he was in charge of a platoon, and carried out a number of difficult rearguard actions most skilfully. Although greatly outnumbered he, with his platoon, frequently held up the enemy and successfully covered the withdrawal of the other units. By his gallantry and devotion to duty he set a fine inspiring example to his men.

Sergeant Charles Henry Boote, 35th Divisional Train, ASC
LG, 4 September 1919, Belgian *Croix de Guerre*

Driver (acting Lance Corporal) Walter Oxford, 510th (London) Field Company, RE (TF)
LG, 4 September 1919, Belgian *Croix de Guerre*

Armourer Staff Sergeant A.G. Hammersley, AOC
LG, 22 September 1919, Meritorious Service Medal (Basra, Mesopotamia)

Lieutenant William Henry Westhead, RGA (Special Reserve)
LG, 24 October 1919, Belgian Order of the Crown

Lieutenant William Henry Westhead, RGA (Special Reserve)
LG, 24 October 1919, Belgian *Croix de Guerre*

The following awards were recorded in the *Stafford Roll of Service in the Great War – 4 August 1914–28 June 1919* (1920) but have not been traced:

Private Frank Joseph Bates, Bedford Regiment (formerly 1st Battalion, North Staffordshire Regiment)
Distinguished Conduct Medal (KIA, 2 December 1917)

Corporal John Tomkinson, 1st Battalion, North Staffordshire Regiment
Distinguished Conduct Medal

Corporal Charles Middleton, RFA
Military Medal

Corporal J. Rochell, South Staffordshire Regiment (formerly of the Coldstream Guards)
Military Medal
Also reported to have been Mentioned in Despatches, when it was stated that he was only the second Stafford Gas Works employee to be awarded the MM. Rochell was presented with a gold half-hunter watch by his employer. He served for three years in the Coldstream Guards.

T. Winnard (no further information)
Military Medal

Sapper Andrew T. Crighton, RE
Mentioned in Despatches

Private George Bernard Bruce, 1st South Wales Borderers
In late 1916 it was reported that Private George Bruce, 1st Battalion, South Wales Borderers had received a head wound and was in Queen Mary's Hospital, Whalley, Manchester. He was thrice Mentioned in Despatches, first for gallantry at Loos, for carrying messages under heavy shellfire from the enemy; second said to have been earned at 'Colone' for good patrol work; third at Mametz for devotion to duty. The latter 'Mention' was reported as having been 'for bringing in a wounded comrade who had been gassed'.

Leading Telegraphonist A.H.G. English, RN
Mentioned in Despatches

Second Lieutenant William J. Leckie, 1/5th Battalion, North Staffordshire (attached to the Manchester Regiment)
Mentioned in Despatches

Lieutenant Henry Williams, Worcester Regiment
SC, 2 June 1916, announcement of the death of Lieutenant Henry Williams who was Mentioned in Despatches as a QMS with the RE 'For exceptional gallantry' in France, following which he was commissioned into the Worcester Regiment.

Private Henry Evans, 4th Battalion, South Staffordshire Regiment
Recommended for Bravery (twice wounded)

Gunner D. Barclay, RHA
French *Croix de Guerre* (wounded)

CHAPTER 25

Memorials to the Dead

❖

News of local war casualties began with reports in the press of the deaths among the Regulars and Reservists from the town during the retreat from Mons and the subsequent battles of the Aisne and the Marne. The casualty figures quickly increased as the first of the Volunteers and then the Territorials entered the theatre of war. The papers carried weekly updates, details of casualties filtering through from relatives and official channels.

Families made their own memorials, while schools, workplaces and churches all played their part in remembering the dead. With over 1,165 fatalities, it is only possible to touch on a few of the many notices that appeared in the press. These must be seen as representative of the many announcements that were featured throughout the four years of hostilities.

A cemetery at the front.

STAFFORDSHIRE TEACHER KILLED IN FRANCE.

TRIBUTES TO THE LATE SERGT. ARROWSMITH.

" Everyone thought well of him, and the news of his death cast a gloom over all." This kindly message from his platoon officer in France has been a great consolation to the parents of Sergt. Edgar Arrowsmith, of the 8th North Staffordshire Regiment, whose death on Nov. 6 from a German sniper's bullet was reported in out last issue.

The eldest son of Mr. and Mrs. D. Arrowsmith, of Claremont, Stone-road, Stafford, he was only 24 years of age, but had entered upon a very promising career in the teaching profession. He received his early education at Corporation-street Council School, Stafford, and, winning a County Council scholarship, he proceeded to Stafford Grammar School, where he passed the Junior and Senior Cambridge Local examinations with honours on each occasion. He subsequently entered the Dudley Training College to complete his studies, and six months after leaving that institution he was appointed assistant to Mr. J. Southworth, head-master, when the new Council School at Baddeley Green, near Stoke-upon-Trent, was opened. In the interim he had taken relief duty at St. Luke's School, Leek, and Knightley School, near Eccleshall.

THE LATE SERGT. E. ARROWSMITH.

Sergt. Arrowsmith responded to the call for recruits early in August of last year, and joined the 8th South Staffords. Being proficient in Swedish drill, he qualified for the post of instructor by examination at Lichfield, and was awarded a certificate. He acted as instructor to some of the troops on Salisbury Plain from March until July last, and the authorities wished to retain his services, but he was anxious to help the lads in the trenches, and crossed to France during the latter month. He had previously been promoted to the rank of sergeant, the intimation reaching him while he was home at Easter. The last communication his parents received from him was a field card on Nov. 2, with the simple message "I am well." Four days later he fell a victim to an enemy sniper. Sergt. Bannister who was a couple of yards behind, caught him, as he fell, and rendered what assistance he could, but death came very quickly. 2nd-Lieut. A. N. Westlake, writing to the deceased's parents, says—"I feel that little I can say will lighten the burden of your grief, but I am sure you would like to know that he was liked and respected throughout the company. The Major said he was one of the N.C.O.'s he could spare the least. I was his platoon officer for two months, and cannot speak too highly of his efficiency. I got to know him in that time, and I can truly say that the better I knew him the more I respected him as man to man." The writer added that anyone would be proud to have such a son, who died the best of all deaths—as a soldier fighting for King and country.

The first intimation of Sergt. Arrowsmith's death was sent by Co.-Sergt.-Major J. H. Clarke, whose home is at Stafford, and who wrote :—" He died, as he lived, for the benefit of others. His loss has cast a gloom over the whole of his company, as he was beloved by everyone, from his commanding officer down to the humblest man in the company. Always a cheerful smile and a helping hand, under most trying circumstances, he always did his best to brighten the lives of his less cheerful companions." L.-Corporal J. Beetlestone, of the same regiment, writing on behalf of the members of D. Company, says : "He (Sergt. Arrowsmith) was always willing to do any of us a good turn if it lay in his power. He was not only a sergeant but a gentleman, and his loss will be greatly felt amongst us." Sympathetic letters have also been received from Principal Forster, of Dudley Training College ; Mr. J. Wheeldon, Headmaster of Corporation-street School, Stafford, and the Headmaster of Baddeley Green School, who wrote :—" Your son was loved by us all—teachers and scholars alike." The Chairman of the School Managers, Mr. F. Green, also sent a message of condolence, stating that they valued Edgar's services and considered him a painstaking and devoted teacher. Perhaps the most touching of all the tributes to the late Sergt. Arrowsmith are the many letters received from the scholars, which show that their late teacher will live in their memories.

Whilst in North Staffordshire, Sergt. Arrowsmith took great interest in swimming. He was a member of the Harley Water Polo team, and at a gala held in Hanley Baths in the summer of last year he was awarded the certificate and medal of the Royal Life Saving Society for a practical exhibition. Mr. D. Arrowsmith, his father, is clerk and schoolmaster at H.M. Prison, Stafford.

The announcement of the death of Sergeant E. Arrowsmith.

On 11 December 1915, the *Staffordshire Chronicle* reported that on the previous Sunday (5 December) a memorial service had been held at the Primitive Methodist church for two former members of the congregation. One of those being remembered was Sergeant Edgar Arrowsmith of 'D' Company, 8th Battalion, North Staffordshire Regiment, who was killed by a sniper near Festubert on 6 November. Arrowsmith was a former Corporation Street School pupil who earned a scholarship at King Edward VI Grammar School. His platoon officer later wrote: 'Everyone thought well of him and the news of his death cast a gloom over all.'

In a separate service, held at St Thomas' Church, Lance Corporal Joseph Lowndes Weaver, Wireless and Cable Section, Royal Engineers was remembered. Weaver, it was reported, was formerly a sidesman of the church and a Sunday School teacher. He worked for the Post Office and his name is recorded on a plaque at the Newport Road Depot.

With 1916 drawing to an end there was scarcely a street in the town that had not lost at least one serviceman killed, with many more gassed or wounded. As early as August Captain Levett, of Milford Hall, had suggested the creation of a parish memorial, at Walton-on-the-Hill, recommending that plans be made 'so that when the inestimable blessing of peace does come we shall not be unprepared'.

In late October 1916 a letter written by Mrs Conway Morgan, of Queensville, Stafford, appeared in the *Staffordshire Chronicle* under the heading 'Suggested Shrine for the Departed':

Private Arthur Venables.

A 'Widow's Penny' issued to the next of kin of Arthur Venables.

It seems rather sad that Stafford has not got a shrine like other towns for those who have given their lives for their King and Country. I feel sure that some public place could be selected, so that all who passed by could read the names of the Stafford heroes. The shrine need not be costly, it ought to be beautiful, but very simple, just a record that shall never fade in memory of our brave men.

In response to public demand a number of temporary memorials did evolve, including the one at Christ Church. This took the form of two lists of the fallen flanking a central inscription.

Periodically the press made attempts to alphabetically serialize nominal lists of the dead, but these very quickly became out of date. Meanwhile, an announcement In the *Staffordshire Chronicle* of 8 August 1917, read: 'Relatives of soldiers killed at the war are requested to send photographs to the Free Library, for insertion in the Memorial Album, which can be seen at the Library any time.' However, it wasn't until the end of the war that a concerted effort could be made to record the names of every local man (and one woman) who had lost their life as a consequence of the hostilities.

On 4 January 1919, the *Staffordshire Advertiser* carried the following announcement: 'Stafford Roll of Honour. A list is being compiled with the sanction of the Mayor, Councilor J. Rushton, for issue in booklet form of all those Soldiers, Sailors and Airmen (Officers, NCOs and men) who served in the Great War.' The list was based on information gleaned from completed forms which were returned to the offices of the *Staffordshire Advertiser* at 39 Greengate Street. The process of collecting information was very ad hoc and consequently the booklet that was eventually published was greatly inferior to those produced elsewhere. Only a fraction of the reported 6,500 Staffordians who served during the Great War were recorded at all, while many of the entries were basic, lacking details of the men's service record, or even their unit. In some instances only the men's surnames and initials were recorded, while many men's names were omitted completely.

NOVEMBER 3 1917

STAFFORD SOLDIERS KILLED IN ACTION.

Official intimation has this week been received by Mr. and Mrs. W. T. Heath, of 127, Sandon road, Stafford, that their only son, Pte. Albert H. Heath, of the South Staffordshire Regiment,

THE LATE PTE. HEATH.

was killed in action on Sept. 26, aged 30 years. Before he joined the Army in 1916, Pte. Heath was the manager of the Newtown branch of the Co-operative Society, and was much respected. A comrade who was with him when he was killed writes :—" He died a brave soldier's death, fighting for his King and country. All the officers and men of his company send their deepest sym-

A news article about the death of Private Arthur Heath.

A second appeal was made, this time for the details of the town's war dead. Again, the information that resulted from these enquiries varied in detail and accuracy. This allowed for over 430 names (out of a total of around 1,165 fatalities) being omitted from the final publication, entitled *Stafford Roll of Service in the Great War – 4 August 1914 – 28 June 1919*, and the Corporation War Memorial.

With the signing of the Versailles Peace Treaty in July 1919, the war was finally brought to an end and the last servicemen and women were demobbed the following year. Since the November Armistice many of the troops and the German POWs in France and Flanders had been employed in clearing the battlefields of munitions and bodies. The British Sector was divided into zones, each of which was searched by a dozen-strong team. Through this meticulous process a total of 200,000 bodies were recovered over a period of 2 years; most could not be identified.

From 1916 every serviceman was issued with two identity discs, one of which was removed on death in order to aid the reporting process; prior to this date a soldier's only ID disc was removed on burial, which often took place in a mass grave. Therefore, if a grave marker was destroyed due to military action, the casualty became anonymous.

Tens of thousands of graves were lost in this way, in the ebb and flow of the front. One such example was the last resting place of Private Arthur Lawton, 1st Battalion, Grenadier Guards. In late June 1915 it was reported that the American Embassy had received notification that Lawton, who had died on 9 April, had been buried by the Germans near Auchy-les-Mines, south-east of Cuinchy. Lawton's grave may never have been marked and its precise location became lost due to military action. Today, Arthur Lawton is remembered on the Le Touret Memorial.

After the war there was a call for the remains of the dead to be brought back to Great Britain, to be interred in parish churches or family vaults. On 4 May 1920, however, the House of Commons ruled

Notification of the death of Private S. Lloyd.

Rifleman Dean's funeral in Stafford. Abraham Dean was wounded at the Hohenzollern Redoubt on 25 September 1915 and died at home.

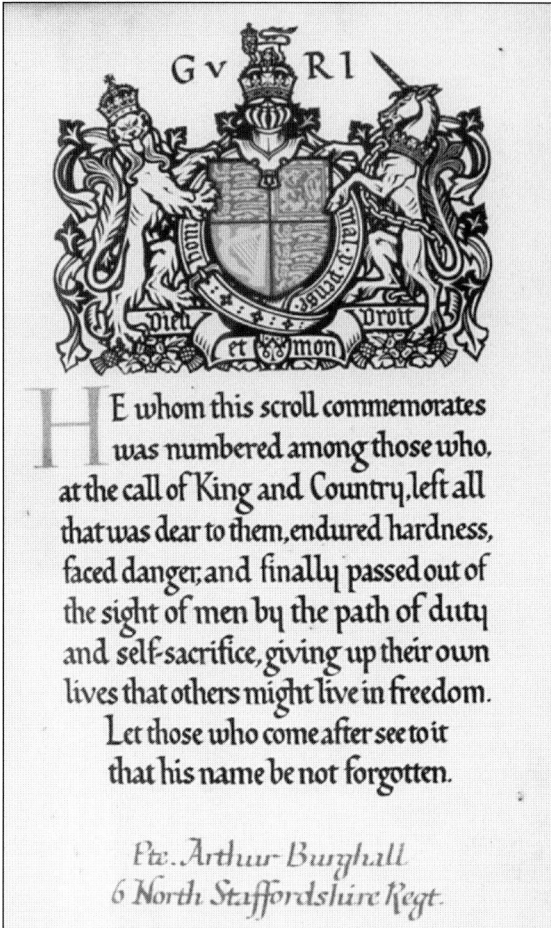

A Memorial Scroll to Private Burghall, 6th North Staffs.

HE whom this scroll commemorates was numbered among those who, at the call of King and Country, left all that was dear to them, endured hardness, faced danger, and finally passed out of the sight of men by the path of duty and self-sacrifice, giving up their own lives that others might live in freedom. Let those who come after see to it that his name be not forgotten.

Pte. Arthur Burghall
6 North Staffordshire Regt.

that the bodies of the dead would not be repatriated, and that memorial stones to all of the war dead would be standardized. Each one bore the casualty's service details, along with their unit badge, and Rudyard Kipling's words: 'Their name liveth for evermore'. There was provision for a family inscription to be added at the foot of the gravestone, but at a cost of 3s. ½d. per letter. The cemeteries themselves were standardized too, the central monument taking the form of a Cross of Sacrifice composed of a Sword of War sheathed by a cross (designed by Brookfield).

Many men were originally buried close to where they died, often at Dressing Stations or other temporary medical posts, and so it was decided to exhume these smaller groups of graves which were reburied in newly created Commonwealth War Graves cemeteries. There was often no rhyme or reason for their location. For instance, the Tyne Cot Cemetery eventually held 12,000 interments, having grown from a handful of graves clustered around a German bunker which had later become a First Aid Post.

ROLL OF HONOUR UNVEILED.—A memorable service was held at the Primitive Methodist Church on Sunday afternoon, when a roll of honour, on which was inscribed the names of all the Primitive Methodist Sunday School boys who had answered their King and country's call, was unveiled. The Rev. B. B. Portnell (circuit minister) presided over a large gathering. Rifleman T. Feist and Rifleman C. Murch (of the New Zealand Rifle Brigade), Corp. H. Wetherbed (Notts. and Derby), L.-Corp. H. R. Freebury (Notts and Derby), Pte. Arthur Preston (signaller, Sherwood Foresters), and Pte. Frank Hulme (Leicestershire Regiment) formed a guard-of-honour during the unveiling ceremony, which was performed by Councillor H. Hulme, who has four sons in the Army and one in the Navy. As the Union Jack, which covered the roll of honour, was withdrawn, the congregation rose, the male portion saluting the roll. The Rev. B. Portnell presented certificates to the fathers of those who had fallen in the war. A short but very touching address was given by the Rev. B. Portnell, who impressed the congregation by saying that he believed the spirits of the boys who had given their lives for their country were present at the unveiling. Councillor H. A. Roberts sang with much feeling, "Nearer, my God, to Thee," Mrs. Pyett accompanying on the organ. After the Benediction the congregation filed reverently past the roll of honour.

Sep 22ⁿ 1918.

News of a Primitive Methodists' Roll of Honour.

In the immediate post-war era few people were able to afford to visit war graves in France and Flanders. Instead war memorials were erected across the country, each of which bore the names of the local community's war dead. Many of the more important Stafford factories including Edwin Bostock & Co., W.H. Dorman & Co. Ltd and Siemens Brothers Electrical Engineering Works (soon to be re-named English Electric Co.) all erected their own memorials bearing the names of their workmen who were killed in action, as did the Stafford and District Post Office and King Edward VI Grammar School. Other memorials included those of the parishes of St Mary's, Christ Church, St Alban's and the roadside cross at Weeping Cross, to name but a few.

The Stafford Corporation 1914–19 War Memorial, located in Victoria Square, bears the names of over 600 of the town's casualties and is surmounted by the bronze image of a British Tommy holding his rifle and raising his helmet in salute of the hard-won victory. The figure, sculpted by Joseph Whitehead, originally faced the railway station where Staffordians entrained following their enlistment. With the later development of the County Court site the view of the station was interrupted and the figure was turned to face St Mary's Church.

The original dedication ceremony, like the annual Remembrance Day services to follow, was conducted by Lionel Payne Crawfurd, Bishop of Stafford, supported by the Mayor of the Corporation and representatives of the military. These units included the North and South Staffordshire Regiments,

The Stafford Corporation Memorial.

The County War Memorial.

the re-formed Stafford Battery and the Staffordshire Yeomanry. Also in attendance at the all-ticket unveiling were hundreds of veterans, along with the next of kin of the fallen. Corporal Sutherland, who was badly wounded in action, was given the honour of unveiling the memorial. The service closed with the sounding of the Last Post and the words: 'They shall not grow old like we grow old. At the going down of the sun and in the morning, we shall remember them' (Lawrence Binyon, September 1914).

A second memorial built to honour the county's war dead was constructed at the edge of the Victoria Pleasure Gardens. Around the monument may be found the badges of the North and South Staffordshire Regiments, Staffordshire Yeomanry, Royal Army Medical Corps, Machine Gun Corps and the Royal Artillery, along with those of the Royal Navy and the Merchant Navy (later supplemented by plaques relating to the county's role in the Second World War). The names of many of the battles in which the various battalions of the North and South Staffordshire Regiments fought are carved into the ashlar blocks of the wall built around the monument. These include the battles of Ypres, Loos, Marne, Gallipoli, the Somme and Passchaendale, along with the Royal Navy's actions at the Falklands and off Jutland.

Of the memorials to individuals, there are a number of graves in Stafford Cemetery (mainly of non-local men who, presumably, died of wounds at Stafford Hospital) and in the parish churchyards dotted around the town, most notably at Castle Church; all are of the standard Commonwealth War Graves type.

There were a small number of privately commissioned memorial tablets dedicated to officers, including one to Second Lieutenant Richard Wilton in Baswich church, and another to Brevet Major William Congreve, VC, DSO, MC, *Légion d'honneur*. One memorial, that to Second Lieutenant Richard Levett, which may be found at St Thomas' Walton Church, Walton-on-the-Hill, is reminiscent of the alabaster altar tombs of the Middle Ages.

Erected in 1920, the Weeping Cross War Memorial was designed by a Mr Evans (of the Wayside Cross Society) and sculptured by Robert Bridgeman & Sons of Lichfield. The Memorial commemorated the twenty-four men of the parish who died during the conflict (along with VAD Nurse, Marjorie Gibson) and was dedicated on 1 November 1920 by Dr. J.A. Kempthorne, Bishop of Lichfield.

The Cenotaph

Nationally the war dead of the Great War and later conflicts are remembered at the Cenotaph in Whitehall, where the reigning monarch and senior British and Commonwealth servicemen and politicians lay their wreaths on Armistice Day. The annual ceremony is marked by a march-past of war veterans. It is a sobering thought

The Cenotaph originally a temporary feature of wood and plaster, later rebuilt in Portland stone.

that if the Empire's dead were to march four abreast past the Cenotaph, the procession would take three-and-a-half days.

The Cenotaph was originally designed as a temporary construction made of wood and plaster. It was to be a place of homage to the dead during the Victory Parade of 19 July 1919. However, public opinion led to it being made a permanent memorial and so the great pylon was later rebuilt in Portland stone on the same spot.

The Unknown Warrior

In France and Flanders vast war cemeteries began to be created from 1918 onwards, and plans were drawn up for the cathedral-like memorials to the missing. There was a pressing need to mark the deaths of the hundreds of thousands of men who had no known grave. Many families had had to wait over a year before their loved ones were officially announced as 'missing presumed dead' and remained in a state of limbo.

Nationally it was recognized that these families needed a burial and a grave to help them with the grieving process. Two years after the original ceasefire, on 11 November 1920, the body of a serviceman, the Unknown Warrior, was laid to rest at the west end of the nave of Westminster Abbey. The mortal remains of four unidentified British servicemen were exhumed, one each from the four battlefields of the Aisne, the Somme, Arras and Ypres. The anonymous coffins were taken to the chapel at St Pol on the night of 7 November 1920, where one was selected at random. The other three bodies were re-interred.

The next day the coffin was placed inside another made of 2in-thick oak from Hampton Court, lined with zinc, sent over from England. It was covered with a Union Flag which had been used at the front as an altar cloth (known as the 'Ypres' or 'Padre's' Flag). The coffin plate bore the inscription 'A British Warrior who fell in the Great War 1914–1918 for King and Country'.

In a ceremonial procession witnessed by up to a million family and friends of the country's war dead, the coffin was drawn on a gun carriage to Whitehall. Here His Majesty the King unveiled the Cenotaph before placing a wreath of red roses and bay leaves on the coffin. The most senior commanders of the armed services acted as pall bearers. At Westminster Abbey, the coffin was borne to the west end of the nave through a guard of honour composed of 100 holders of the Victoria Cross.

The burial service was read and the coffin, bearing a Crusader's sword, was lowered into the grave, the King following the ritual of throwing a handful of French soil onto the coffin lid.

The grave was filled in, using 100 sandbags of French earth, before being covered by a temporary stone with a gilded inscription on it: 'A BRITISH WARRIOR WHO FELL IN THE GREAT WAR 1914–1918 FOR KING AND COUNTRY. GREATER LOVE HATH NO MAN THAN THIS.'

On Armistice Day the following year, 1921, the present black marble stone was unveiled at a special service.

The memorial stone on the Grave of the Unknown Warrior is inscribed:

BENEATH THIS STONE RESTS THE BODY
OF A BRITISH WARRIOR
UNKNOWN BY NAME OR RANK
BROUGHT FROM FRANCE TO LIE AMONG
THE MOST ILLUSTRIOUS OF THE LAND
AND BURIED HERE ON ARMISTICE DAY
11 NOV: 1920, IN THE PRESENCE OF
HIS MAJESTY KING GEORGE V
HIS MINISTERS OF STATE
THE CHIEFS OF HIS FORCES
AND A VAST CONCOURSE OF THE NATION
THUS ARE COMMEMORATED THE MANY
MULTITUDES WHO DURING THE GREAT
WAR OF 1914–1918 GAVE THE MOST THAT
MAN CAN GIVE LIFE ITSELF
FOR GOD
FOR KING AND COUNTRY
FOR LOVED ONES HOME AND EMPIRE
FOR THE SACRED CAUSE OF JUSTICE AND
THE FREEDOM OF THE WORLD
THEY BURIED HIM AMONG THE KINGS BECAUSE HE
HAD DONE GOOD TOWARD GOD AND TOWARD
HIS HOUSE

Around the main inscription are four texts:

THE LORD KNOWETH THEM THAT ARE HIS [top]
UNKNOWN AND YET WELL KNOWN, DYING AND BEHOLD
WE LIVE [side]
GREATER LOVE HATH NO MAN THAN THIS [side]
IN CHRIST SHALL ALL BE MADE ALIVE [base]

General Pershing, on behalf of the USA, had earlier (on 17 October 1921) conferred his country's highest gallantry award, the Congressional Medal of Honor, on the Unknown Warrior and this hangs in a frame on a pillar near the grave.

On 26 April 1923, Lady Elizabeth Bowes-Lyon (later Queen Elizabeth) married the Duke of York (later King George VI) at Westminster Abbey. The Duchess, who had lost a brother during the war, placed her wedding bouquet on the Grave of the Unknown Warrior, which began a tradition upheld by royal brides to this day.

The Poppy Appeal
Over 2,000,000 British servicemen suffered wounds or were gassed during the war.

Many were unable to work again and remained in need of financial support for the rest of their lives.

The choice of poppies as the symbol of a lost generation was inspired by the poem 'In Flanders' Fields' written during the Battle of Ypres (22 April–25 May 1915) by John McCrae. He penned the poem on a page torn from a despatch book. Sadly, McCrae became one of the war's many casualties when he died of wounds in a French hospital within sight of the White Cliffs of Dover in May 1918. His final words came from the last verse of his poem: 'If ye break faith with us, we shall not sleep.' A reply to the appeal made in McCrae's poem was written by the American Miss Moina Michael, who poignantly marked Armistice Day 1918 by selling twenty-five poppies, the profits from which she gave for the aid of wounded soldiers. The first official sale of poppies to remember the dead and to help raise money for the country's invalided servicemen coincided with Armistice Day 1921. Since then the Poppy Appeal has become a key annual event in the nation's calendar, raising millions of pounds to help support men and women who have suffered through service to their country.

Missing Casualties

❖

ABBOTTS, Victor Cumberbatch, 14343 Pte, 8th Battn, North Staffs Regt
ADDISON, Frederick William, 11408 Pte, 1st Battn, Coldstream Guards
ALLCOCK, Alfred, 4187 Pte, 2nd Dragoon Guards (Queen's Bays)
ALLSOPP, Ernest, 2649 Pte, 10th Battn, Royal Warwick Regt
AMISON, T., Labour Corps
ANDREWS, William John, 120668 Cpl, 1st Aircraft Supply Depot Repair Park, RAF
ARROWSMITH, Hubert, 66825 Cpl, 161st Siege Battery, RGA
ARUNDALE, George Henry, 122128 Pte, MGC (Infantry); formerly 239157, Hereford Regt

BACKLER, Thomas, 4528 Gnr, 'C' Battery, 34th Brigade, RFA
BAGNALL, Harry, G/13145 L/Cpl, 6th Battn, The Buffs (East Kent Regt); formerly G/12830 9th Battn, Royal West Surrey Regt
BAGNALL, James Wright, 688 Gnr, 6th (Stafford) Staffs Battery, 3rd North Midland Brigade, RFA
BAGNALL, William Thomas, 11591 Pte, 1st Battn, Coldstream Guards
BAILEY, Albert, 241254 Pte, 1/6th Battn, South Staffs Regt (TF)
BAILEY, J.V.
BAKER, Frank, 657228 Gnr, 23rd Battery, RFA
BATES, Frank Joseph, DCM, Pte, Bedford Regt; formerly 1st Battn, North Staffs Regt
BATES, Frederick Edward, 241340 Pte, 1/6th Battn, North Staffs Regt (TF)
BEARDMORE, John T., 149276 Dvr, 'D' Battery, 293rd Brigade, RFA
BECKETT, Cpl, ASC
BEECH, Charles, S/12781 L/Sgt, 8th Battn, Rifle Brigade
BELFIELD, John, 20834 Pte, 2nd Battn, Manchester Regt
BELLAMY, Claud Cecil, 15169 Sgt, 4th Battn, Bedford Regt
BENNETT, Charles Sydney, 241708 Pte, 1/5th Battn, Leicester Regt (TF)

BENNION, Percy, 14638 Pte, 16th Battn, Royal Warwick Regt

BENTLEY, H., MM, 282087 L/Cpl, 7th Battn, Highland Light Infantry

BERRY, Frederick Reginald

BEVAN, George, 14932 Sgt, 18th Battn, King's (Liverpool) Regt

BIRCH, Edward, 1st Battn, Coldstream Guards

BLACKWELL, J.

BONNER, Alfred H., 41900 Pte, 12th Battn, Sherwood Foresters (Notts & Derby Regt)

BOON, Ernest, 242521 Pte, 1/5th Battn of the King's Own (Royal Lancs Regt) (TF)

BOOTH, John, L/16522 Pte, 9th Battn, Royal Fusiliers

BOSTOCK, Hugh William, 2nd Lt, 1/6th Battn, South Staffs Regt (TF)

BOSTOCK, Humphrey Thomas, MC, Capt, 6th Battn, North Staffs Regt

BOULT, George, 726 Pte, 2/6th Battn, North Staffs Regt (TF)

BOULTON, John, 3184 Pte, 1st/5th Battn, North Staffs Regt (TF)

BOURNE, Richard Augustus, 16479 Pte, 2nd Battn, Lancs Fusiliers

BRAGG, Alfred, 34122 Pte, 5th Battn, Alexandra Princess of Wales' Own (Yorks) Regt; formerly 215223, North Staffs Regt

BREEZE, Donald H., RFA

BRINTON, Eric

BROADHEAD, Leonard V., 595 Pte, 3rd County of London Yeomanry (Sharpshooters)

BROMLEY, Frederick, 13434 Pte, 12th (Service) Battn, Hampshire Regt; formerly 16661, Worcester Regt

BROMLEY, Noah, 6380 Pte, 1st Battn, South Wales Borderers

BROMLEY, William, 9704 Pte, 2nd Battn, South Staffs Regt

BROWN, Alexander M., 1277 –, 'A' Battery, 232nd Brigade, RFA

BULBROOK, Samuel, R/3535 L/Cpl, 13th Battn, King's Royal Rifle Corps

BULL, A.

BUTCHER, Alfred, 300485 Cpl, Staffs Yeomanry

BUTCHER, Charles, 1966 Pte, 'B' Coy, 2nd Battn, Manchester Regt

BUTLER, Alfred, 22297 Pte, 'C' Coy, 11th Battn, Leicester Regt

BUTLER, John, MM (alias for BUCKLEY, John T.), 49339 Bdr, 126th Battery, 29th Brigade, RFA

BUTTERFIELD, Charles William, 2nd Lt, 5th Battn, North Staffs Regt

CALEY, George, 151509 Gnr, 99th Siege Battery, RGA

CAPPELL, James L., Chaplin's Forces

CARLETON-SMITH, Beaven, 2nd Lt (Observer), No. 100 Squadron, RAF

CARMICHAEL, G.

CARTWRIGHT, Albert, 7657 Rflm., 2nd Battn, Royal Irish Rifles; formerly 9914, RFA

CARTWRIGHT, Ernest, 8858 Pte, 3rd (Special Reserve) Battn, South Staffs Regt

CASEY, William, Gnr, RFA

CASHMORE, Harold, 265394 Pte, 10th Battn, Cheshire Regt

CHAMBERLAIN, P., Dvr, RFA

CHAPMAN, Donald

CHARLESWORTH, Henry, Colour Sgt, 'late of the Leicestershire Regt'

CHEADLE, Henry Richard, G/13936 Pte, 7th Battn, The Buffs (East Kent Regt.)

CLAYTON, Charles Harrall, 119095 L/Cpl, 16th Battn, Northumberland Fusiliers

CLAYTON, William Henry, 91290 Ftr, 56th Battery, 34th Brigade, RFA

CLEMENTS, William Bayley, WO, Corps of Army Schoolmasters

CLEWLOW, Harry, 3350154 Pte, 9th (Glasgow) Battn, Highland Light Infantry (TF)

CLEWS, W.

COLCLOUGH, W.

COLES, Samuel Ernest, 9719 Rflm., 3rd Battn, King's Royal Rifle Corps

COOKE, Sydney Stevenson, 9 Pte, 1st Brigade Australian Headquarters

COOKE, William Henry, 163345 A/CSM, 12th Labour Coy, RE

COOPER, Charles

COOPER, James, 40191 Pte, 1st Battn, Dublin Fusiliers; formerly 22819, North Staffs Regt

COPE, William, 17838 Pte, 10th (Service) Battn, Yorks and Lancs Regt

CORFIELD, John Henry, 34625 Pte, 3rd Battn, Manchester Regt

COUZENS, Algernon George, 2811 CQMS, 1/5th Battn, North Staffs Regt (TF)

COWEN, Patrick, 15171 Pte, 2nd Battn, Lincoln Regt

COX, George, 6443 Pte, 2nd Battn, South Staffs Regt

CREED, Benjamin Robert, 46932 Pte, 32nd Station Hospital, RAMC

CRESSWELL, John, 9038 Pte, North Staffs Regt

CRUTCHLEY, Frederick, 40193 Pte, 1st Battn, Royal Dublin Fusiliers; formerly 22568, North Staffs Regt

CRUTCHLEY, John, 71560 Dvr, 103rd Brigade, RFA

CUMMING, Colin Edward, Lt, 103rd Battery, RGA

DACY, John, 18209 Pte, 2nd Battn, Cheshire Regt

DALE, James, 28567 Pte, 8th Battn, King's Own (Royal Lancs Regt)

DALE, Stephen, 531553 2nd SBS PO, RAMC; served onboard HMS *Birkenhead*

DAVEY, Harry, 35055 Pte, 11th Battn, Cheshire Regt

DAVIES, Harold George, 29754 Pte, 22nd Battn, West Yorks (Labour Corps)

DAVIES, John Charles

DAVIES, William, Pte, Royal Welsh Fusiliers

DAWSON, Edward John, 46598 Pte, 18th Battn, Durham Light Infantry

DEAKIN, Frederick, Pte, 1/6th Battn, North Staffs Regt (TF)

DEAKIN, Frederick (Belgian *Croix de Guerre*), 241691 L/Cpl, 2/6th Battn, North Staffs Regt (TF), attached 176th Light Trench Mortar Battery, RFA

DEAKIN, Thomas, 18382 Pte, 12th (Service) Battn, King's Shropshire Light Infantry
DEAN, Arthur
DEAN, Francis, 47437 Rflm, 1st Battn, Royal Irish Rifles; formerly 28623, ASC
DEAVALLE, George Henry, 53319 Pte, RAMC
DEAVILLE, Richard, 810003 QMS, 232nd Brigade, North Midland Division, RFA
DEVLIN, Hugh, 446222 Pte, 10th Battn, Alberta Regt, Canadian Infantry
DODD, William George, 10870 Pte, 7th Battn, North Staffs Regt
DOUGLAS, John William, L/39189 Gnr, 'B' Battery, 175th Brigade, RFA
DOUGLAS, William Henry, DCM, 17706 Sgt, 'D' Coy, 9th Battn, Loyal North
  Lancs Regt
DRAPER, D., Bdr, RA
DUDLEY, William, 26421 Pte, 6th Battn, King's Shropshire Light Infantry

EGERTON, Frank Rowland, 3037 Pte, 14th Battn, King's Own Hussars
EGERTON, William Webster, 493066 Pte, 13th (Kensington) Battn, London Regt
ELLEMENT, Henry Victor, Pte, 1/5th Battn, South Staffs Regt (TF)
ELLERTON, Sidney, 6763345 Gnr, 'Y' Battery, 59th Trench Mortar, RFA
ELSMORE, Thomas Charles, 3592 Gnr, 'A' Battery, 63rd Brigade, RFA
ELVERTON, Sidney, 67345 Gnr, RFA (TF)
EMBERTON, William Henry, 201393 Pte, 1/4th Battn Northumberland Fusiliers
  (TF)
EVANS, H., ASC
EVANS, H.L. or H.J., L/Cpl, North Staffs Regt
EVERALL, Thomas Henry, 203103 Pte, 2nd Battn, King's Own Regt; formerly
  23156, Northumberland Fusiliers and 144912, RFA

FALLOWS, James, 40616 Pte, 9th Battn, North Staffs Regt
FAULKNER, Albert Edward, 816 L/Cpl, 4th Battn, Seaforth Highlanders
FAULKNER, Samuel John, 25370 Pte, 2nd Battn, Worcester Regt
FEAKLEY, George Thomas, 9337 Pte, 2nd Battn, Leicester Regt
FERRAN, Maurice A.M., MC, 2nd Lt, Royal Irish Rifles
FINLOW, John Charles, 53843 Pte, 15th/17th Battn, Prince of Wales' Own Regt
FISHER, R., North Staffs Regt (TF)
FISHER, Thomas, 16904 Pte, 11th Battn, Cheshire Regt
FOLLOWS, A.
FOLLOWS, John
FORD, F., 226235 Pte, 7th Battn, North Staffs Regt
FORD, Fred, 2632 L/Cpl, 1/6th Battn, North Staffs Regt (TF)
FOSTER, Ernald William, C/6180 L/Cpl, King's Royal Rifle Corps
FREEMAN, John Thomas, 308122 Pte, The King's (Liverpool Regt)
FROST, Thomas James, S/9086 Rflm., Brigade

GARDINER, Thomas Alfonzo, 37006 Pte, MGC (Infantry); formerly 3708, Seaforth Highlanders

GARLICK, Charles, 291522 Pte, 1/7th Battn, Cheshire Regt (TF)

GARNER, William Herbert, 13/378 Pte, 13th (Service) Battn, Yorks and Lancs Regt

GASK, William, 205712 Pte, 6th Battn, King's Own Yorkshire Light Infantry

GERRARD, Percy, 2392 MG Sgt, 1/6th Battn, North Staffs Regt (TF)

GIBSON, Marjorie, VAD

GILL, George William, 32035 Pte, 12th Battn, Northumberland Fusiliers

GODRIDGE, Albert, 44526 Pte, 1st Battn, Somerset Light Infantry; formerly 12626, Shropshire Light Infantry

GOSS, Herbert, 3035 Pte, 1st Battn, Royal Munster Fusiliers

GRAINGER, Frederick Thomas, 556982 Rflm., 16th Battn, London Regt (Queen's Westminster Rifles)

GRATTIDGE, Bernard George, 78565 Spr, Class 'W' Army Reserve, RE

GREEN, Alan F., 28465 Pte, 2nd Battn, 3rd New Zealand Rifle Brigade

GREEN, John, 20371 Gdm., 3rd Battn, Grenadier Guards

GRIFFIN, Edwin, 18436 Pte, 1st Battn, Northampton Regt

GRIFFITHS, Edward, 8269 Pte, 9th (Service) Battn, Yorks and Lancs Regt

HACKETT, Albert Edwin, 49527 Sgt, 92nd Field Coy, RE

HACKETT, William P., Motorized Transport, Royal Army Service Corps, attached 91st Siege Battery, RFA

HALL, Daniel, 40478 Pte, 2nd Battn, Prince of Wales' Own Regt (West Yorks); formerly 30995, Leicester Regt

HALLETT, Francis John Leese, 9830 Cpl, 1st Battn, Northamptonshire Regt

HAMMOND, A.T., Cpl, Canadian Forces

HAMMOND, C.D.

HANCOX, Albert Frederick, 44736 Pte, 2nd Battn, Lincoln Regt; formerly 37105, Leicester Regt

HARDING, Bertram Henry, 61562 Spr, No. 208th Field Coy, RE

HARDING, S.F., 1/4th Battn, Duke of Wellington's Regt

HARRIMAN, Frank, 118263 Pte, MGC (Infantry)

HARRIS, Charles, S/10539 Pte, 2nd Battn, The Buffs (East Kent Regt)

HARRIS, Fred, 10280 Pte, 7th Battn, North Staffs Regt

HARRISON, Charles H., 202953 Pte, Depot South Staffs Regt; formerly 3546, Staffs Yeomanry

HARRISON, Frank, 118263 Pte, MGC (Infantry); formerly 89947, Sherwood Foresters (Notts and Derby Regt)

HARVEY, Richard Walter, G/92854 Pte, Royal Fusiliers; posted 2/2nd Battn, Royal Fus.; formerly T/4/061630, ASC

HARVIE, Edward Alexander Gordon, Temp. Sub Lt, Anson Battn, RN Division, RNVR

HAUGHTON, L.

HAYNES, Henry Hillas, 240764 Cpl, 1/5th Battn, Loyal North Lancs (TF)

HAYWARD, John, 334010 Pte, 9th (Glasgow) Battn, Highland Light Infantry (TF)

HAYWOOD, Joseph George, 202956 L/Cpl, 1/5th Battn, South Staffs Regt

HEAPY, Ralph, T2/SR/02673 Dvr, ASC

HEBBERT, F. Victor, 612522 Pte, 2/19th Battn, London Regt

HICKINBOTHAM, Noah, 4954 Pte, 6th Battn King's Own (Royal Lancs) Regt;
    formerly 850, RGA

HIGHFIELD, Ernest Thomas, 12637 Pte, 5th Battn, King's Shropshire Light
    Infantry

HIGSON, A.W.

HILL, Charles, T/207078 Sgt, 8th Battn, The Queen's Regt (West Surreys); formerly
    North Staffs Regt

HILL, Eli, 145324 Spr, 155th Field Coy, RE

HINDE, John William, 29287 Pte, 2/5th Battn, King's Own (Royal Lancs) Regt (TF)

HODGETTS, William, 5623 Rflm., 7th Battn, King's Royal Rifle Corps

HODGKINSON, James, 81016 Pte, 1/7th Battn, Durham Light Infantry (TF)

HODSON, T., 436633 Pte, 49th Battn, Canadian Infantry (Alberta Regt)

HODSON, Thomas, 31469 Dvr, RFA

HODSON, William Arthur, 15655 Pte, 'B' Coy, 9th Battn, Leicester Regt

HOLDEN, Harry, 240040 Pte, 1/6th Battn, North Staffs Regt (TF)

HOLDFORD, Charles, 12358 Cpl, MGC (Infantry); formerly 21819, Leicester Regt

HOLLAND, Thomas, 7473 Sgt, 11th Battn, Royal Fusiliers; formerly 3555,
    Middlesex Regt

HOLLINS, Albert, 15456 Sgt, 8th Battn, Somerset Light Infantry

HOLLINS, Benjamin

HOLLINS, Percival Byron, 256153 Pte, Labour Corps; formerly 17721, 3rd Battn,
    King's Shropshire Light Infantry

HOLLINSHEAD, Sion George, 13278 Pte, 9th Battn, Alexandra Princess of Wales'
    Own (Yorks Regt)

HOLLOWAY, John Thomas, TI/2116 Dvr, 2nd Division Train, ASC

HORDERN, Charles John, 58116 Gnr, 56th Battery, RFA

HORNE, Fred, Gloucester Regt

HOUGH, Arthur, MM, 22011 A/Sgt, 11th Field Coy, RE

HUGHES, Alfred, 260016 Cpl, 2/5th Battn, Lincoln Regt (TF)

HUGHES, Lionel Holford, 2nd Lt, 3rd Battn (attached to 1st Battn), North Staffs
    Regt

HUTCHINSON, Thomas, 20/251 Pte, 20th (Tyneside Scottish) Battn,
    Northumberland Fusiliers

ILIFFE, Hardy H. (served under the alias WILSON, G.H.), 430229 Pte, 48th Battn,
    Canadian Infantry

JACKSON, A.

JACKSON, Frank, MI/5889 S/Sgt, Mechanical Transport, ASC, attached to 28th Divisional Field Ambulance, RAMC

JACKSON, Samuel, 8452 Pte, Coldstream Guards

JACKSON, Tom, 50644 Pte, 2/5th Battn, Lancs Fusiliers (TF)

JAMES, Albert, 72 Cpl, 16th Lancers, later 42nd Canadian Dragoons, Royal Canadian Forces

JAMES, Geoffrey Cecil James, Capt, North Staffs Regt

JAMES, Richard, 35060 Pte, 7th Battn, King's Shropshire Light Infantry

JEFFREY, Albert, 18173 L/Cpl, 2nd Battn, Coldstream Guards

JEFFRIES, John, 5974 Pte, 9th Battn, Royal Warwick Regt

JENKINSON, William James, 202497 Pte, 10th Battn, Durham Light Infantry

JOHNSON, Frederick Edward, 283626 Pte, 1/4th Battn, Royal Fusiliers; formerly 4066, 26th Cycle Battn

JONES, A.

JONES, Arthur George, 47357 Pte, Bedford Regt; formerly 1861, RAMC

JONES, Charles, 9307 L/Cpl, 7th Battn, King's Shropshire Light Infantry

JONES, Harold Ashton, 16231 Pte, 3rd Battn, Worcester Regt

JONES, Harry, 14854 Pte, 10th Battn, Cheshire

JONES, Henry, 23494 Pte, 15th Battn, Sherwood Foresters (Notts and Derby Regt)

JOWETT, John William, 122730 L/Cpl, 'C' Coy, 8th Battn, Leicester Regt

JUDSON, Stephen, 102957 Spr, 177th Tunnel Coy, RE

KENNY, A., Royal Welsh Fusiliers

KEY, William, 863 Pte, 1st Battn, Lincoln Regt

KIDWELL, Ormond, 429060 Pte, 7th Battn, Canadian Infantry (British Columbia Regt)

KIRKLAND, Arthur, 241377 Pte, 2/6th Battn, North Staffs Regt (TF)

LATHAM, Albert Ernest, 95926 Sgt, 46th Brigade Ammunition Column, RFA

LATHAM, John, 5253 Pte, 1st Battn, North Staffs Regt

LAWLEY, Victor, 5891 Pte, 8th Field Ambulance, RAMC

LAWRENCE, Arthur, 278168 Cpl, 10th Battn, Essex Regt; formerly 11317, Royal Berkshire Regt

LAWTON, Bertie, 54468 Bdr, 105th Battery, 22nd Brigade, RFA

LAWTON, Frank Clements, Drmr, 'late of 1/3rd Battn, Herefordshire Regt'

LAWTON, William, 10675 Pte, 15th Battn, Lancs Fusiliers

LEA, Samuel Thomas, 9778 Pte, 4th Battn, Worcester Regt

LEIGHTON, Harry, 39145 Pte, 2nd Battn, Highland Light Infantry; formerly T/I/2014, RASC

LEVETT, Richard William Byrd, 2nd Lt, 1st Battn, Kings Royal Rifles

LEWIS, G.C., 50652 Sgt, RHA

LINDSAY, Alexander James, 20765 Pte, 5th Battn, King's Shropshire Light Infantry; formerly 26354, Suffolk Regt

LLOYD, Harry, P/8186 L/Cpl, Corps of Military Police (Foot Branch); formerly 12417, Leicester Regt

LLOYD, James Thomas, 6294 A/Sgt, 9th Battn, Royal Welsh Fusiliers

LLOYD, Samuel, 5331 Pte, 2nd Battn, Coldstream Guards

LODGE, Geoffrey Brettingham, 6353 Pte, 50th Battn, Australian Infantry

LOVATT, Edwin, 79952 Spr, 176 Tunnel Coy, RE

LOWE, Harry, 73431 Pte, 2nd Battn, Royal Welsh Fusiliers

LYCETT, William Arthur, 42254 Pte, 2nd Battn, Royal Inniskilling Fusiliers

LYCETT, William Philip Thomas, 40365 Pte, 2nd Battn, South Staffs Regt; formerly 28717, North Staffs Regt

LYONS, William Francis, MM, 49040 L/Cpl, 103rd Field Company, RE

McFERRAN, Maurice Anderson, MC, 2nd Lt, 5th Battn, attached to 2nd Battn, Royal Irish Rifles

McGRANE, W., 5450 Pte, 1st Battn, Irish Guards

McGREGOR, Robert, 324 Pte, 2nd Battn, Seaforth Highlanders

McNAIR, James, 9043 Cpl, 2nd Battn, Princess Louise's Argyll and Sutherland Highlanders

McPHEE, William Hay, S/9451 L/Cpl, 9th Battn, Gordon Highlanders

MADDEN, William Henry, Capt, 16th (Pioneer) Battn, Royal Irish Rifles

MANNION, John, 10204 Pte, 1st Battn, King's Own Regt (Liverpool Regt)

MANSELL, William, 687062 Dvr, 'D' Battery, 285th Brigade, RFA

MARSH, William, 37131 Pte, 2nd Battn, Lancs Fusiliers; formerly 23128, North Staffs Regt

MARSHALL, Thomas, S/333 Rflm., 9th Battn, Rifle Brigade

MARTIN, Arthur Edward, 11509 Pte, 3rd Battn, Coldstream Guards

MARTIN, Arthur James, 39151 Pte, 1st Battn, Princess Charlotte of Wales' Regt

MATHER, William Hubert, 421029 Cpl, 1/3rd (North Midland) Field Ambulance, RAMC (TF)

MAYBE, Frederick Thomas, 6376 Pte, 1st Battn, North Staffs Regt

MEARS, Percy, 20334 Pte, 1/8th Battn, King's Own Regt (Liverpool Regt) (TF)

MEESON, George, 72666 Pte, 1st Battn, Sherwood Foresters (Notts and Derby Regt)

MELLOR, James William, 40027 Pte, 1st Battn, North Staffs Regt

MILES, Clarence, 240510 L/Cpl, 1/6th Battn, North Staffs Regt (TF); formerly Oxford and Bucks Light Infantry

MILES, F., Machine Gun Corps

MILLWARD, George, 13173 Pte, 8th (Service) Battn, South Staffs Regt

MORETON, Percy, 202491 Pte, 1/5th Battn, North Staffs Regt (TF)

MORRIS, Edwin A., G/13948 Pte, 7th Battn, The Buffs (East Kent Regt)

MORT, Paul John, J/41552 AB/S, HMS *Ghurka*, RN

MORTON, Thomas, 15100 L/Cpl, 8th Battn, Northumberland Fusiliers

MOSS, John Holmes, 69170 Pte, 1/5th Battn, Northumberland Fusiliers (TF); formerly TR/5/62470, Ter. Res. Battn

MOTTASHAW, William Henry, MM, 8620 WO II, 7th Battn, The Duke of Cornwall's Light Infantry

MOULD, John Henry, 58383 Pte, 1/4th Battn, Royal Warwick Regt (TF)

MOULD, W., 29317 Pte, 1st Battn, East Lancs Regt

MOUNTFORD, Benjamin, 805132 Gnr, 'A' Battery, 232nd Brigade, RFA

MOUNTFORD, James, 3912 Pte, 2nd Royal Warwick Regt

MOUSLEY, Samuel Charles, 45500 Pte, 6th (Service) Battn, South Staffs Regt; formerly P/2777, MFP

MULLARKEY, Alfred John, 139722 Chief PO, HMS *Bulwark*, RN

NEVILLE, William Henry, 7751 Sgt, 8th Battn, North Staffs Regt

NORMAN, Aubrey L.W., Lt, HMS *Newmarket*, RN

NORMAN, Basil Chamberlin Qu'appelle, Lt, 4th Battn, North Staffs Regt

OWEN, Harold Ernest, 53034 Pte., 2nd West Yorks Regt (Prince of Wales's Own)

PADDISON, George Henry, 29235 Pte, 1st Battn, East Yorks Regt; formerly 21853, North Staffs Regt

PARKER, Alfred, 11578 Pte, 8th Battn, South Staffs Regt

PARKER, John, 19025 L/Cpl, 1st Battn, Grenadier Guards

PARKER, William, 24215 L/Cpl, 1/4th Battn, King's Own (Royal Lancs Regt) (TF)

PARKES, George Nathaniel, 76038 Dvr, 'D' Battery, 112th Brigade, RFA

PARTRIDGE, Ernest John Henry, 10097 Bmn, 2nd Battn, East Surrey Regt

PAYNE, Bertram, 45483 Sgt, 254th Tunnel Company, RE

PEARSON, Alexander William Thomas, 5563 Rflm., 6th London Regt (City of London Rifles)

PEARSON, Alfred, 92759 Pte, Royal Fusiliers; posted 2/2nd London Regt

PEARSON, John, 17457 Pte, 15th Battn, Royal Scots Regt

PENNIFER, Henry John, G/52118 L/Cpl, 12th Battn, The Duke of Cambridge's Own Regt; attached to 18th (Entrenching) Battn, Middlesex Regt

PERKIN, William, 55099 Pte, 22nd Battn, Manchester Regt

PERKS, Arthur Edgar, 42431 L/Cpl, 13th Battn, Alexandra Princess of Wales' Regt; formerly 164213, RFA

PHILIPS, Mark Hibbert, 2nd Lt, 4th Battn, (attached 1st Battn) South Staffs Regt

PHILLIPS, Thomas Howard, 94832 Pnr, N.N. Cable Section, RE

PICKERSGILL, Sydney, 50075 Pte, 11th Battn, Essex Regt; formerly 65018, North Staffs Regt

PIGGOTT, Harold John, T1/1876 L/Cpl, 6th Cavalry Divisional HQ, Army Service Corps

PLANT, Alfred Thomas, K/18237 1st Class Stoker, HMS *Invincible*, RN

PLANT, A.S., 47730 Pte, 10th Battn, Essex Regt

PLANT, Charles Henry, 11908 L/Cpl, 1st Battn, South Staffs Regt

POOLE, George, 29443 Pte, 11th Battn, Yorkshire Regt; formerly 28626, Sherwood Foresters (Notts and Derby Regt)

POOLE, Harry, 14530 L/Cpl, 7th Battn, North Staffs Regt

POTTS, D.

POTTS, S.

POWELL, Edward, 12201 Pte, 2nd Battn, Cheshire Regt

POWELL, George Thomas, 16776 Sgt, 7th Battn, North Staffs Regt

PRICE, Frederick George, 19722 Pte, 7th Battn, King's Shropshire Light Infantry

PRICE, John Thomas, 242416 Pte, 2/5th Battn, North Staffs Regt (TF)

PRIME, William, 202410 Drm., 2/6th Battn, North Staffs Regt (TF)

RAWLINSON, J.J., Royal Canadian Forces

REDFERN, John George, 9445 Pte, B' Coy, 1st Battn, North Staffs Regt

REECE, Arthur Eber, 16929 Gdm., 1st Battn, Grenadier Guards

REYNOLDS, John William, 27782 Pte, 10th Battn, Lincoln Regt

REYNOLDS, Wilfred, 90966 Gnr, 'A' Battery, 190th Brigade, RFA

RICE, Joseph, 35397 Pte, 15th Battn, Sherwood Foresters (Notts and Derby Regt)

RIDGEWAY, Charles F., 24369 Pte, 56th Battn, MGC (Infantry); formerly 1723, Border Regt

ROBERTS, Zachariah Male, 17760 Pte, 12th Battn, Sherwood Foresters (Notts and Derby Regt)

ROCHELL, Edwin Thomas, 7491 Pte, 1st Battn, North Staffs Regt

RODGERS, Edward Gordon, 12/767 Pte, 12th (Service) Battn, Yorks and Lancs Regt

ROGERS, Arthur, 83654 Bdr, 'D' Battery, 256th Brigade, RFA

ROGERS, Ralph, 111843 Sgt, 226th Siege Battery, RGA

ROOKER, Charles W.H., 9090 L/Sgt, 1st Irish Guards

ROWLAND, A.E., 2nd Lt, 2/6th Battn, North Staffs Regt (TF)

RUSSELL, Charles, G/64180 Pte, 4th Battn, Royal Fusiliers

RUSSELL, William Henry, 198128 Spr, 36th Field Coy, RE; formerly 8437, Royal Warwick Regt

RYLANDS, Percy Harold, Z/202 Rflm., 1st Battn, Rifle Brigade

SALT, Robert, 29432 Pte, 15th Battn, Yorkshire Regt

SALT, Walter Petit, Temp. Capt., 2nd Battn, Lancs Fusiliers

SANDERS, Arthur, 40040 Pte, 10th Battn, Worcester Regt

SARGENT, John Henry, 38272 Pte, 2/5th Leicestershire Regt (TF)

SAVAGE, Joseph Henry, 33273 Pte, 11th Battn, South Wales Borderers

SCARROTT, Arthur, 20280 Sgt, 10th Battn, Canadian Infantry (Alberta Regt)

SCOTT, Harry, 304547 Gnr, 11th Brigade, Canadian Field Artillery
SCOTT, R., 12571 Sgt, 6th Battn, King's Shropshire Light Infantry
SEVILLE, William, 7410 Cpl, 1st Battn, King's Shropshire Light Infantry
SHAW, Thomas, 5348 Pte, 2nd Royal Welsh Fusiliers
SHONE, Robert, 10407 Pte, 7th Battn, North Staffs Regt
SILLITO, Charles Orlando, 122723 Gnr, 323rd Siege Battery, RGA
SILVESTER, Herbert, 20156 Pte, 2nd Battn Yorkshire & Lancashire Regt
SLACK, Cyril Hamden, 2/2263 Gnr, New Zealand Field Artillery
SMALL, Harry, 200653 Pte, 1/4th Battn, Royal Scots (TF)
SMALLWOOD, George, Gnr, 182nd Battery, RGA
SMITH, A., SM, MGC (Motorised)
SMITH, Bert, 32042 Pte, 2nd Battn, Northampton Regt
SMITH, Ernest, R/910 Rflm., 12th Battn, King's Royal Rifle Corps
SMITH, James William
SMITH, Richard Edwin, MM, 17579 A/Sgt, 1st Battn, South Staffs Regt
SMITH, Stanley Clarence, 3526 Sgt, RAF
SMITH, Sydney, 10542 Pte, 2nd Cheshire Regt
SMITH, William Frederick, 2020858 Pte, 5th Battn, Princess Charlotte of Wales'
    Regt
SMITH, William Henry, Gnr, Canadian Regt
SMITH, William John, 219560 Dvr, 49th Ammunition Column, RFA
SPEARING, Harold, 119389 Gnr, 59th Brigade, RFA
SPRONSON, J.C., Pte, London Regt
SPRONSTON, Herbert William, 91505 Gnr, 'C' Battery, 183rd Brigade, RFA
SPROSSON, George
STANLEY, William, 260023 Pte, 1/5th Battn, Leicester Regt (TF)
STANTON, George, 21972 Pte, 9th Battn, King's Own Yorkshire Light Infantry
STEVENTON, Henry E.
STOTT, Ernest, 75950 Pte, 9th Battn, Northumberland Fusiliers
STUBBS, A.J.
STUBBS, Frank Wibberly Done, 44277 Sgt, 74th Field Coy, RE
SUTTON, Bert
SUTTON, Frederick James, 58521 Pte, 1st King's Own (Liverpool) Regt; formerly
    28630, Manchester Regt
SWINGLEWOOD, Jacob, 75844 Dvr, 119th Battery, 27th Brigade, RFA

TALBOT, Thomas Henry, 9772 Pte, 11th Battn, Lancs Fusiliers
TAYLOR, Arthur William, 20032 Pte, 12th (Service) Battn, Highland Light Infantry
TAYLOR, William, 18445 Pte, 9th Battion, Leicester Regt
THOMAS, Albert, 2192 Pte, 9th Battn, Lancs Fusiliers; formerly 15168, South
    Staffs Regt
THOMPSON, Frank, 49245 Pte, 13th Battn, Cheshire Regt

THORNTON, Charles, 15090 Pte, 'D' Coy, 1st Battn, Sherwood Forester (Notts and Derby Regt)
THORNTON, Harold, M/286216 Pte, Base Depot, Army Service Corps
THORPE, Thomas, R/6839 Rflm., 11th Battn, King's Royal Rifle Corps
TIDESWELL, Percy, 22275 Gdm., 4th Battn, Grenadier Guards
TILDESLEY, Albert Edward, A/2971 Rflm., 8th Battn, King's Royal Rifle Corps
TILDESLEY, William Bernard, 39421 Gnr, 5th Brigade, RFA
TILL, Samuel J., 90948 Gnr, 9th Battery, 56th Brigade, RFA
TILSTONE, Leonard, 1326 Pte, 9th Battn, Warwickshire Regt
TOMKINSON, Joseph
TURNER, E.W., North Staffs Regt
TURNER, Samuel, T4/062147 Dvr, ASC
TWIGG, Frank William, Lt (A/Capt.), 1st Battn, Northants Regt

VENABLES, Arthur, 176214 Spr, 5th Field Company, RE
VERNON, Arthur, 10482 Pte, 7th Battn, North Staffs Regt

WAGSTAFF, John Carleton, 2nd Lt, 8th Battn, South Staffs Regt
WALKER, John Edward, WO, Corps of Army Schoolmasters
WALTHO, D. Charles, 91582 Dvr, 19th Divisional Ammunition Column, RFA
WALTON, A., Pte, North Staffs Regt
WARD, John T., 18189 Pte, 8th Battn, East Yorks; formerly 8838, North Staffs Regt
WARD, Sydney John, 1849 Pte, 1/5th Battn, North Staffs Regt (TF)
WATSON, William, 285894 Pte, Queen's Own Oxfordshire Hussars
WEBB, Albert James, 169664 Shoe-Smithing Cpl, Fort Garry Horse
WEBB, Henry
WELCH, George, 243217 Pte, 2/5th Battn, Lancs Fusiliers (TF)
WELLS, Albert, 4643 Pte, 1/5th Battn, Northumberland Fusiliers (TF)
WENLOCK, William, 8455 Pte, 1st Battn, South Staffs Regt
WHEAVER, Joseph Lowndes, 78175 L/Cpl, Wireless and Cable Section, RE
WHEAVER, W., RE
WHITEHOUSE, Ernest, 50636 L/Cpl, 10th Coy, Imperial Camel Corps; formerly 30380, Hussars
WHITFIELD, Jack, S/3147 Rflm., 11th Rifle Brigade
WHITFIELD, William George, M/16855 Cook's Mate, HMS *Eden*, RN
WHITGREAVE, Henry Egerton, Temp. 2nd Lt, 1st Battn, Somerset Light Infantry
WHITTLE, Stanley Westwood, 213 Cpl, 'F' Coy, 1/5th Battn, Manchester Regt (TF)
WIGGIN, H.
WILLIAMS, W.A., Spr, RE
WILLIAMSON, Henry, Lt
WILSON, A.
WILSON, Thomas, 18677 Pte, 8th Battn, Cheshire Regt

WOOD, Samuel, 300539 Pte, 1/1st Battn, Staffs Yeomanry
WORRALL, William, 2631 Pte, 1/6th Battn, North Staffs Regt (TF)
WRIGHT, Frank, 12/229 Cpl, 12th Battn, King's Own Yorkshire Light Infantry
WRIGHT, Thomas Burnett, 12368 Pte, 18th Battn, Royal Welsh Fusiliers
WRIGHT, William, 17009 Pte, 9th (Service) Battn, South Staffs Regt
WYNNE, Arthur, 10730 Pte, 'B' Coy, 1st Battn, Royal Scots Fusiliers

YEWBERRY, Harry, 43322 Pte, 7th Battn, South Staffs Regt

Index